A MAN
OF BAD
REPUTATION

A MAN OF BAD REPUTATION

The Murder of John Stephens and the Contested Landscape of North Carolina Reconstruction

DREW A. SWANSON

THE UNIVERSITY OF NORTH CAROLINA PRESS

Chapel Hill

This book was published with the assistance of the Z. Smith Reynolds Fund of the University of North Carolina Press.

Designed by Jamison Cockerham
Set in Arno, Scala Sans, Gatlin Bold, and Fell DW Pica
by codeMantra

Manufactured in the United States of America

Cover art: *Caswell County Courthouse, Main Street, Yanceyville, Caswell County, NC.*
Courtesy Historic American Buildings Survey, Library of Congress Prints and
Photographs Collection; tobacco field, 1899, courtesy iStock.com/THEPALMER.

Complete Library of Congress Cataloging-in-Publication Data
is available at https://lccn.loc.gov/2023023183.

ISBN 978-1-4696-7470-4 (cloth: alk. paper)
ISBN 978-1-4696-7471-1 (pbk: alk. paper)
ISBN 978-1-4696-7472-8 (ebook)

To Margaret, Ethan, and Avery,

who all have sterling reputations

Contents

Illustrations

Acknowledgments

Acknowledgments are difficult when you have been working on a project for as long as I have tinkered with this book—more than ten years now. I apologize in advance to anyone I omit, and please know that your contribution likely made this a better work.

A range of institutions provided funding and time that supported my research and then helped shepherd this book to the finish line. The Southern Historical Collection at the University of North Carolina awarded a Joel Williamson Visiting Scholar Grant, and the University of Georgia's Willson Center for Humanities and Arts assisted with early research, as did the support of an Andrew W. Mellon Fellowship at Millsaps College. Regular professional development funds from Wright State University and then a year of leave to finish up the research and drafting were instrumental in the later stages. A course release granted by the Jack N. and Addie D. Averitt Distinguished Professorship in Southern History at Georgia Southern University provided assistance as the book made its way through production.

I presented work at several conferences and workshops where audiences and fellow panelists posed thoughtful questions and helpful suggestions. These venues included annual meetings of the Agricultural History Society; the American Society for Environmental History; the National Council on Public History; the Southern Forum on Agricultural, Rural, and Environmental History; and the St. George Tucker Society; special workshops of the Filson Historical Society and the Center for the History of Agriculture, Science, and the Environment of the South at Mississippi State University; and invited talks at Duke University, Georgia Southern University, and Wright

State University. Various deans and chairs over the years endorsed and supported this work, including Linda Caron, David Davis, Kristin Sobolik, Bill Storey, and Jonathan Winkler. Carol Herringer deserves special notice (and maybe some sort of award for patience), having now served as my department chair at two different institutions.

As always, archivists and librarians were indispensable allies. I owe a great deal to the staffs at the University of Georgia, Millsaps College, the Southern Historical Collection, Duke University Special Collections, the North Carolina State Archives, the Chautauqua County Historical Society for their digitization efforts, and the Morrow branch of the National Archives. Wright State University librarians helped me maintain momentum despite the unprecedented hurdles posed by COVID-19 shutdowns.

Many colleagues read portions of this work, listened to me ramble on about tobacco and violence, and offered helpful advice over the past decade. I took some of it and probably ought to have embraced more of their words of wisdom. They include Jim Giesen, Mark Hersey, John Inscoe, Paul Lockhart, Erin Mauldin, Samuel McGuire, Noeleen McIlvenna, Keri Leigh Merritt, Tiya Miles, Sarah Milov, Barton Myers, Steve Nash, Tom Okie, Dwight Pitcaithley, John Sherman, Bill Storey, Paul Sutter, Dan Vivian, and Bert Way. Bruce Baker and Adrienne Petty gave the manuscript a careful evaluation for the press and greatly strengthened it with their feedback, graciously revealing themselves after the fact: I could not ask for better readers. University of North Carolina Press editorial director Mark Simpson-Vos initially encouraged the project, and Brandon Proia was an enthusiastic acquisitions editor, believing that the book belonged at UNC Press and offering a number of useful suggestions. He was also patient and supportive as my first deadline came and went. Andrew Winters then graciously stepped in as the book moved into production. Carol Seigler and Mary Carley Caviness steered the project through submission and production with aplomb. And Julie Bush worked hard to save me from myself in copyedits. This was my first time working with the folks at UNC Press, and they have proven wonderfully efficient.

With each book, I appreciate the love and support of family more and more. To dedicate so much time and attention to such a project requires a sacrifice—and it primarily comes at the expense of those we love. This book thus belongs to Margaret, Ethan, and Avery as much as to me; however, I own all its mistakes.

A MAN
OF BAD
REPUTATION

Introduction

PREMEDITATION

A foul mark on the reputation of the County of Caswell.

RICHARD PEARSON, in "State vs. F. A. Wiley and Others" (1870)

N ot every day did a visitor to the office of the North Carolina Historical Commission in Raleigh confess to a crime, much less to an infamous and long-mysterious murder. But an elderly man making his way down the commission's hallways in the summer of 1919 would do just that. He had an appointment to tell a story dating from his youth, during the state's Reconstruction era. John G. Lea had kept his role in the assassination of a state politician secret for nearly half a century, but the time had arrived to come clean. His was a tale that connected past to present, with confidence in the shape of the future. In it, Lea confessed to helping murder Senator John Walter Stephens in Caswell County in 1870. He calmly, even proudly, explained that the killing had been the work of the county's chapter of the Ku Klux Klan, the deed undertaken for the good of his community. No mere participant, he claimed to have been the architect of the assassination. Lea believed his actions had laid the groundwork for the white supremacy that ruled North Carolina in the early twentieth century, and he was unapologetic about it. He chose to tell this story on July 2, just two days before Independence Day.

John G. Lea testified to being head of the Caswell County chapter of the Ku Klux Klan and orchestrator of the assassination of Senator John Walter Stephens. "Lea, John G.," in the Portrait Collection #P0002, North Carolina Collection Photographic Archives, Wilson Library, University of North Carolina at Chapel Hill.

The officials hearing Lea's confession—some of the state's most prominent keepers of public memory—hardly needed convincing that the event had been of great importance. The murder of so long ago had far-reaching effects, echoing beyond the courthouse basement where the senator was killed and linking events in his small town of Yanceyville to state and national upheavals as the meaning and results of the Civil War were still being contested. It had provoked North Carolina's governor, William Woods Holden, to declare part of the state in insurrection and impose martial law in an effort to stamp out the Klan. When Holden ordered troops to Caswell and neighboring Alamance County to arrest suspected Klansmen, it launched weeks of conflict that came to be known as the Kirk-Holden War (Colonel George Kirk was the commanding officer of the state forces). When this effort to root out the Klan fell apart, Holden's political opponents used the debacle to impeach the governor in an effort to "redeem" the state from Republican governance. The effects rippled outward. The killing and the state's political struggles featured prominently in the US Congress's investigation of Klan activities in the South, a review that eventually led to the Enforcement Acts that all but ended the first Klan's organized domestic terrorism. But it also factored in a chain of events that resulted in the entrenchment of Jim Crow in the state, a new and even more effective form of white supremacy that used "soft" terrorism in place of the Klan's overt violence.

John Stephens's death deserves a more prominent place in our Reconstruction histories, not because he was an exemplary statesman or principled leader (there is reason for doubt on both fronts) but because the circumstances of his murder and its aftermath contributed to momentous shifts in the policies and tactics of the time. Within the state, the assassination and the Kirk-Holden War that followed became a hinge: the door to a postwar North Carolina of full black citizenship and more democratic politics had seemed partially open, but it began to swing closed in 1870, in part because of the blood spilled in that Caswell County Courthouse basement. And North Carolina Conservatives' model of violent resistance to Republican governance, followed by political backlash against any effort to circumscribe those attacks, was representative of strategies across the South. The Stephens murder was a seminal early moment in North Carolina's Redemption and part of a wave of kindred regional violence that struck a crucial blow to Reconstruction writ large. It was both unique and typical, as contradictory as such a claim may seem on its face. Lea and his co-conspirators did not make the failure of the state's Reconstruction inevitable by shedding Stephens's blood, nor were they sanguine about shaping state and national discourses, but their violence became a spark that contributed to a great conflagration.

Competing stories were born in the same room where Stephens died. The memory of the event, shaped and reshaped in the decades that followed, became over time at least as important as the deed itself. John Lea's interview with the Historical Commission was neither the first nor the final account of the murder, and the killing became a touchstone in the tales that North Carolinians told themselves and others about Reconstruction in the state. Who Stephens was and why he was killed proved malleable in public memory. He alternately fit the role of heel and martyr, and his killers—even during the long years in which their identities remained unknown—were likewise cast as both heroes and villains, depending on who was telling the story. These narratives shifted to suit the times, helping us trace the evolution of local and national ideas about Reconstruction, race, and reconciliation. Like all history, each account revealed as much about its teller and era as it did about the murder and subsequent mystery. For example, Lea's choice of moment and audience reflected the politics of the time. He opted to go on record near the height of Jim Crow and at a date when a second Ku Klux Klan was emerging and to speak to public officials who had important roles in establishing the Lost Cause and the notion of a tragic and corrupt Reconstruction in North Carolina. Lea felt comfortable that he was among friends, or at least kindred spirits, and that conditions were right for North Carolinians (white ones, anyway) to appreciate his story.

The ghost of John Stephens has long haunted Reconstruction historiography. His contested memory swirled around the trial to find his killers and the impeachment proceedings that deposed Governor Holden, which were both judgments of reputation as much as fact. His life and death were woven into North Carolina apologists' explanations of Klan violence and likewise featured in the Dunning School and Lost Cause portrayals of Reconstruction as a corrupt era. Later, national scholars would rehabilitate Stephens and prop him up as an early civil rights hero, even as many state histories clung to older visions of an abusive and greedy politician. Today, prompted by a renewed racial justice movement's frank reassessment of the nation's failure to live up to the fullest promises of Reconstruction, Stephens's story might reclaim its past importance. Hints of this can be found in North Carolina, for example, in a multipart collaborative journalism project published by ProPublica and the *Raleigh News and Observer* exploring how current activists are drawing on Alamance County's troubled racial legacy to shape its present.[1]

By tracing Stephens's death, we can follow the tale of Reconstruction violence from a dusty courthouse basement through the fields of the rural South to the North Carolina capital and on to Capitol Hill. But his death and memory also serve as reminders of the importance of local factors in shaping Reconstruction. For example, the details of rural and agricultural history—what David Harvey calls a community's "socio-ecological order"— are crucial in explaining much of southern Reconstruction.[2] Scholars are still unpacking the ways Reconstruction played out across the rural South, adding to better-known histories of urban places like Memphis and New Orleans.[3] In this stretch of countryside, race and politics were central to the killing, but so was tobacco. The region relied on the crop from the early years of its colonial settlement, and it remains important to local agriculture to this day. The plant shaped the landscape: tobacco culture guided the clearance of forests, the siting of towns, the construction of railroads, and the size of farms. It set the rhythm of seasons, bending human bodies to its botanical needs, even as farmers used breeding and cultivation to shape it. At various points in their lives, both Stephens and Lea bought and sold bright leaf, the desirable local variety of the crop, and many of the senator's other killers also relied on tobacco to make their livings. Among other things, the Klansmen accused the senator of encouraging African Americans to demand higher wages for their farm labor, to file lawsuits over the division of crops, and to burn tobacco barns as a method of political intimidation. The substantial wealth that bright tobacco could generate gave economic weight to these accusations and actions. No understanding of how Reconstruction played out in North Carolina's northern Piedmont can be complete without taking tobacco agriculture into account.[4]

We likewise can grasp only part of the following story unless we remember the intrinsic and lasting messiness of the Civil War. In North Carolina, as in the rest of the South, this had meant a divisive and violent home front that tore families and communities apart, even as it mussed long-tangled state and local politics into a snarl. At war's end the Confederate dream of a southern slave republic lay shattered; only the debris remained. North Carolina had been slow to join the Confederate cause but suffered a full measure of devastation just the same. Veterans returned home, often with their bodies or minds mangled. Widows found new husbands, or did not. Sons assumed the mantles of fallen fathers—or rejected their course. Fallow fields needed tending. There were fences to mend and barns to rebuild. And much of this work entailed continued fighting: with oneself, with expectations, against other people. In recent years historians have rightly highlighted how the violence of the Civil War bled into the 1870s, both in racially motivated massacres and violence at the polls and in the nation's accelerating expansion westward. Former Confederates waged war on freedpeople, some African Americans took up arms to secure their new rights, and the Union army turned its full might on Native Americans.[5] Indeed, as Justin Behrend observes, the "fighting during Reconstruction was not all that different from irregular warfare during the Civil War."[6] This internecine warfare was quite often as much a community struggle as a national one, something fully revealed in the pages that follow.

Part of what makes Stephens's case so fascinating is the way in which his life, death, and memory serve as a window into the nation's Reconstruction experience. Stephens and his killers were in turns noble and petty, loyal and opportunistic. They were driven to better their situations and fearful of what change might bring. They were willing to mete out violence to serve their ends, and in the end, they tasted violence as well. Like the United States of the second half of the nineteenth century, they were neither innocent nor rotten to the core. Small-scale history (or "microhistory," as it is sometimes called) has the power to furnish names and faces to these seemingly impersonal forces and to remind us of the humanity and contingency of past events. Its focused and narrative form has been used to good effect in explaining the centrality of race in southern history, from the struggles of free black landownership in the early Chesapeake, to the convolutions of slavery on the colonial frontier, to the workings of the judicial system in the antebellum cotton South, to the construction and challenging of Jim Crow in the Yazoo-Mississippi Delta.[7] Indeed, southern historians seem particularly drawn to this form to illuminate episodes of racial violence, perhaps from a desire to find in personal stories some explanation for a region that seemed especially inhumane.[8] Closer to this tale, a set of microhistories of North Carolina's and Virginia's Piedmont in the nineteenth and twentieth centuries proved notably influential on the pages that follow, including the work of Bryant Simon, Claude Clegg III, Suzanne Lebsock, Henry Wiencek, Eric Rise, and Richard Sherman.[9]

And Stephens's assassination is quite a story, dramatic in its own right. The killing and its aftermath contain all the elements of a Faulkner novel. People with a deep-rooted sense of place, the tragedy of southern race relations, the long shadow of the Civil War, dependence on a demanding staple crop, the omnipresence of the past, the continuous rewriting of what "actually happened": these forces were all at play in Caswell County. The tale also comes with a plot, something absent from much historical work. Drawing on this, there is an element of murder mystery in the story that follows, a structure rooted in contemporary events as much as a literary device. Sadly, like most Faulkner novels and other southern gothic works, the tragedy in the tale threatens to overwhelm the glimmers of hope.

Also akin to the fluid nature of Faulkner's writing, it is difficult to pin down exactly what "type" of history best explains Stephens's life, death, and afterlife. His is a story of race in the American South. Even though he and his killers were white, the political and social questions of the place and the age were almost always inflected with racial animosity. Stephens may have been a "scalawag" (a white Republican), but his political power was rooted in newly enfranchised African American men. It is a Civil War era tale— as noted above—and participants grappled with the war and its outcomes. Agriculture and the environment furnish the history's backbone, as the soil and its dominant crop lured Stephens to the region and helped convince Lea and his co-conspirators that there were opportunities worth killing for at stake. This is also political history, of course: How could the assassination of a politician by his opponents be otherwise? And it is public history, once Stephens's death entered the realm of memory, transmuting into ink on the page, lines carved in stone, and letters cast in iron. What follows is each of these sorts of histories, but best understood as a fusion of them all.

So many elements each being their own portion of the total tale are in this volume fused together to better understand all elements

This small-story form does more than just make for engaging narrative; it also captures something essential yet often overlooked in our Reconstruction histories. The struggles and violence of the era were not solely the product of big historical events, like the war and emancipation, or the broad political frameworks of Republicans and Democrats. They were also enmeshed in the personal relationships of the people involved, the product of their daily lives. They came out of mud and blood as much as elections and state constitutions. In this story, who was killed and who killed him owed as much to individual aspirations and animosities as to the big forces at work in the state and nation. It was memory, memorialization, and, finally, the writing of history that compressed the messiness of multiple lives into a comprehensible narrative and tested meanings, much as a man might try on several jackets in search of just the right cut for the times.

PERSONAL

Indeed, Stephens's story that follows is an account of two lives. The first is one man's experience in the tumult and possibility of the years that followed on the heels of the Civil War. Stephens's life embodied the nation's Reconstruction experience. While alive, his actions were always contextual, guided and embedded within his personality, experiences, and place. Like

*2 Themes
How he lived his life*

the experiment of Reconstruction itself, his deeds seemed at times a contradictory stew: noble, ambitious, foolish, avaricious, brave, magnanimous, vindictive, unfinished. From our distant perspective, Stephens might appear both admirable and distasteful. Stephens's second life is found in his memory, how his actions and killing came to be interpreted in the wake of his death: his "afterlife," if you will. This, too, is instructive in considering the American experience. As Stephens was transformed from martyr to devil and back again, his legacy paralleled white Americans' perceptions of the Reconstruction era.[10] The senator's story is a reminder of the symbolic power of individual lives, especially when those lives coincided with seminal historical moments. Stephens will never be as famous as Thomas Jefferson, John Brown, or Robert E. Lee, just to name three men whose memories have proved at least as significant and contested as the lives they led.[11] Yet the malleability of his legacy is in many ways akin to theirs, his symbolic meaning overlapping his actual actions. The result is a historical figure who may not bear a great deal of resemblance to the actual man.

Which leads to some necessary caveats. Not all meanings are fully recoverable. For example, black voices are crucial to the story that follows, although they are still underrepresented in the source material. African Americans were perhaps more deeply invested in Reconstruction than any other portion of the nation's people, and freedpeople actively worked to shape the meaning of emancipation, to make it mean more than just freedom. In Stephens they found, and then lost, an important ally. As much as they offer this story through actions and testimony, there are disproportionately few black voices preserved in the record to give full accounting of that hope and loss. In a few spots they speak out—for example, in the words and works of dynamic individuals such as Wyatt Outlaw, Wilson Carey, and Patsie Burton, and in the later writing and memory-making of scholars like W. E. B. Du Bois and John Hope Franklin—but in other places their actions and desires are filtered through impersonal records or the voices of whites. The silences in the archives, the monuments not erected—these gaps in the past must be considered as carefully as what made it onto the page or was carved into stone.[12] This tale is thus rooted in the white experience of North Carolina's Reconstruction, perhaps more than readers might wish. Still, in this flawed seed is perhaps a useful germ. In historians' extensive and laudable recent work in highlighting the black Reconstruction experience, the scholarship has turned away from the old political stories of white squabbles. This is understandable, given the real and crucial racial turmoil of the era and earlier histories' penchant for omitting or disparaging African American aspirations and deeds. Yet North Carolina's Reconstruction experience was grounded in real political and social divisions among whites as well as blacks, a fractured landscape long in the making, and these divisions deserve a fresh look in conjunction with fuller treatment of the African American experience. Stephens's death is a story that might unite these two historiographies.[13]

If our knowledge of contemporary black perceptions of these events is incomplete, there are also limitations on how perfectly we can understand even the central figures of Stephens and Lea. There is only so far we can go down the rabbit hole. Microhistories are reconstructions rather than revelations, and individuals are ultimately unknowable. When trying to breathe life back into Stephens, Lea, the Piedmont's rural freedpeople, and Yanceyville's townsfolk, we can read the scraps of their written words that survive and judiciously weigh what neighbors said about one another, and, perhaps most importantly, we must place these interpretations in the context of place and time as best we can rebuild them. This context is multilayered and includes local communities, Caswell County, North Carolina, the South, and the nation on the morning after a cataclysmic war. But, despite the most strenuous efforts, we can never truly know what is behind the mask of another's face. It is only in the moments where we look at someone else and for a fleeting second realize that his or her life is as intense as our own that we recognize the depths of our inability to truly commiserate. And, as Robert Penn Warren notes, even this brief recognition that strangers, too, are "complete and individual, the center of a world as real and important" as our own, is always incomplete and fleeting.[14] This is the vicarious pleasure of biography after all: to know the unknowable, or for a moment to pretend that we do. But in the end we must acknowledge that, no matter how hard the historian digs, much of the past remains only a short step beyond an educated guess. Still, moving forward starts with taking a step.

One

PROMISE

The soil itself soon sickens and dies beneath the unnatural tread of the slave.

Hinton Rowan Helper, *The Impending Crisis of the South* (1857)

t was an unlikely place for a boom. The rolling red clay hills of the North Carolina and Virginia line, part of the Piedmont between the flat coastal plain and the Appalachian Mountains, had never been the center of anything important, at least from a Euro-American perspective. Settlers began trickling into the region in the mid-eighteenth century, more than a hundred years after Jamestown's founding, despite its close proximity to colonial beachheads. The Chesapeake Bay lay just a hundred miles to the east, but the Piedmont had long served as its western frontier. Patrician planter William Byrd provided the first detailed description of the region when his party, tasked with surveying the state line, trekked through its forested hills in 1728. He reported that this stretch of the Piedmont was a landscape of clear rivers and streams, thick forests, and rich bottomlands of black soil covered in a luxurious growth of river cane. Bears, deer, and wild turkeys were present in abundance, and Byrd also observed creatures that were soon to disappear. Sandhill cranes flew over his party, mountain lions and red wolves screamed and howled in the night, and even a few buffalo trotted through the woods. It seemed a fat land, and Byrd claimed a large tract of it on speculation. He called his portion of the newfound paradise "Eden."[1]

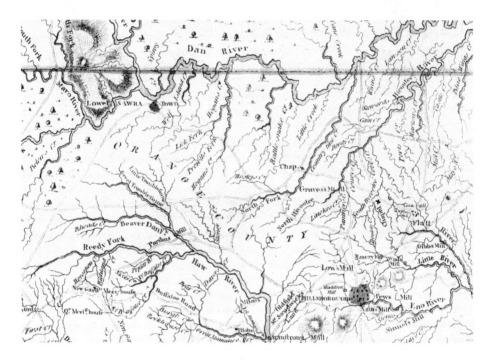

This detail from a 1770 map highlights the numerous waterways that bisected the land that would become Caswell County. Detail from John Collet and J. Bayly, *A Compleat Map of North-Carolina from an Actual Survey* (London: S. Hooper, 1770), Library of Congress.

It turned out that this Eden was not quite the land of milk and honey it seemed at first sight. Indeed, the name had more to do with Byrd's hopes to sell tracts of his real estate venture to European settlers than with any intrinsic qualities of the land; if it took visions of paradise on earth to turn heavenly profits, so be it.[2] The Piedmont's steep hills and their sandy topsoils, which were vulnerable to gullying erosion once they were cleared for agriculture, did not prove very tempting to colonial farmers. Only once the coastal regions of both colonies had filled in with plantations and steady tobacco cultivation had led to soil exhaustion did settlers begin to make their way into the Piedmont in significant numbers. Second sons, the poor, land speculators, and recent Scots-Irish immigrants carved out farms in the pines and oaks in the years leading up to the Revolution, first taking up tracts in the more fertile bottomlands along the region's numerous small rivers and creeks and then in the sandier, less-productive uplands.[3]

Nature may have extended only a modest welcome, but from the colonists' perspective the land appeared to be virtually free for the taking. The

Chapter One

Piedmont where North Carolina and Virginia met was a land with very few Indian peoples by the early eighteenth century. The region existed in the space between the once-powerful Native American federations of the Chesapeake and societies like the Catawba and Cherokee to the west. The Occaneechi, Saura, and other peoples had once lived along the border rivers, which the English would name the Dan and Staunton upstream from their merger to form the Roanoke River. But the epidemic diseases that came with cultural contact and the bloody work of earlier colonial conflicts, like the attacks on the Occaneechi orchestrated by Nathaniel Bacon in the 1670s, had killed or driven away most Indigenous people a generation prior. Settlers staked out their land claims in a man-made wilderness.[4]

Some of those settlers who did find their way into the Piedmont—a place often styled the "backcountry," highlighting its secondary qualities and consideration—found themselves in a new North Carolina county: Caswell. It was carved from the northern side of Orange County in 1777 and named for then governor Richard Caswell. After a further division in 1792 created Person County from the eastern half of Caswell, the county's final borders formed a slightly imperfect square a little over twenty miles to a side, with the Virginia line forming the northern boundary and the county seat located in the middle. In Caswell and adjoining counties these settlers replicated the social and cultural patterns of the Tidewater, if in more meager forms. Tobacco became the main cash crop with wheat a distant second. This was simply practical. Tobacco sold for a relatively high price per weight, while wheat and other grains hardly covered their transportation costs in a land of poor roads and shallow, rocky rivers. Corn and oats fed man and beast. Hogs and cattle were numerous but ill-attended, spending most of their lives foraging and multiplying in the woods that served as fuel lots, hunting grounds, and common livestock range. This truncated plantation complex brought with it enslavement. From the very first settlement of the region, wealthier whites brought bound African Americans with them, a stream of forced migration intermingled with the voluntary one, and many poor whites aspired to one day own slaves of their own. The nation's first census following the Revolution, taken in 1790, recorded that more than a quarter of Caswell County's 10,096 people (2,736) were enslaved. Sixty years later, enslavement had increased in importance, and bound people now outnumbered free in the county: 7,770 to 7,076.[5] It may not have been a place of grandee planters, but Caswell was firmly wedded to enslavement from its colonial days.

If the Piedmont as a whole was no promised land, Caswell County was one of its more out-of-the-way corners. In general, North Carolina's Piedmont counties trailed their Virginia neighbors in population, development, and prosperity into the mid-nineteenth century. Poor transportation networks were a factor in this slow growth. A modest tributary of the Roanoke River, the Dan, snaked back and forth across the state line, but its shifting sandbars and rocky riffles inhibited the traffic of boats larger than slim bateaux, and even those small canoe-like craft floated well in dry seasons only with the help of regular channel improvements. Below the Dan's and Staunton's juncture, the Roanoke River was still choked by rapids and sandbars. Compounding the problem, the Roanoke emptied not into the deep water of the Chesapeake Bay, one of the world's best natural harbors, but instead into North Carolina's Albemarle Sound, a broad but shallow body of water that lacked a safe outlet to the Atlantic for large ships. Seventy-five miles to the north, in the valley of the James River, which flowed into the mighty Chesapeake, farmers had much better transportation prospects, reducing the incentive to settle on the Roanoke's branches. Throughout the Piedmont, towns were rare and dispersed settlement the norm.[6] Much of Caswell's land seemed as unpromising as its rivers: its forests of pines and scrubby oaks, its steep hollows and sloping uplands, and its sandy topsoil underlain with stiff red and yellow clays were all marginal in farmers' eyes.

Still, by 1800 the place seemed safely settled. At the county seat of Caswell Court House (eventually to be renamed Yanceyville), citizens conducted court business, paid taxes, voted, and shopped in a few stores. Farmers made substantial tobacco crops and rolled their cured leaf north in wooden barrels, known as hogsheads, to the warehouses in Danville, Virginia, or to river landings where they could be shipped east.[7] And the population grew steadily, especially the number of enslaved people, most of whom labored at growing tobacco. As the Tidewater faded under the burden of depleted soils and cutover forests, scrub pines waving over its abandoned fields like natural flags of surrender, the Piedmont seemed in the process of absorbing the old district's losses.[8] Missionaries evangelizing in the county professed shock that at least one-third of the more than 1,300 families they visited in Caswell in 1829 had no Bible in their homes, but residents' secular interests seemed on surer footing.[9] Tobacco raised on a mixture of small farms and larger plantations, cultivated by both free and enslaved labor, promised a path to prosperity. For a generation or two, modest success seemed to be Caswell's future.

Then this footing quickly began to give way. The restless western movement that spilled farmers into the Piedmont just before the Revolution only accelerated in the new nation, as the violent displacement of Native Americans in the mid-continent and the technological innovations of the Industrial

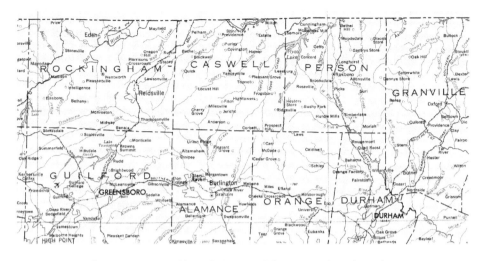

Caswell County's eventual boundaries. Detail from *State of North Carolina, Base Map* (Reston, VA: United States Geological Survey, 1972), Library of Congress.

Revolution opened the vast Midwest and the Gulf South in great chunks to the sons and daughters of the old colonies. Accounts of the cheap and fertile lands of Ohio and Alabama, with their miraculous stands of corn, cotton rows vanishing against the horizon, and vast hardwood river bottoms, were the stories on every tongue, and they drew eastern people like iron filings to a magnet. By the early 1840s the whispers of "Gone to Texas" were everywhere spoken out loud. The dream of a new frontier was a nightmare for the old coastal South.[10]

In Caswell, planter George Jeffreys felt the pull that fresh land exerted on local farm families. In response Jeffreys embraced agricultural improvement, a national movement then sweeping the Piedmont that promoted the idea that more intensive cultivation (in his case relying on enslaved laborers) could renew old land and restore agrarian prosperity.[11] He wrote a farming manual, joined the county's Red House Agricultural Society, and even corresponded with Thomas Jefferson on agricultural subjects. But all of Jeffreys's work failed to keep his family together in North Carolina. His son-in-law, seemingly so well positioned for local success, purchased land in Louisiana, where sugar and cotton promised greater profits than did tobacco, and was preparing for a move that would take that branch of the family far from home. Jeffreys lamented in his diary, "My Lord has it come to this[?]"[12]

H. P. Womack also fled Caswell for fresh land in Tennessee, writing his relative Pleasant back home of the freedom and opportunity he found in the

West.[13] Many others followed Jeffreys's son-in-law's and Womack's paths westward. Some planters mimicked Jeffreys, seeking to improve local farms with more intense agricultural work and soil conservation measures, in hopes of stemming the tide.[14] Meanwhile, other county residents, like Joseph Totten, saw ways to profit from the exodus. Totten sold black Caswellians to buyers in the Deep South as a slave trader between the 1830s and 1850s and invested some of the resulting profits in Mississippi land.[15] In his specialization in selling people "down the river" in order to buy his own share of the promised land, Totten exemplified a form of slavery that was at least as capitalist as it was "feudal."[16] And so Virginians and North Carolinians, both white and black, headed over the mountains to the new lands by the tens of thousands, and the backcountry became a place to the "back" of two regions instead of just one.[17]

In Caswell, some observers saw local people themselves to blame for this erosion of land and human capital, believing that migration stemmed from "push" as well as "pull" factors. Improvident farming had undermined the system, they argued, sending the county's precious and fragile topsoil downhill and then downstream, leaving a wasteland of gullies and galled fields in its place.[18] And tobacco came in for the severest indictments, since reformers saw in its intense cultivation the worst soil wastage.[19] Jeffreys, the county's most vocal agricultural sage who wrote agrarian tracts under the pseudonym "Agricola," had published a book-length jeremiad in 1819 predicting the depopulation of the Piedmont if serious reform did not occur. He declared regional farming to be "a land-killing system," one that could result only "in want, misery and depopulation."[20] This grasping agriculture was, ultimately, "a crime of the first magnitude."[21] Caswell's sons and daughters were not so much lured away as driven by the sins of their fathers, and even Jeffreys's foresight failed to prevent his own family from following the same path.

Then came the discovery of gold . . . of a sort. Piedmont tobacco growers tinkered with and then mastered techniques for producing a form of yellow cured tobacco. This "bright leaf," as it came to be known, was an especially mild and sweet tobacco that became wildly fashionable for chewing tobacco in an age when many Americans chewed twists and plugs. (Later in the century it would also become a main ingredient in cigarettes.) Wrapped around the outside of a piece of chewing tobacco, a fine bright leaf served as both flavoring and an advertisement of the quality ingredients that manufacturers promised lay within their product. Caswell was the cradle of this bright tobacco boom, with the first reliable crops coming from its tired and gullied fields. The crop's origin myths vary, but most attribute the pioneering work to the planter Abisha Slade and his relatives and often credit an enslaved man, Stephen, with the accidental discovery of the best curing method. If the details are fuzzy, the mix of forces at work seems clearer: planters, relying on enslaved labor, pursued some way to make a familiar crop and tired land pay better. They sought a miracle from a crop that had driven Piedmont plantation culture for more than a century. The precise date the variety came to be is also hazy, but by 1850 Caswell landowners had full-fledged bright tobacco fever, and the affliction was spreading to adjoining districts. The crop offered hope that the Piedmont had found a staple that might rival the profitability of Deep South cotton.[22]

Like antebellum gold rushes, golden tobacco simultaneously came from paying close attention to the land and from ignoring its environmental limits. The landscape was a benefactor to be read and studied as well as an object of pillage to be plundered of its tightly held resources. The smoothest, mildest, and brightest yellow tobacco crops came from fields that farmers had all but given up on as worthless. In what seemed like a miraculous twist of fate, these crop qualities were in part the result of nutrient starvation. Low nitrogen levels, normally a detriment in agricultural soils, instead proved a boon for creating desirable bright leaf. Old fields became renewed sources of farm profit, and Caswell's farmers cut more and more forest to transform it into yellow tobacco land. Even the old labor-intensive work of manuring the land to maintain soil fertility fell by the wayside. That these practices defied old rules concerning wise cultivation was troubling for some farmers, but in the face of promised wealth they often proved willing to set aside such concerns.[23]

This seemingly providential crop did come with challenges. It required farmers to master complicated curing techniques and new forms of cultivation and encouraged them to build new tobacco barns and, as the technology advanced, to purchase or build curing furnaces. It also posed conservation hazards. Wood disappeared by the thousands of cords into curing fires, further deforesting an intensively farmed countryside. And the soils beneath the tobacco fields and cutover land proved quite fragile. The topsoil was thin and sandy, and under it in most areas lay a stratum of slick red or yellow clay. In heavy rains, water cut through the sandy upper layer and, striking the impermeable clay below, sheeted downhill sideways carrying liquified topsoil with it. Especially on Caswell's characteristic hillsides, the county's farmland literally melted away under intense summer thunderstorms and winter's cycles of freeze and thaw. Farmers struggled to come to grips with these contradictions: poor land made good crops, but only until that poor land was gone, run downhill to choke the region's creek bottoms and rivers. Above those now swampy waterways lay denuded and gullied clay ridges, bare and red like the ribs of some great carcass. Faced with these scenes, how might Caswell's tobacco growers imagine that bad stewardship made for a good farmer?[24]

Still, the abusive cultivation produced tidy profits for a time, fattening wallets even as it spent down soil. New endeavors swept the county, a buzz of energy that echoed the call of tobacco auctioneers selling another hogshead of bright leaf. Tobacco manufacturing facilities organized in the small town of Milton on the Dan River in the northeastern corner of the county, producing twists and bars of chewing tobacco, each wrapped with a "fancy" yellow leaf that promised smooth yet flavorful interiors. Other small tobacco factories popped up across the countryside; eleven were in operation by 1860. Collectively the county's tobacco industries employed 352 people that year, putting them and more than a quarter of a million dollars in invested capital to work to produce $345,400 worth of twists and plugs.[25]

Other businesses emerged as well. Gristmills and sawmills were at work at the falls of streams, and shoe and saddle makers, tanners, machinists, carriage builders, a blacksmith, and foundries sold products and services across the county. None was particularly large, but all relied on the growth brought by the tobacco economy. Aside from the tobacco interests, the most important local industry was the Yarborough foundry on Country Line Creek, which turned out agricultural implements for wealthy farmers, as well as iron spoons, stoves, and kettles. The Yarborough complex included a flour mill, wood shop, and machine shop in addition to the foundry.[26] Farmers sometimes doubled as manufacturers or retailers, blurring the lines between agriculture and industry. Philip Howerton and Thomas Easley, for example, were licensed to construct and sell "Dr. Clark's patent threshing machine" in Caswell and surrounding counties. Howerton also contemplated constructing a commercial charcoal kiln to produce tobacco-curing fuel for the district, and many of the tobacco factory owners also raised the crop that supplied their manufacturing.[27]

In the countryside surrounding Yanceyville and Milton, famed architect Dabney Cosby worked to build homes for newly affluent planters.[28] Enterprising tobacco growers took city newspapers and state or regional agricultural journals and read classic agronomy texts like John Taylor's *Arator*—along with the work of their own George Jeffreys—to keep abreast of the news and experiments in cultivation.[29] Some of them sent their daughters to the Somerville Female Institute in Leasburg, on Caswell's eastern edge, where principal Solomon Lea assured parents that "probably there is no other community in which a School could be located for the training of youth, that exerts so little of unfavorable influence, and affords greater facilities for forming virtuous principles and correct habits of life."[30] And growers throughout Caswell kept in touch with William Sutherlin, of Pittsylvania County, just across the Virginia line. Sutherlin was the driving entrepreneurial force behind the region's most substantial tobacco factory, Sutherlin and Ferrell, and an influential booster of the railroad then extending tie after tie from Richmond toward Danville. Along with prominent Caswell planters he worked to improve regional transportation networks in order to bring bright tobacco more easily to market.[31]

More than any other phenomenon, the increase in local land prices demonstrated planters' belief that tobacco would pay, and pay handsomely. In an age when farmland from Maryland to South Carolina seemed old and worn-out in comparison to tracts in the southwest, Caswell and the few border counties surrounding it saw prices inflate as if they were in the Gulf South. These valuations started early in the boom: in 1846 Caswell was forty-fifth in the state in population out of seventy-seven counties, but its land was the sixth highest in total value. These prices continued to climb in the 1850s, with the result that farms that a short time prior had brought just fifty cents per acre jumped in value nearly a hundredfold, with some selling for as much as fifty dollars per acre on their promise for producing bright leaf.[32] Some people who had emigrated seeking brighter agrarian frontiers came back to the county. H. P. Womack planned his return from Tennessee in 1853, and John Flintoff, who first left the North Carolina Piedmont for Mississippi in 1841, moved to Caswell in 1854 and finally found profitability in tobacco cultivation.[33] As two nineteenth-century agricultural writers observed, "The yellow-tobacco interest of North Carolina proved far more beneficial to the whole population than the finding of gold would have been."[34]

This "gold rush" thesis paid no attention to the fate of enslaved people, of course. Some county families realized great wealth, but at the expense of human bondage as well as exploitation of the land. Enslavement expanded as fast as or faster than the increase in tobacco acreage. Between 1850 and 1860, the enslaved population grew by more than 1,500 people, even as the white population shrank by about 500, as wealthy planters squeezed out smaller farms.[35] By 1860 only five North Carolina counties were home to more enslaved people than Caswell, all of them to the east and longer settled.[36] Some plantations had grown quite large. Isabella Glenn, for example, owned

Handwritten margin note: Land prices / larget became / perceived / they believed / the Tobacco / would be / King Forever.

108 people when she passed away in the late 1840s.[37] In 1860, J. L. Garland laid claim to 116 people, and W. L. Stamps held another 115 individuals in bondage. Samuel Hairston owned 45 slaves who labored in the county, but that substantial workforce was but part of a sprawling plantation empire that spread across Virginia and North Carolina (Hairston himself lived across the state line in Virginia), altogether drawing on the bound labor of more than 1,000 human beings. The average county slaveholder owned more than 12 people, and nearly one in five masters held 20 or more people in slavery, the latter a figure historians often use to denote a "planter." Caswell County's devotion to slavery thus exceeded the state's average.[38]

Wealth and enslavement concentrated in particular families, such as the Leas. In the 1860 census, James, S. L., and Sidney Lea each owned between 50 and 60 enslaved people, and their relatives John, "W.," and William Lea possessed between 20 and 50 people each.[39] The Leas had long been influential figures in Caswell, amassing capital in the form of land and human beings and translating that wealth into political and social power. The first Lea arrived in the region during the colonial era, and a William Lea helped organize the first county seat and operated the jail in the years after Caswell's initial borders were drawn in 1777. In recognition of his service, William was made a town trustee and the village was named Leasburg. Another Lea, Solomon, built a reputation as an educator. He taught at Virginia's Randolph-Macon College, became president of Greensboro (NC) Female College, and then opened the Somerville Female Institute in his hometown of Leasburg in 1848.[40]

Planters may have dominated public life, but there were some free people of color in Caswell who carved out their own lives in the narrow space between enslavement and true freedom.[41] By far the most successful was Thomas Day, a cabinetmaker in the small town of Milton. Day opened a workshop in the 1820s and gained renown for his fine furniture and architectural carpentry that adorned regional plantation houses throughout the Dan River valley. By 1850 Day himself owned 13 slaves, some working on a farm he owned outside of town and the others laboring in his cabinet shop. He earned the business and, it seems, the admiration of many white neighbors, who welcomed him as a member into the town's Presbyterian church.[42] In 1830 a number of white Milton residents also petitioned the state's General Assembly on his behalf. North Carolina had recently passed legislation that sought to make the immigration of free blacks difficult. Day had married Aquilla Wilson of nearby Halifax County, Virginia, and naturally wished his new wife to join him in Milton. The petitioners pled that the assembly make an exception to the immigration statute in this case, waiving all "fines and

**Thomas Day operated his woodworking shop from this building in
Milton.** Thomas T. Waterman, *Union Tavern, Main Street between
Lee Street & Farmer's Alley, Milton, Caswell County, NC*, Historic
American Buildings Survey, 1940, Library of Congress.

penalties" since Day was "a first rate workman, a remarkably sober, steady
and industrious man, a highminded, good and valuable citizen, possessing a
handsome property in this town." Day would remain locally prominent into
the 1850s, before the financial panic of 1857 and failing health undermined
his business.[43]

Day was exceptional. A few of Caswell's black people were free and found
economic and social stability, but they were a decided minority as the Civil
War approached. The county's free black population shrank from 423 in 1850
to just 282 in 1860, even as the enslaved population and the number of tobacco
planters grew.[44] Slaveholding produced the wealth that built county seats and
planters' big houses and funded educations at schools like Somerville, and it
came at an enormous human cost. Here, as elsewhere across the South, the
potential for extraordinary violence lurked underneath the surface of the
system. Masters may have argued for the pacific, even beneficent, nature of
southern slavery, but fears of rebellion and the realities of abuse were never
far from mind. One particularly dramatic tale might stand in for this lurking
evil. Dave Lawson, once enslaved in North Carolina's northern Piedmont,
remembered some of the worst aspects of bondage in his stories of a particularly cruel and avaricious master named Drew Norwood. Many years later
an oral historian collected Lawson's memories, recording them in the racially

charged dialect often used to represent the speech of black southerners in the early twentieth century. An element of visceral fear remained in the tales he related more than a half century after slavery's end.[45]

Norwood operated a plantation, Lawson remembered, but the bulk of his fortune came from trading in slaves. Rumors circulated that he even stole slaves from other masters—and, like the chattel the law said they were, "fatten[ed]" them up—for sale to the Deep South. The accusations of cruelty piled up. Norwood beat his own slaves, going so far as to kill a woman he caught fleeing to a neighboring planter in an attempt to expose her abuse. Inverting the common contemporary trope of slaves as bestial, Lawson recalled that Norwood physically resembled "a mad bull." "De debil done lit a lamp an' set it burnin' in his eyes," which glared out from above teeth "like a mad dog's." His cruel reputation grew until his name was used to scare misbehaving slave children.[46]

Lawson went on to describe how his own grandparents Cleve and Lissa had put an end to Norwood's terror by breaking the cardinal rule of enslavement—they had violently rebelled. Norwood came to take Lissa to sell in South Boston, a tobacco town just across the Virginia line in Halifax County. But the couple fought back against this separation. They subdued and tied up the slave trader and then killed him by pouring boiling water down his throat through a funnel. In an act that mirrored Norwood's cruelty, they burned up a man who had an insatiable hunger for turning slaves into money. But Cleve and Lissa's escape was fleeting. Their crime was discovered, and they were arrested by the local sheriff and then seized by an angry mob, which killed them. In Lawson's tale the crowd lynched his grandparents with the very rope they had used to bind Norwood. Lawson's message was plain: Cleve and Lissa had thwarted an abusive master but could not fully escape the bonds of enslavement, at least not in life. The system was even more voracious and powerful than the cruelest individual man.[47] Real, embroidered, or imagined, Lawson's story captured the ragged edges of enslavement. It was a world in which masters feared bloody rebellion from the people they claimed were content, while slaves rightly feared greedy masters who might "put them in their pocket." Worse yet was mob violence, which might put them in their graves.

Indeed, in its drive for quick wealth made from bright tobacco, Caswell seemed determined to remake itself in the image of the Deep South. There is much in its antebellum economy and society that resembled the cotton southwest, the booming frontier of Alabama's Black Belt, the alluvial bottomlands of the Mississippi Delta, and the sugar districts of Louisiana's German

Coast.[48] Caswell would never be dominated by a planter aristocracy to the same extent as those newer southwestern frontiers, but the 1850s did see the county's reliance on slavery expand, presumably at the expense of yeomen and the landless poor. And the tobacco that lay at the heart of this economy of sweat and blood and soil piled up in more and more barns and warehouses each year. In 1849 Caswell's planters, farmers, and slaves produced just under 2.3 million pounds of the yellow weed. Ten years later, riding the wave of bright leaf profits and an expanding network of boosters, warehousemen, and manufacturers, the county cured more than 4.6 million pounds, the third highest total in North Carolina and roughly 14 percent of the state's total crop despite Caswell's small physical area. It was almost certainly the largest producer of the lucrative bright leaf variety, although census takers did not differentiate between tobacco types. Expanding tobacco production turned soil into a commodity as well. Farm values tripled over the decade leading up to the Civil War, and tracts well-suited to bright leaf cultivation continued to sell for even higher prices.[49]

The golden tobacco boom in Caswell both illustrated and defied the concerns of North Carolina's most infamous antebellum critic of slavery and the plantation economy. Piedmont native Hinton Rowan Helper's *The Impending Crisis of the South* (1857) blamed slavery and paternalist planters for what he saw as the region's shortcomings. Human bondage was a destructive and backward system that kept his state and the rest of the South in a condition of underdevelopment. In particular Helper argued that tobacco and cotton plantations relying on enslaved labor were less productive than northern agriculture, with its foundation in free labor. Only the traffic in human misery and exploitation of the soil resources of the South kept the slave system afloat. Helper sketched a vicious circle: "The diabolical institution subsists on its own flesh. At one time children are sold to procure food for the parents, at another, parents are sold to procure food for the children. . . . The soil itself soon sickens and dies beneath the unnatural tread of the slave."[50]

Despite this admission of the human miseries of slavery, Helper cared little for the fate of enslaved people. Indeed, he was virulently racist even by the standards of his time and place. What motivated Helper instead was a concern for the harmful effects he believed slavery had on North Carolina's poor whites and small farmers. This rift between the state's planters and its small landowners and landless whites was a long-standing source of political contention, with yeoman farmers concentrated in North Carolina's western half resenting the political power of predominantly eastern planters. Unlike contemporary apologists such as Virginia's George Fitzhugh, who praised the institution of slavery as natural and healthy, Helper believed a slavocracy and staple agriculture were sowing the seeds of North Carolina's destruction.[51] Slavery was certainly not a positive good, he wrote, and not even a necessary evil.

For Helper and others contemplating slavery and politics in the state, the Piedmont seemed to exist between two imaginary poles: the small yeoman farms of the western mountains and a planter-dominated coastal plain to the east. (These characterizations hid as much as they revealed, but they nonetheless carried a great deal of rhetorical power.) In Caswell, bright tobacco did increase the traffic in slaves and a staple crop. It did add to the wealth and political power of an elite planter class, exemplified by such families as the Garlands, Hairstons, and Leas. And yet the economic boom was a rising tide that also held the potential to benefit middling white farmers as their land values increased and the county's tobacco crops sold for strong prices. They made money on farming, opened small businesses, and reinvested some of the profits in purchasing more land and enslaved people. Helper might have called it all a sham, an agrarian gold rush as hollow as the metallic version, and likely to ruin more men in the end than it enriched. (Helper had himself been to California as a "forty-niner" only to return to North Carolina still a man of modest means.) But many Piedmont whites saw the situation differently. They hoped bright tobacco could make the Old South new again and that they might move into the planter class.[52]

That promise was chiseled in stone in the heart of the county just after Helper published his jeremiad. The crowning jewel of Caswell's antebellum prosperity was a new courthouse in Yanceyville. The old structure had burned down in the midst of the economic boom, and in 1858 construction began on an elaborate pile of stone and brick on a rise in the middle of the town, facing the square. The architect, John William Cosby, seemed determined to pay homage to every building style then fashionable; the structure's walls, roofline, columns, and eaves sported Victorian, Gothic, and even Italianate elements. The courthouse was three stories tall including an elevated basement, and it sat on a granite base and was crowned with a dramatic cupola with a clock face on each of its four sides. The interior housed barrel-vaulted ceilings, elaborate plaster work, and a pair of intricate spiral staircases. A graceful wrought iron fence manufactured at the county's Yarborough foundry surrounded the grounds in a display of local industry, the stone came from a local quarry, and the bricks were also manufactured nearby. Hiring Cosby reflected the county's affluence. The editor of the nearby *Milton Chronicle* praised the architect's work on other public buildings, including "the assylum [*sic*] for the Mutes in Raleigh and other grand monuments." Erected at a final cost of nearly $30,000 and completed by 1861, the impressive structure was a tribute to local wealth and optimism regarding the future. The architecture also made clear the agrarian roots of Caswell's newfound prosperity. Citizens who entered the courthouse for legal proceedings, to pay their taxes, or for political meetings passed under a row of columns topped with brightly painted metal capitals formed in the shape of tobacco leaves.[53] Tobacco had built the county, even this hall of government, the motif implied, and its white leaders believed Caswell's future would remain rooted in tobacco culture.

As cannons boomed in Charleston Harbor in the spring of 1861, Caswell was a landscape swept by its own paroxysms of creative destruction. Farmers carved new fields from pine and oak woods, moving onto ridges once thought useless for farming, while downhill old fields abandoned to soil exhaustion and erosion sprouted crops of weeds. Ax-wielding men, both enslaved and free, cut forests to burn for charcoal to feed tobacco-curing fires, and spirals of smoke reached heavenward from innumerable barn flues. Gullies grew like living beings, stretching their fingers steadily up slopes, disgorging their sandy loads in creek and river bottoms, literally turning the earth upside down one particle of soil at a time. On certain days coffles of slaves might be seen marching along county roads, traveling either from the Tidewater toward the labor camps of the cotton South or on their way for sale to the county's tobacco planters. Amid these ruins of landscapes and human lives, monuments to wealth arose. Milton and Yanceyville expanded, adding businesses catering to the tobacco trade and bringing town life to a rural county. Internal improvements of roads and river channels promised ever-increasing commerce. White-columned board and brick planter homes conveyed the power and prestige of prosperity. Prognosticators hailed this as a golden age, but the coming war threatened it all.

As the Deep South broke away from the Union in early 1861, Caswell County—like the rest of North Carolina—was initially torn in its allegiances. Many of the county's planters had Whiggish impulses, invested as they were in tobacco manufacturing and internal improvements, but they were also increasingly wedded to the defense of slavery. They hoped for a continuation of slave labor but also wanted to sell the tobacco that those bound workers produced to northern consumers and do business with New York banks. Historian William Powell believed Caswell's white population to be strongly Unionist and reluctant to contemplate secession on the eve of war, but that seems something of an exaggeration. White Caswell residents resoundingly supported a convention to consider the issue of secession when North Carolina polled its voters, approving the measure by a count of 692 to 137.[54] And, once the state did leave the Union, Caswell's white men of military age volunteered for Confederate service at rates above the state average. As a consequence, the eventual draft took only a small portion of the county population: just 1.5 percent.[55] If their allegiance was initially divided, most whites in Caswell quickly chose to follow the Confederacy into rebellion, marching off to war of their own free will.

Once secession took place, mobilizing for war consumed citizens' energy. Six companies of Caswell men organized during the first spring and summer of the conflict, and over the course of the war county men made up all or most of a total of thirteen companies, including one unit of Home Guards. The early companies were organized by prominent community members, typically drew their soldiers from a single neighborhood, and took pride in distinctive local names. Among them were the Milton Blues, Yanceyville Grays, Leasburg Grays, Caswell Boys, Caswell Rifles, and Caswell Rangers. At first equipped by their organizers, some marched off to war in showy uniforms more suited to parade than combat. A soldier in the Milton Blues described his outfit as "quite pretty. Dark gray Pants with blue stripe, and a blue shirt trimmed with black." Over it he wore "a gray coat that hangs loosely, after the gown style, with box-pleats and belt."[56]

After they marched or rode the rail lines out of the county, these nattily dressed volunteers were incorporated into North Carolina's state forces, in the case of the Milton Blues and Leasburg Grays as companies in the 13th North Carolina Regiment. It was a unit that would see extremely heavy combat over the course of the war. The 13th fought in Gen. Robert E. Lee's Virginia campaigning of 1862, took heavy losses at Antietam, and clashed with the Army of the Potomac again at Fredericksburg, Chancellorsville, and Gettysburg, before bleeding across Virginia in 1864 and 1865 in the face of Gen. Ulysses S. Grant's Overland Campaign and in the siege of Petersburg. Having seen a full share of war, the surviving Caswell men were among the members of the 13th Regiment who surrendered at Appomattox in April 1865.[57]

It was not all glory, honor, and death on the battlefield for Caswell's soldiers. Farmer Bartlett Yancey Malone of the Caswell Boys Company, which was attached to the 6th North Carolina Regiment, saw combat in most of the battles in the eastern theater through Gettysburg. Then, in November 1863, he was captured and spent most of the remainder of the war in a federal prison at Point Lookout, Maryland.[58] Along with thirty other Caswell prisoners of war from his unit (including his brother), Malone endured months of poor food, cold weather, illness, and boredom. The dull stretches were broken by occasional moments of sadness, horror, and terror, as when friends died of sickness or guards killed and wounded prisoners who violated the rules. Recording one of these moments, Malone wrote in his prison diary that "a Yankey shot one of our men the other day wounded him in the head shot him for peepen threw the cracks of the planken." After less than two months in the camp, Malone gloomily speculated on New Year's Eve 1863, "Maby I will never live to see the last day of 64." He would survive. Malone was paroled in late February 1865 and was home in Caswell on furlough when the war ended.[59]

Malone and the members of his company were not alone in spending time in a federal prison. Maj. John Graves, of a prominent county family, was captured at Gettysburg and imprisoned at Johnson's Island in Ohio, where he died less than a year later. The county also sent men into varied military roles. Some served in the signal corps and others in the Confederate navy. And even more residents were pulled into service, if only for a few months near the end of the war, as a desperate Confederacy expanded the draft to capture younger and older men. Some of the county's boys ended up in a company of Junior Reserves in 1864, composed mostly of seventeen-year-olds, while Company F of the 77th North Carolina was a Senior Reserves unit, enlisting men between forty-five and fifty years of age. Still others served in a company of Home Guards, securing important sites in the county and searching for deserters and draft dodgers.[60]

White Caswell's allegiance to the Confederacy seemed to remain strong or even grow during the conflict, which was relatively unusual in the North Carolina Piedmont. Although the state contributed more soldiers than any other to the rebel cause, it was also home to more deserters than any other, a sign of its citizens' somewhat tenuous allegiance to the Confederacy. Unionism within the state, or at least resistance to the authority of the Confederate government, is most associated with the mountain counties and the coastal portion of the state that spent a good part of the war under Union control, but the central Piedmont saw a good deal of opposition to the war as well.[61]

There were several reasons for this. Most of the Piedmont's central counties were not economically reliant on the staple crop and slavery system present in the region's southern tier, where cotton flourished, or in its northernmost counties like Caswell, where bright tobacco had proved lucrative. Outside of the cotton and tobacco districts, the Piedmont was a blend of corn and livestock agriculture, contained an antislavery streak rooted in Moravian and Quaker religious traditions, and was home to a few abolitionist intellectuals like Helper. As a result, the central Piedmont was primed to resent what some of its citizens saw as a war to preserve slavery. Only about one-fifth of eligible Piedmont men enlisted in Confederate service prior to implementation of a draft, and the region became a hotbed of internal dissent, draft dodging, and skirmishing between citizens, especially after Confederate conscription began in 1862. Counties with a high percentage of Quakers saw a correspondingly high percentage of their population drafted rather than volunteering for Confederate service, indicating a degree of forced allegiance to the rebellion. Indeed, some Caswell Home Guard units were dispatched to central Piedmont counties to help round up deserters in 1864. John Flintoff served as a member of the Home Guard group styled the "Caswell Cavalry," for instance, and described more than a month of service that fall in Randolph and adjoining counties in which his unit helped capture more than 300 deserters.[62]

And it must not be overlooked that many of the region's enslaved African Americans actively resisted the war effort, most notably by escaping the Piedmont for federal lines in the eastern part of the state.[63] Some of them not only fled for freedom but also fought. Roughly 6,000 North Carolinians of color served as Union soldiers, filling four regiments recruited from the state.[64] People who did not risk the flight to Union lines might still employ all of the means of resistance honed during decades of enslavement: work slowdowns, breaking tools, feigning illness, and similar steps to challenge the war effort. Even if they chose not to actively pursue these "weapons of the weak," masters often feared that resentment and even rebellion bubbled under the surface.[65] They were loath to leave plantations without overseers or the presence of other white men, a reluctance that itself undermined the Confederate cause. These realities made life on the Caswell home front tense, even though its white Confederate sympathies were strong, since more than half of the county's population was enslaved at the start of the war. With these numbers in mind, the reality was that Caswell was in fact a majority Unionist county, if not in the way Powell once envisioned.

Although white Caswell itself was strongly Confederate, it also had ties to one of the state's most vocal opponents of the war, William Woods Holden. Holden was a native of the Piedmont, born near Hillsborough in Orange County, between Yanceyville and the capital in Raleigh. He entered the newspaper business as a teenager, working first for a paper in Danville, Virginia, and then at Caswell's *Milton Spectator* in the mid-1830s before he found work as a printer.[66] When Holden became involved in politics in the 1840s, he did so first as a Whig but then quickly switched allegiances to become a stalwart Democrat. In 1843 Holden purchased the *Raleigh Standard* and as its editor became one of the most influential political voices in the state. Historian Paul Escott argues that "more than any other individual he had resuscitated the Democratic party of the 1840s and guided it to a position of dominance in the 1850s."[67] In the antebellum years he was a firm supporter of both slavery and white supremacy, and Holden reviled the new Republican Party and its determination to limit slavery's spread. The new party was, he declared, "the largest installment of perdition that ever came up to afflict this planet." Abraham Lincoln's election thus unsettled Holden. Faced with a dreaded Republican in office, he at first publicly supported the prospect of North Carolina's secession and the rebellion.[68]

These opinions would change once the war broke out. Holden quickly grew disenchanted with both the Confederate and state governments and eventually became one of North Carolina's leading peace advocates. His personal experience might have influenced these shifts. Holden's son Joseph volunteered for Confederate service, was captured at Roanoke Island, and spent a number of months languishing in a northern prison until his exchange in 1863, a process no doubt worrying for his father and perhaps one that helped sour him on the war effort. If love of family potentially was one motivating factor, ambition surely was another, and Holden had a healthy measure of it. As editor of the *Standard*, Holden had a visible platform for his opinions, which he soon used to direct a peace campaign within the state. The culmination of his disaffection came with his gubernatorial campaign against the incumbent, Zebulon Vance, in 1864, although Holden lost the election in a landslide.[69]

Holden's criticism of the war attracted some sympathy in the state—Vance himself was a persistent thorn in the side of the Confederate government seated in Richmond—but it also contributed to a growing public opinion that he was an agitator and an opportunist. Rumors circulated that Holden was a member of the Red Strings, also known as the "Heroes of America," a secretive loyalist organization dedicated to restoring the Union. The Red Strings numbered perhaps as many as 10,000 in North Carolina, and Holden's public statements on the conspiracy did little to disavow its aims even as he claimed ignorance of its existence. (An outsized belief in the importance and power of the Red Strings persisted into the early Reconstruction period, when national portrayals imagined that the shadowy organization worked to ensure Republican dominance across the South.) The Red Strings may even have operated in Caswell County, despite its strong Confederate leanings.[70] Holden's gubernatorial defeat stemmed in large part from his unpopularity with the state's Confederate soldiers who, despite finding some appeal in his peace platform, came to view Holden as traitorous. Expressing the belief that Holden's brand of politics was undermining the war effort in dangerous ways, one soldier on the front wrote home that "I think the N C soldiers passing through Raleigh on Furlough ought to stop and hang the old son of a bitch." Troops of the Army of Northern Virginia marching through Raleigh on their way to the western front in September 1863 took this attitude to heart. They missed catching Holden himself, but they destroyed the *Standard*'s office in an effort to silence the peace press.[71]

Disgruntlement extended beyond a few politicians and deserters as the war grew longer. The conflict created mental hardships for people on the home front, as family and friends awaited news of the fates of their loved ones in service, and it generated economic difficulties as well, especially in its final two years. The prices of everyday goods, especially food and salt, skyrocketed, and supplies were short as the Union secured control of southern agricultural land and the Confederate government scrambled to supply its soldiers in the field. State and Confederate "taxes in kind" seized a share of farm products for the war effort, and to make matters worse, Caswell suffered three years of bad weather in a row, which led to poor crops.[72] Across the Piedmont some towns, including Salisbury and High Point, saw bread riots led by women as the deprivations of war forced ever greater belt tightening on the home front.[73] Charles Evans, editor of the Milton newspaper, blamed the high prices and shortages on local farmers' slavish devotion to raising tobacco even in the face of war. A crop that had once been an opportunity seemed now a curse. "It would be a glorious deed for this Southern Confederacy if every Tobacco Factory in it were burnt to the ground and their very ashes scattered to the four winds of heaven," he wrote in the autumn of 1863, for "our idea is that the people can do better without tobacco than meat and bread."[74]

Highlighting the unsettled nature of the Piedmont home front, a relative wrote to past and future governor Jonathan Worth of the hazards present in the region in the late winter of 1865 as the crumbling Confederate war effort broke down law and order. Deserters prowled the region's roadways, he warned Worth, and "there is not a day or night passes but what some one is robbed of all the parties can carry away."[75] The final months of the war saw more than deserters moving through the region. Whereas Piedmont Unionists and escaping slaves had earlier fled toward federal lines in the eastern part of the state, the tide of displaced people reversed late in the conflict. As the Union army conquered more and more of the Confederacy, thousands of rebels sought safety in the North Carolina Piedmont, often bringing enslaved people with them.[76]

Hardship characterized North Carolina's interior in 1864 and 1865, and its young men fought and died in large numbers on the bloody fields of eastern Virginia, but the war's main currents would never flow over Caswell's soil. It remained a "backcountry" during the Civil War, just as it had before the conflict. Vital supplies moved toward Richmond on a new branch of the Richmond and Danville Railroad (which had been built in wartime with the impressed labor of county slaves), and news of dead and maimed loved ones flowed home with saddening frequency.[77] But no real battle was fought in the county. Perhaps the closest Caswell came to the "glory" of the Army of Northern Virginia was in the fall of 1863, when Stephen Dodson Ramseur married Ellen Richmond and briefly honeymooned at her family's Woodside plantation near Milton. (The groom's mother's family was from Caswell, and Richmond was a cousin.) Ramseur was a rising military star, soon to be a major general at the tender age of twenty-seven before he was killed in action at Cedar Creek.[78]

In the war's final weeks, it seemed possible that the front would reach the county. General Lee's Army of Northern Virginia had abandoned its trenches around Petersburg and Richmond, fleeing southwestward with General Grant's army in pursuit. And Jefferson Davis's crumbling government evacuated Richmond and established itself in Danville, just across the state line, designating the tobacco town the new capital of the Confederacy. To the south, Gen. Joseph Johnston's disintegrating force faced the Union columns led by Gen. William T. Sherman. There were vague hopes that Johnston and Lee might unite and turn on their pursuers, snatching victory from the jaws of defeat somewhere in the North Carolina Piedmont. And a cavalry raid led by Union general George Stoneman penetrated the region from the west, with the aim of tearing up a portion of the rail line that connected Danville to Greensboro, North Carolina.[79] But all of these arrows that seemed aimed straight at Caswell fell short of the mark. Grant brought Lee to bay at Appomattox Court House, the Confederate government dissolved as Davis and other officials fled Danville, Johnston surrendered to Sherman near Durham, and Stoneman found other ripe targets with the result that his troopers never made it to the northern Piedmont. All of a sudden the war in the eastern theater was over.

The curtain closing on four years of war offered Caswell hope and fear in equal measure. White citizens who by and large had supported the Confederacy worried about the end of the world as they knew it. Some no doubt relished the prospect of peace, even if it meant a new social order, for the war had been long and bloody. Would the prosperity that tobacco had promised return in the postwar period? African Americans embraced emancipation and hoped for a future where some version of equality—economic, political, even social—might be in the offing. But they too had worries: Would military peace equal social tranquility? Would they be equal players in postwar Caswell? The war was over, defining its legacy was just beginning, and it would be an effort written in both blood and ink.

End of War with everyone having hopeful prospects HOPEFUL — Some feared Reprisals and the end of that life or the power it.

Two

PERDITION

The Constitution of our fathers, the constitution of our happiness, we
drop a Tear of remembrance for thy many blessings and now bid thee
a long farewell. We turn with fearful forebodings to the future.

CASWELL COUNTY COURT OF PLEAS (1868)

he whole world was up for grabs. Or so it seemed in the weeks
following Appomattox. It was too late for Thomas Day to see: he
had passed away in 1861. But for free black artisans like the cabinetmaker, perhaps social and political opportunity would come to the communities where they had carved out economic niches. For those who had
been enslaved, the revolution that was emancipation promised even greater
things: a leap from bound to free, and maybe even some sort of equality.
Maybe land. Some freedpeople left rural Caswell County for the promises
of other places, like the nearby city of Danville, Virginia, while many more
stayed in the county and there held on to hopes for a better future. More
than half of the county's population mulled these prospects with a degree of
optimism, as rumors swirled across the South about some division of land
come Christmas.[1]

For their part, many Caswell whites feared the changes. Their world
seemed to be collapsing in on itself rather than expanding. The promises of
the Confederacy and the wartime state government had proved hollow, the

forced labor that had been the flesh and backbone of the tobacco economy was gone, and the same questions of landownership and political power also echoed in their houses. Mastery had slipped through their fingers; might the soil itself be the next to go? Spoken by black mouths in hopeful tones, these questions were perhaps hushed and fearful coming from the old masters.

This turmoil created opportunities, as uncertainty is wont to do. Ambitious and enterprising people can often turn a world in flux into a path to advance, and the postwar South was full of individuals on the make. Freedpeople sought property to secure their independence, establish families, and build wealth. They knew better than anyone that control of land that could grow tobacco equated to power. Planters looked to reestablish their perquisites, and, despite losing the recent war, they still held many advantages. Middling whites imagined that now was finally their time to lead North Carolina. And some northerners saw promising prospects in the conquered region, whether from altruistic or acquisitive motives. When much is uncertain, dreams have few limits.

If North Carolina loyalties had been a tangled web during the war, they remained at least as complicated in its aftermath, as rebels and loyalists sought to understand the new lay of the land. From outside the state, the dynamic looked even more confusing. President Andrew Johnson hoped that the state's Unionists would seize the reins of power when he extended an official invitation for North Carolina to rejoin the Union on May 29, 1865, the first of his state reconstruction proclamations. To that end he appointed the wartime peace candidate William Woods Holden as provisional governor, impressed by his history of openly criticizing the Confederate state government. Elections were then held for state and national offices. Johnson was surprised and bitterly disappointed when North Carolina's voters elected former Confederate officials to six of seven congressional seats, as well as sent many men who were not yet pardoned to the state legislature. The state's whites may have been tired of war, but they were not yet willing to embrace the Republican Party, at least not without a political restructuring.[2]

Northern observers who traveled the South in the months after Appomattox also found North Carolina, and especially its Piedmont region, perplexing. J. T. Trowbridge, a novelist of abolitionist sentiment, criticized the state's "stay laws," which forbade creditors from collecting debts and had put a halt on lending, as ruinous economic radicalism. Yet he equally detested the violence directed at freedpeople, declaring that "cases of robberies, frauds, assaults, and even murders, in which white persons were the agents and freed people the sufferers, had been so numerous, according to the State [Freedmen's Bureau] Commissioner, 'that no record of them could be kept.'"[3] John Richard Dennett, on assignment for *Nation* magazine, rode through the Caswell countryside in the late summer of 1865, a journey that left him similarly pessimistic. The land and people looked poor, he wrote, and he spoke with residents who assured him that the county had been the home of Unionists during the war who organized in secret societies to avoid the draft and shelter deserters. But Dennett expressed some skepticism concerning this supposed loyalty, for during the war "the avowal of their sentiments, however, they never attempted," and now that the conflict was over they all claimed to have been secessionists. He thought local allegiance more a matter of convenience than principle.[4] Ohioan Whitelaw Reid also noted the contentious and conflicted politics of a state that had resisted the Confederate government's power and now seemed equally intent on bucking Washington's authority. Much of this rebelliousness centered on white efforts to control the black population, Reid believed. Like Dennett, he disparaged North Carolina's loyalty as self-serving, nothing but "Cracker Unionism."[5]

Exactly who governed various corners of North Carolina, and under what terms, also seemed uncertain immediately after the war. The Union armies had clearly been victorious, and part of the restoration of peace would entail military occupation. To that end, the federal government placed an officer over the state, Maj. Gen. Dan Sickles (who was succeeded in 1867 by Maj. Gen. Edward R. S. Canby). Governor Holden headed the layer of civil government as President Johnson's temporary appointee. But the elections to take place in short order were supposed to restore a more democratic political arrangement.[6] Within the state the Democrats and the portion of former Whigs who had allied with them to control the war effort imagined that they would continue their leadership in peace and, to distance themselves from the stigma of rebellion, came to call themselves "Conservatives," while white and black Republicans imagined their own coalition for the future.[7]

Another layer of bureaucracy participated in daily life in the state. Tasked with overseeing the transition of African Americans from enslavement to freedom, the Bureau of Refugees, Freedmen, and Abandoned Lands (commonly known as the Freedmen's Bureau) established offices across North Carolina. Formed during the war to operate in portions of the South that had been conquered by the Union army, the bureau was placed on a more regular footing in 1865. The first head of the bureau in North Carolina was Eliphalet Whittlesey, who had been a minister and professor at Maine's Bowdoin College before the war. Whittlesey established the state bureau's headquarters in Raleigh on June 22, 1865. His intention was to place an agent in every county, but he lacked the manpower to do so; he instead established "sub-districts" that grouped together between two and eight counties under the supervision of an agent, with the hopes of eventually expanding staffing. The shortage of agents in the early North Carolina bureau was dire: at no point in the first year could Whittlesey count more than twenty men operating in the field. Few in number, bureau employees were nonetheless tasked with enormous responsibilities and often wielded a good deal of discretionary authority. As part of their work, they distributed food and medical care, approved interracial labor contracts, oversaw the operation of schools, supervised child apprenticeships, and ruled in court disputes that involved freedpeople. They often functioned as quasi judges, sheriffs, wardens of the poor, and school commissioners, as well as agents of federal power. Across the South, Freedmen's Bureau agents came from varied backgrounds and held equally diverse motivations. Some were soldiers, placed in the posts fresh from the field, while others were civilians, both northern and southern. Almost all were white. In various times and places they were paid both by salary and by fees generated in the course of their duties. Some bureau agents believed in full black citizenship, while others seemed intent on restoring a captive agricultural labor force.[8]

Whittlesey's administration was troubled from the start. He struck some northerners as well as white southerners as a radical (his critics came to include his boss, bureau commissioner Oliver O. Howard). Within a year he was arrested at President Johnson's order, court-martialed, and convicted of corruption and profiteering along with a handful of other state bureau officials. Whittlesey's administration was perhaps a victim of Washington infighting, as Johnson worked to undermine an agency he saw as a tool of his political opponents, but the effect of its collapse was that bureau leadership in North Carolina would remain unsettled. There were six assistant commissioners in charge of North Carolina in the three years that followed Whittlesey's arrest, starting with Thomas Ruger and concluding with Charles Compton. Despite rapid turnover in the North Carolina bureau offices, its agents at the subdistrict level wielded real influence in the early shape of Reconstruction. They served as intermediaries between the federal and state visions of the process, as well as mediators between white and black citizens on the ground.[9]

For prominent North Carolinians, the upset of the war and the equally uncertain landscape produced by Reconstruction caused them to rethink their economic paths, social connections, and political allegiances. Politicians often switched sides: Opponents of secession turned Confederate officials during the war, only to become Republicans once the federal government began Reconstruction in the state. Others who had pushed for peace during the war turned into embittered opponents of Radical Republicans in Washington after emancipation, sometimes motivated by a genuine belief in the right of home rule, and sometimes from careful calculation of self-interest. Layered on top of the state's tumultuous antebellum politics, the shifting stances of the times became a thicket of competing allegiances and ideas. What did it mean to have been a Whig or a Democrat? Were the former rebels loyalists to the state or traitors of the nation?

Hinton Rowan Helper, whose 1857 book, *The Impending Crisis of the South*, had done so much to inflame North Carolinians' debates over slavery, epitomized these mercurial sentiments. An enemy of the Confederacy, he quickly grew disillusioned with Reconstruction. Driven from the state before the war for his abolitionist ideas, from a distance he had adamantly opposed secession, supported the state's peace movement, and viewed the Republican Party as the natural political home of North Carolina's poor whites. But as Congress increasingly took the reins of Reconstruction with an eye toward advancing the prospects of freedpeople in the South, and seemingly with little concern for the region's poor whites, Helper reacted in disgust. His vision was that of a prosperous, free, and *white* South, not one of social, political, or economic equality regardless of race.[10] To that end, by the late 1860s he was publishing attacks on Congressional Reconstruction and envisioning a racial purge of the United States. In the preface to the first of these books, Helper declared that "the primary object of this work is to write the negro out of America, and that the secondary object is to write him … out of existence."[11] In another tome "in behalf of a Free and White America," he worried that the Republican Party aimed for "the forced political, religious, civil, and social equality of the white and black races," which could only result in "the ultimate degradation, division, and destruction of the Republic."[12] Ultimately he rejected the "Ethiopian Radicalism" of the party for which he had sacrificed so much and called for a new political body dedicated to white workers and a white nation.[13] The war had ended slavery, an institution that Helper had despised, but he liked what he believed to be emerging in its place no better.

William Woods Holden continued his circuitous political path as well. First a Whig and then a Democrat, for secession and then for peace, framed as a patriot and a traitor, at the war's conclusion he became a Republican. This shift seemed to pay off. As noted, in a remarkable stroke President Johnson appointed Holden provisional governor of North Carolina in May 1865, likely because of Holden's strident anti-war message (and perhaps some appreciation for his class leanings and brash style, similar as they were to Johnson's own traits). Holden envisioned a state controlled by white Republicans of his mold, and he initially opposed any form of African American enfranchisement. Only when he came to believe that black voters held the key to Republican political power in North Carolina did he slowly come around to expanding voting rights. A later critic noted that by the end of 1866, Holden "promoted negro suffrage as violently as he had opposed it in the past." Despite Holden's finger to the wind of state politics, he again lost the governor's office when elections were held in November 1865. Former governor Jonathan Worth was the victor, even though he had served as a state official during the rebellion. Worth was hardly a fire-eater: he had been a Unionist going into the war but found himself opposed to Holden and Republicans coming out of the conflict. Worth's budding conservatism was of the old Whig style, opposed to rapid social change and for political home rule, and he increasingly viewed Holden as an opportunistic pawn of Washington and the Republican platform as radical. Worth's middle-of-the-road approach held solid appeal for the fractious mass of North Carolina's white voters in the months after surrender. Holden thus found himself once again on the outside of political power and hungry to return to the office he had held for a few months.[14]

Although he was much less famous than Helper or Holden, John Walter Stephens was another man on the make whose world was transformed by the outcomes of the Civil War. Through a series of unlikely events, his life and death became central to North Carolina's hotly contested Reconstruction. Few records remain of Stephens's life before the war. Like many poor-to-middling southern whites, he was born and grew up on the margins of the plantation economy that was central to regional prosperity. He entered the world in the mid-1830s, born in either 1834 or 1835. His parents were Absalom and Letitia Stephens, who were probably living in Guilford County, just southwest of Caswell, at the time. Soon after John's birth the family moved to the tiny Wentworth community in Rockingham County (west of Caswell) and then on to the hamlet of Leaksville in the same county. Absalom was a successful tailor, but he died when John was young. The boy had some education—a census taker listed him as attending school at the age of fifteen—and he grew up in a household with four younger siblings.[15] At adulthood he was five-foot-ten and slim, just 140 pounds. He found work as a harness maker, was a member of the Methodist Church, and in 1857 married Nannie Walters. The couple had a daughter, but by 1859 Nannie had died and John was recorded as living in a boardinghouse in northern Rockingham

William Woods Holden's career epitomized the shifting and contentious political terrain of North Carolina's Civil War and Reconstruction. "Holden, William W.," in Portrait Collection #P0002, North Carolina Collection Photographic Archives, Wilson Library, University of North Carolina at Chapel Hill.

(it is unclear where his young daughter was staying). He was poor as well as bereaved—the census taker listed him as possessing no real estate or personal items worth valuing. In 1860 he remarried, this time to Martha Frances Groom, often called Fannie.[16]

To this point, Stephens's life seemed unremarkable. It had included modest opportunity but also hardships, and it had produced no tangible wealth and little written record. But the war changed Stephens's prospects, as it did for so many southerners. There is no evidence of whether Stephens actively supported or opposed secession, and given his lowly place in society such stances would have carried little weight beyond their personal consequences.

So substitute all the ledger that would have been his name.

It does seem that Stephens made no effort to join Confederate military service. His brother William served with the Confederacy, enlisting in Rockingham on May 10, 1861, as a private in Company H of the 13th Regiment of North Carolina Infantry. Many other Stephenses joined rebel service as well in Rockingham and Caswell Counties, four in Company D of the 13th alone, a unit primarily composed of Caswell men. John it seems avoided a uniform for the duration of the conflict—one unsubstantiated source holds that he hired a substitute to serve in his place when drafted—although he did work as an impressment agent late in the conflict, seizing horses for the Confederate war effort.[17]

At the conclusion of the war, Stephens and his family moved to Yanceyville, likely motivated by its tobacco economy. He may also have had relatives in the county, as the 1860 census takers recorded dozens of Stephenses living scattered across Caswell, including near the Yanceyville post office. Stephens had done some business in buying and reselling tobacco in South Carolina before or during the war, and he continued that work as a "tobacconist" in Caswell.[18] The future there, as elsewhere across the South, was uncertain. Caswell faced hard times immediately following the war—notes from the Bank of Yanceyville were "almost worthless" into early 1866, and in the spring of the following year there were still dozens of white and black residents who relied on food aid from the Warden's Court to keep starvation at bay—but bright tobacco offered some economic promise. The crop continued to command high prices and seemed poised to spread to other parts of the South, but at the moment its center of cultivation remained in North Carolina's upper Piedmont. The nicotine addiction that was so harmful to tobacco's consumers provided its growers and resellers in places like Caswell with a measure of economic security.[19]

Stephens soon advanced his prospects by securing an appointment as a justice of the peace in the county. It seemed an odd post, given his lack of experience or county connections. The position came from a rather unlikely relationship that Stephens formed with Albion Tourgée. Tourgée was an Ohio-born Union veteran who had moved to Greensboro, North Carolina, after the war, where he practiced law, dabbled in raising fruit, served as a superior court judge, and advocated for freedpeople's political rights. He came to know Stephens through their mutual Union League work, and Tourgée apparently tutored Stephens in the law and remained his confidant as he faced the hazards of political work in Caswell. Tourgée also oversaw Stephens's bar examination. Stephens had begun Reconstruction as a Democrat, but around 1867 he switched his allegiance to the Republican Party. The transition may have come from a personal change of heart, from Tourgée's influence, from Stephens's sense that the political winds were shifting in the state, or from some mixture of these forces.[20]

It also appears that Stephens worked for a time for the Freedmen's Bureau, serving as a county-level agent. The first bureau employee in Caswell seems to have been W. B. Bowe, hired as a local agent of the subdistrict office in Alamance County. Bowe was dismissed in the summer of 1866 because of his ties to the former Confederate government and his failure to swear the required loyalty oath.[21] At some point after that, Stephens began acting as the county's agent and ruling on disputes between black and white residents. When Lt. F. W. Liedtke took charge of the bureau office overseeing Alamance and Caswell in May 1868, he dispatched his own agent to Caswell, W. J. Dawes. Faced with Stephens's claim to the post, Liedtke seemed uncertain of the legitimacy of Stephens's position. Civilian agents like Bowe and—perhaps—Stephens operated under a fee system, collecting payment from parties for the cases they heard, which often led to poor central record keeping and a great deal of dissatisfaction between military and civilian bureau personnel. Liedtke questioned Raleigh headquarters about whether Stephens had a legitimate appointment and, apparently not receiving a satisfactory answer, shortly thereafter instructed him to quit representing himself as a bureau employee and collecting fees. If Stephens failed to do so, Liedtke warned, "I will cause your arrest."[22]

Loss of the bureau post failed to dim Stephens's political star. Part of the state's political changes came from the efforts of the Union League, the organization that first brought Tourgée and Stephens together. Originally a northern organization intended to support the Union war effort, after the war it expanded into the South and increasingly embraced African American membership. The southern Union League would eventually be devoted to securing black voting rights and providing freedpeople social and economic support.[23] Initially labeled Loyal Leagues in North Carolina, reflecting an effort to appeal to the state's numerous opponents of the Confederacy, chapters first appeared in 1866 and then grew in number the following year. Tourgée was active in the early North Carolina Union League, and the state's first Union League president was none other than William Woods Holden, who used the organization to promote Republican political gains.[24] Caswell was the site of Union League organization at an early date. Among the county branches was one in Leasburg, once a heart of tobacco planter power. In 1868 the small village had a league chapter with twenty-nine African American members. Many of them were related, part of the extended Yancey family, and they worked as house servants, blacksmiths, farm laborers, and in a local tobacco factory.[25]

These Union League chapters, along with the Freedmen's Bureau and other organizations, such as churches, sought to advance black economic prospects, among other aims. Emancipation had ended slavery, but a range of other less-than-free work arrangements arose in its place. In the early years of Reconstruction, annual labor contracts for modest cash wages, share wages, and sharecropping intersected with Black Codes, which among other provisions criminalized unemployment, leading to restricted options and debt peonage.[26] The coercion of black labor could be even more direct, as with the apprenticeship laws established across the South as part of the postwar Black Codes. North Carolina county officials—sometimes with the approval of Freedmen's Bureau agents and sometimes over their protests—bound out African American children as "apprentices," ostensibly to provide them care in the absence of parental support. Relatives of apprentices frequently protested that the system was rife with abuse, virtually re-enslaving black children until the age of twenty-one, even in instances where there was familial support. A Freedmen's Bureau agent charged with investigating apprenticeships in Caswell noted in the spring of 1867 that "the court there had bound in a few cases children not orphans without the consent of their parents."[27] Freedpeople ultimately had some success in North Carolina's state-level courts in dismantling the worst excesses of the apprenticeship program, but for many black Tar Heels it epitomized the limits on freedom that bound their lives.[28] Caswell's freedpeople also envisioned opportunities in tobacco, but their path toward prosperity held even more obstacles than the one Stephens traveled. As a pair of economic historians famously framed it, the Civil War had produced but "one kind of freedom" for freedpeople.[29] Or as a Freedmen's Bureau agent tasked with supervising labor arrangements in Caswell more bluntly put it, here "a poor [black] man has no chance of obtaining justice."[30]

Much of the everyday tension in the county centered on making a living. The Freedmen's Bureau office in charge of Caswell fielded numerous complaints about pay and contracts. Often freedpeople claimed that landowners failed to pay them what was promised, be it daily wages or a share of the crop at season's end, or that they had been driven off the land before payday under some false pretense. Landowners countered that freedpeople stole livestock, abused the land, shirked work, and failed to pay their bills. The bureau agents duly adjudicated these disputes, in many cases, we might imagine, leaving one party happy and the other disgruntled.[31] These important yet quotidian economic contentions also found expression in violence in Caswell. Peace was, perhaps, a lofty goal after four years of war. In the months following Appomattox, sporadic violence flared across North Carolina as contesting parties sought to control the peace process and define the terms of emancipation and reunion. Much of this violence came from white landowners who desired continued control of black labor. Slavery might be gone, its death finalized by ratification of the Thirteenth Amendment in late 1865, but many planters believed law made in Washington did not have to equate to truly free African American labor. If legal structures like apprenticeships and vagrancy laws failed to supply a tractable work force, violence remained another tool in the kit of mastery.

By the end of that first year of peace, Maj. Gen. Thomas Ruger, a military commander on the ground in North Carolina, reported to Washington on the simmering violence he observed. In the six months following the South's surrender he documented ten racially or politically motivated murders and more than 120 assaults.[32] Such events only increased in the months that followed. Across the South, similar violence against freedpeople flickered, so common that bureau offices kept a category of files devoted to such attacks, often labeled "record of murders and outrages." For their part, Conservatives argued that these claims were inflated, if not entirely fabricated, for political purposes, but the truth on the ground was that the Civil War's violence had not entirely dissipated; it had only changed form and targets.[33]

Not every freed person experienced physical threats. Some Piedmont African Americans carved out relative prosperity in the postwar years, dodging the dangers of debt and violence, like Porter Scales in Rockingham County. A wagoner during the Civil War, he drew a state pension for his service to the Confederacy and parlayed that money into purchasing a 130-acre farm near the Dan River.[34] In the same county, Charles Lee Dalton recalled a postwar life of steady farm work and the occasional factory job, enriched by family and religious communities. The result may not have been wealth, but it was relative comfort.[35]

For many black people, threats of violence interlaced these threads of tranquility, however. Beatings and bloodshed touched numerous Caswell lives, in part because Freedmen's Bureau officials were spread so thin on the ground. Across the South, the bureau's power tended to diminish outside of towns with offices, and in counties like Caswell—officially supervised by the agent in Graham, one county over—there was what historian Gregory Downs has called "a catastrophic lack of manpower" on the ground.[36] Fanny Cannady could remember little about the end of the war—she was just six in 1865—but one memory cut through the years to stay with her into old age: "I do 'member how Marse Jordan Moss shot Leonard Allen, one of his slaves. I ain't never forgot dat."[37] Julia Ware was crossing Thomas Ware's plantation with a group of other freedpeople in 1867 when the landowner opened fire on them for being on the place without his permission. One man was grievously wounded, and Ware was struck in the head and arm, lucky to survive.[38] Another unnamed freedman brought suit against Thomas Slade, claiming that Slade had attempted to stab and shoot him in a disagreement over work in the planter's tobacco crop. Slade said only that he offered hard words when the hired hand refused to follow the terms of a labor contract. Jesse C. Griffith, county sheriff, assured the Freedmen's Bureau after the fact that Slade had been found not guilty in a fair trial.[39] Perhaps the bureau agents were skeptical of this explanation, since one noted a few months later that "white men who openly assaulted colored men with knives and clubs in the presence of the Sheriff [Griffith] were not arrested."[40]

Another example of the way everyday interactions could turn into struggles for mastery or respect took place in August 1865, when freedman Edward Glass was sentenced to thirty days of hard labor with a ball and chain for assaulting his former master, Iverson Glass. Angry that Edward refused to serve as his carriage driver, Iverson attacked him with a hammer. The freedman fought back with his fists and then a shovel. It is unclear if Iverson faced any charges for his part in initiating the fracas. Complaining of the injustice, one Freedmen's Bureau agent noted that "in this part of the Co[unty] many outrages are perpetrated upon freedpeople, of which no notice is taken by the civil authorities."[41] In another instance, farm manager Edward Self lay in wait for a freedman named Bouldin in the early months after the war, shooting and killing him from ambush. When questioned by federal officials he admitted to the murder but argued that it was warranted because of Bouldin's "impertinence" and "roguery" in questioning how Self managed the farm.[42] Less than two years later, another bureau agent wrote of continued local violence. A freedwoman had been shot in northern Caswell, and Thomas Ware was accused of what appeared to be another racially motivated shooting.[43]

As the Glass fight suggests, even if most violence was implemented by whites against blacks, in certain situations bloodshed could flow both ways. Many freedpeople refused to passively accept the prospect of physical harm or continued subservience. Union League members sometimes armed themselves and visibly demonstrated their willingness to defend their rights and liberties. Freedmen's Bureau agent Charles Wolff noted in July 1867 that "lately several complaints are made by the whites of Caswell Co that the f[ree]d people there neglect their duties & disturb the peace of the country."

What most disturbed the complainants, Wolff observed, was that league members "went armed with guns to their meetings & made some noise which frightened white people there." The agent warned the freedpeople to avoid arming themselves and escalating racial tensions, but they perhaps felt that being unarmed in the face of potential violence was the greater hazard.[44]

Sam Allen's story reinforced the notion of the local spread of violent intimidation and resistance. Recorded by New Deal oral historians in the 1930s, the tale perhaps included some apocryphal elements, but it demonstrated the legends that could build around African American resistance to vigilante violence. In the account, a party of 100 Caswell night riders visited Allen's house one evening, intent on either killing him or driving him from the county. They might have been angered by Allen's efforts to establish a school for freed children; in the spring of 1867 a bureau agent had noted that Allen was "persecuted for this" plan and instructed justice of the peace David Burch to ensure his safety.[45] In a calculated act of intimidation, some of the night riders placed an empty casket across two chairs and then instructed Allen to say his goodbyes to his family. Kneeling at his bedside as if to pray, Allen drew a knife from its hiding place under the mattress, leaped up, and killed two Klansmen with the blade before escaping into the darkness. Highlighting the revenge that such acts of resistance often provoked, the mob returned the next evening in an effort to ambush Allen, but in the confusion of darkness they shot a different black man by mistake.[46]

When Congressional Republicans took control of Reconstruction, rejecting President Johnson's actions and taking a harder line on former rebels, it meant dramatic political and social changes for North Carolina. It began with a referendum on a constitutional convention and the drafting of a new state constitution in early 1868. Required by Congress's Reconstruction Acts and overseen by General Canby, the military officer then in charge of Reconstruction in the state, the Republican-dominated convention drafted a much more liberal state constitution. The delegates produced a document that did away with most racial distinctions under the law and favored poorer North Carolinians more than any previous version. It also mandated a free public school system for black and white citizens, increased the number of elected county and state offices, and overall shifted governance powers from the county courts to Raleigh.[47] Caswell sent two delegates, Wilson Carey and Phillip Hodnett, who held polar opposite views on their duties at the convention. A Republican, Carey was a free man of color who had moved to Caswell in the 1850s from Virginia and was one of the relatively few black delegates at the meeting. He voted for the liberalizing provisions of the new constitution, in line with the majority. Hodnett, who went by the nickname "Squire," was a white Conservative who steadily opposed most new articles in a futile effort to derail the proceedings.[48] In their actions in Raleigh the two men represented the divided sentiment on the ground back home.

The new balance of power at the convention signaled broader political changes in the state. With African American men able to vote, many former Confederates temporarily disenfranchised under the terms of Congressional Reconstruction, and Conservatives still somewhat fractured by persistent differences rooted in the antebellum period and wartime, the Republican Party was positioned to assume power in the state. The new constitution would be ratified in the 1868 fall elections, Holden would finally win a gubernatorial race in his own right, and a slate of other Republican officials would find success as well (including Holden's son Joseph, who at just twenty-three years of age won a House of Representatives seat in Wake County, was elected Speaker of the House, became the official state printer, and had for a time assumed his father's position as vocal editor of the *Raleigh Standard*).[49] John Stephens also benefited from these changes. His position as justice of the peace made him an active participant in the county's political and economic reconstruction, and it became clear that he sought even greater influence. In 1868 he ran for the county's state Senate seat as a Republican against Democrat Bedford Brown, who was the incumbent and a heavy favorite.[50]

Brown was in fact a political institution in the county. He had begun service in the North Carolina House in 1815, eventually won election to the state Senate, and spent the entirety of the 1830s as one of North Carolina's US senators and a staunch Jacksonian Democrat. Brown had been a vocal Unionist in the months leading up to the Civil War, but he nonetheless attended the state secession convention and voted to leave the Union after Lincoln's call for volunteers to suppress the rebellion. He then served in the North Carolina Senate during the war.[51] Called to Washington in the spring of 1866 to testify before the Joint Committee on Reconstruction on conditions in the state, he claimed to have accepted Confederate defeat. White North Carolinians wanted peace, he told the skeptical congressmen, and they sought to resume their place in the Union: an equal place, he was quick to clarify. As to race relations, Brown argued that freedpeople in his region had "behaved rather badly after Lee's surrender," but the situation in places like Caswell was now calmer, thanks in part to the work of the Freedmen's Bureau. The bureau had done such good work, Brown added almost as an afterthought, that it was no longer needed in the state and might as well be dissolved.[52] When the votes were initially counted, the 1868 election seemed like yet another victory for

Brown at the polls, but Republicans charged Democrats with voting fraud and intimidation and refused to seat Brown when he arrived in Raleigh.[53]

The contested election brought bubbling animosities in Caswell County to the surface. Protesting the results, Stephens had requested that the Freedmen's Bureau investigate the election, and the bureau complied. Lt. F. W. Liedtke and a secretary left the bureau's office in Alamance County and traveled north to hold a hearing in the Yanceyville courthouse, allowing each party to call witnesses and cross-examine opponents in a forum open to the public. Stephens claimed that Conservatives had controlled the polls on Election Day and suppressed African American voters, and he produced evidence like the sworn statement of freedman Harrison Willis that the landowner he worked for had intimidated him into not voting Republican. Sheriff Jesse Griffith, a Conservative, declared that his party had been rigorously honest. He stated that Stephens himself had served on the board of voter registration and had been physically present when the Yanceyville ballot box was secured at the end of polling. If anything, Griffith argued, it was Republicans who had pressured all African Americans to vote the Republican ticket. Further muddying the waters, Conservatives produced an affidavit from the aforementioned Willis swearing that Stephens had promised to pay freedmen who would claim their employers or landlords prevented their voting Republican in the election. If they would not do so, Stephens supposedly threatened to make sure they were arrested by the county sheriff. (This was a confusing threat, since Sheriff Griffith was a staunch Conservative and unlikely to work in cooperation with Stephens.) Willis claimed that he had accused his landlord of intimidation based on this threat, and the coercion thus came from Stephens and not the landowner.

From there testimony quickly devolved into competing accusations of uncounted ballots, restricted access to the polls, drunken inspectors, and election officials seen entering the courthouse where the locked ballot box was left unattended at night. Freedpeople testified that landowners threatened to kick them off their tenant farms if they voted the Republican ticket, transforming economic power into political leverage. Conservatives accused Stephens of bribery and argued that many black men who tried to vote had been convicted of crimes and thus lost the franchise under state law. (In this they drew on a statewide Conservative pattern since 1866 of weakening the black vote through prosecution of petty offenses with an eye toward disenfranchisement.) Liedtke, faced with this contradictory testimony throughout the hearing, grew increasingly frustrated with what he saw as lying witnesses and a farcical election. He concluded the voting had been terribly, even criminally, mismanaged and recommended that the election "inspectors be brought to trial before a Military Commission." Conservatives had probably gained the most advantage through their machinations, he believed, but despite his Republican sympathies, he also found Stephens's actions suspicious.[54]

Adding to the uncertainty of the election results was the partisan and polarizing Sheriff Griffith, whose testimony and actions featured so prominently in the investigation. Griffith had served as county sheriff before the war and, despite service as a Confederate official, found himself back in the position after the surrender. In the office he seemed unreconstructed. Liedtke himself had to chastise Griffith in 1867 for failing to defend the rights of freedpeople, noting the numerous allegations of violence against African Americans coming out of the county.[55] And he had drawn the ire of Albion Tourgée, who in his capacity as a superior court judge ordered the Caswell sheriff arrested for persecuting a local Unionist. As a result, Griffith had been removed from the state for a time and imprisoned in Charleston, South Carolina, awaiting prosecution. Governor Worth intervened on Griffith's behalf, pleading his case all the way to President Johnson in an effort to thwart Tourgée (whom Worth disliked) and bypass General Canby, who had proved unsympathetic.[56] Returned to Caswell and the sheriff's office thanks to Worth, Griffith's prominence in election matters ensured Republican doubts, even if the bureau failed to find absolute proof of Conservative wrongdoing.

The bureau could recommend corrective action—Liedtke thought the votes of former Confederates should be discarded followed by a recount—but since the investigation did not prove direct intimidation at the polls, it was the state legislature that would ultimately decide on the election's legitimacy.[57] Stephens turned to a new argument in that forum, challenging the results based on a new North Carolina statute barring former Confederate officials from holding state offices. Like Griffith, Bedford Brown's service during the rebellion thus disqualified him. The General Assembly, now in Republican hands, sent its own investigators to Caswell and made repeated calls for federal military authorities to forward their records pertaining to the election. They too found the Caswell election suspicious and, drawing on the power of the new statutes, the assembly ultimately sided with Stephens. Brown's victory was vacated and Stephens took the senate seat.[58] This was a remarkable rise. In a period of roughly a year, Stephens had gone from a small tobacco buyer new to the county to a state senator and acquaintance of the political figures who governed North Carolina. For their part, Conservatives saw not a success story but a cautionary tale of the corruption and incompetence coming to rule the state.

In Caswell, Conservatives bemoaned both the new constitution and Republican leadership as harmful to peace and prosperity. The constitution extended greater state control over county affairs, among its provisions replacing the county court of pleas with a new board of commissioners appointed in Raleigh. As its final act, the outgoing court members issued a statement that summarized the Conservative stance. "The Constitution of our fathers, the constitution of our happiness, we drop a Tear of remembrance for thy many blessings and now bid thee a long farewell. We turn with fearful forebodings to the future. We see general lawlessness, a most fearful disregard of public and private obligations, great demoralization, the marriage not so sacredly regarded and observe a general feeling of uneasiness as to the future and a dread when the vilest of men are exalted the nation will mourn."[59] Their emphasis on lawlessness would be prescient, though perhaps not in the way they then imagined.

Stephin's Mate
Senator through
"dubious" Means

⇒ Is this a moment of
Republican calling Voter
Fraud?

Three

PYRRHIC VICTORIES

Handwritten margin notes: "Starten / VV..." / "History ↳ NEVER A MELODRAMA" / "Brutal Martial Justice ↳ All criminals?"

> If criminals could be arrested and tried before military tribunals
> and shot, we should soon have peace and order throughout all
> this country. The remedy would be a sharp and bloody one, but
> it is indispensable as was the suppression of the rebellion.
>
> WILLIAM WOODS HOLDEN (1870)

Reputation proved crucial in North Carolina's political struggles. Both Conservatives and Republicans claimed the moral high ground, efforts that involved tearing down opponents as much as elevating allies. These campaigns were self-conscious efforts to define the meaning and values of Reconstruction, history written at the same time it was being made. To this end, rumors concerning John Walter Stephens freely circulated as he moved up the political ranks. Many of the tales accused him of pettiness and graft. If Stephens could not be stripped of official power in the form of his offices, his moral authority might be eroded by framing him as a man of bad character. Little did participants know that Stephens's reputation would remain at issue for the century that followed.

The story on the greatest number of lips involved a wartime incident that supposedly demonstrated his selfishness and ill temper. In the latter stages of the war Stephens became entangled in legal trouble over a dispute with a Rockingham County neighbor, Thomas Ratliff. According to one account, Stephens and Ratliff had desired the same Confederate impressment position, with Stephens winning the job, and the competition had generated hard feelings. Compounding the tension, Ratliff's chickens regularly raided Stephens's garden. In frustration Stephens killed two of the chickens and then informed Ratliff's wife of his actions, and Ratliff responded by filing theft charges against Stephens. Stephens was arrested, jailed overnight, and then released on bond. In a rage, Stephens confronted Ratliff on the street and assaulted him, and when passersby tried to intervene, he shot a Confederate official in the head and a magistrate's son in the arm. Both men survived, and the charges against Stephens were ultimately dismissed a year and a half later, with Stephens paying court costs. Although he avoided prosecution for what might have been serious charges, Stephens's Conservative enemies resurrected the wartime story and branded the senator with the sobriquet of "Chicken" Stephens, a name that would live on for decades in disparagement of the controversial politician.[1]

Across the South, Democrats used similar smear tactics in these battles over reputation to portray scalawags, carpetbaggers, and freedpeople as villains.[2] Caswell Conservatives derisively labeled Wilson Carey the "archives of gravity," ridiculing his political speeches as ignorant pomposity.[3] In keeping with the methods used against Stephens and Carey, Conservatives also circulated rumors of Alamance legislator T. M. Shoffner's bad character, in his case claiming that the senator had dug up a slave's corpse when he was living in Guilford County during the Civil War, boiled the skeleton clean, and sold it to a local doctor. Upon public discovery he was supposedly driven from the county only to resurrect his career in Alamance.[4] Stephens's seemingly lukewarm support for the Confederate war effort also provided his political opponents with low-hanging fruit, as they could tar him as a secreted Unionist without too obviously bending the truth. But even the staunchest of rebels could become traitors after the fact for going over to the Republican Party. Perhaps the most famous example was James Longstreet. A corps commander in the Army of Northern Virginia for much of the war, General Lee affectionately referred to Longstreet as his "old warhorse." Longstreet had been in command of the fateful charge on the third day at Gettysburg and had spearheaded the crucial rebel victory at Chickamauga. After the war he settled in New Orleans, first advising acceptance of defeat and moderation and then becoming an active member of the Republican Party. Despite his prominence in the rebellion, white southern Democrats quickly cast Longstreet as the chief scalawag, and Lost Cause writers began to heap blame on him for the loss at Gettysburg and hence for the ultimate defeat of the Confederacy. At the same time that the Lost Cause elevated Lee and "Stonewall" Jackson into the southern pantheon, it cast Longstreet and similar "traitors" into the pit.[5]

It might be noted that regional Republicans gave nearly as well as they got when it came to circulating rumors about political opponents. For example, editor A. B. Chapin of the *Greensboro Register*, a Republican paper, taunted Conservatives with their own race card. In 1869 he criticized Democratic political campaigning that relied on fears of "amalgamation." Chapin fingered Conservatives and especially the increasing activity of a local Ku Klux Klan when he wrote, "Why you know yourself there isn't a mulatto child in town scarcely whose 'daddy' isn't Ku-Klux?" He continued, ridiculing "the beloved offspring of a zealous brother of the white mask, a big bantling in the owl's nest."[6]

The slander flew in every corner of the South, but labeling and shaming scalawags was especially rampant in North Carolina, given the state's persistent squabbles with the Confederate government and its multifaceted wartime peace movement. White Conservatives in the years immediately after the war set about rewriting the state's history, emphasizing its sacrifice for the Confederacy and minimizing the extent to which the state's citizens were divided by the war. Whites who adopted the Republican Party, like Stephens, were always targets of ire. William Woods Holden drew the greatest wrath, as his genuine political power and appeal to a cross section of white and black North Carolinians demonstrated the reality of opposition in the state to Conservative aims. Minimizing Holden's wartime popularity and attributing his postwar success to kowtowing to Washington worked to obscure the genuinely divided nature of the state. Conservative aspirations relied on transforming wartime Unionists into postwar scalawags. As one historian put it succinctly a half century ago, Conservatives reviled Republicans in governance "not so much because they governed badly, but because they were in the positions of power which the old Whigs and Democrats had divided between themselves."[7]

Stephens's term as senator got off to a rough start. When he arrived in Raleigh in July to claim the seat, the Senate had already rejected Bedford Brown's claim to office but was still undecided on the question of whether Stephens was the de facto winner or a new election was needed. They finally found in Stephens's favor on August 22, 1868, and retroactively awarded him a per diem and travel allowance for the time he spent awaiting the decision.[8]

This period of uncertainty resulted in a moderate scandal. The following January an investigation by the state's Senate Committee on Bribery and Corruption revealed that Stephens had bribed Democrat William Robbins of Rowan County in an effort to secure the per diem payments. Essentially Stephens was accused of paying for Robbins's crucial swing vote on the question. Robbins protested that the money covered legal services he provided Stephens and was not a bribe. The Senate found otherwise and censured the Conservative on April 2, 1869, but an effort to expel him from the Senate failed in a close vote. Stephens escaped censure himself through a technicality: at the moment he bribed Robbins he had not yet been confirmed as a senator, and thus his actions were outside of the body's purview. Nonetheless, the incident provided ammunition for his political opponents and set the tone for Stephens's term.[9]

Slipping past censure, Stephens joined a state legislature with a strong Republican majority; the party of Lincoln held an 87 to 39 edge over Conservatives after the 1868 election. Of the Republicans only 18 were African American, but one of those House members, Wilson Carey, represented Caswell County. Carey's position mirrored that of Stephens: he had lost the election to planter William Long, one of the largest antebellum slaveholders in Caswell, but the House disqualified Long and seated Carey in his place. In the state Senate itself, Republicans outnumbered Democrats 38 to 12, with 28 members of the majority North Carolina–born whites like Stephens. This "radical" legislature proved an active group. Historian Allen Trelease notes that, in conjunction with the new constitution, "it created a functioning public school system for the first time in the state's history; adopted a new and progressive civil code; affirmed the legal and political equality of the races; provided at least minimally for the better treatment of the insane, deaf, dumb, and criminal; helped curb lawlessness and violence; and took steps to alleviate economic distress among various elements of the population."[10]

Stephens took part in these endeavors. He consistently voted the party line on issues of education, taxes, and internal improvements. He also introduced a number of bills, including legislation to maintain the free-ranging of livestock, to charter new railroads and a ferry in Caswell, to liberalize voter registration, and to empower justices of the peace to deputize constables in times of crisis.[11] Conservatives saw not progress but corruption in this robust legislative slate, arguing that its purpose was to advance Republican political power and line the pockets of greedy legislators. There was more than a hint of smoke to back up Conservatives' yells of fire, especially when it came to railroads. Milton S. Littlefield, president of the state council of the Union

League, and banker George Swepson were ultimately implicated in payouts and bribes to facilitate state bonds in support of various railroad projects. (It merits noting that corrupt railroad deals had long been of concern in the state and that this Reconstruction-era bribery money flowed to Conservatives as well as to Republicans.) When the scheme began to unravel, Littlefield and Swepson fled the state and worked to avoid extradition.[12] Here, too, critics viewed Stephens as typically self-interested. He consistently voted yes on the railroad charters and acts brought to the legislature, including proposing a number of lines for his home county. (Again, to be fair, the previous Conservative General Assembly had also chartered a railroad to connect Yanceyville to the Virginia state line and granted it broad powers and privileges.)[13] Later testimony claimed that Stephens accepted a loan of $100 from Littlefield in 1869, which he apparently never repaid.[14] He favored tax reductions for tobacco dealers like himself and worked on legislation to shift more policing power from the counties, where Conservatives might serve as justices of the peace, to Raleigh, where Republicans held sway. He also served as an authorized agent to sell stock for the Raleigh and Gaston Railroad, but again, so did several Caswell Democrats. These stances were particularly important in light of Stephens's membership in two powerful Senate fiscal bodies: the Committee on Corporations and the Special Committee on Roads.[15]

When the legislature was out of session Stephens returned to Caswell, where local opposition was stiff and vocal. In addition to his legislative agenda in Raleigh, his past work settling contract and assault cases on behalf of the Freedmen's Bureau had almost certainly generated some enmity. Many prominent Conservative county officials refused to recognize his legitimacy as he continued in the post of justice of the peace, including the sheriff, still Jesse Griffith, who refused to execute his warrants.[16] At least some white Caswell Democrats viewed Stephens's defection to the Republican Party as a betrayal, and in addition to ignoring his authority they worked to intimidate the senator and his largely African American voting base. Perhaps furthering their suspicion was yet another of Stephens's positions: he served as "Colonel" of the county's militia, a body of emergency troops that might be called upon to keep order in Caswell should Raleigh deem the situation there too unruly.[17] Stephens seemed positioned to thwart Conservative efforts to control the county from every post possible.

Stephens's prominent public roles generated tension on the ground. In late June 1868, while the Senate election remained contested, Stephens wrote to Governor Holden about the precariousness of life in Caswell for officials like himself. He noted that his friends disappeared and credit had dried up when he switched parties, although he had done so "becaus I thought it was rite & have never yet Regretted and hope I never Shall." He made no specific requests of the governor but did lament "that I have not means to buy what I actualy kneed for the support of my family. my crediters have pushed on me and taken every thing that the law would allow."[18]

Bureau agent Lt. F. W. Liedtke agreed with Stephens that the situation in Caswell and Alamance had grown more bellicose by late 1868. Whereas a year earlier Liedtke's predecessor could assure Raleigh that county squabbles were largely peaceful disputes over contracts (ignoring the violence noted above), the agent now believed some bolder white resistance was afoot.[19] "Since the election everything seems to have changed," he noted. The two counties seemed full of unrepentant rebels venting "their abominable hatred and desire of revenge, not to the Government directly because these miscreants dare not, but to the poor, ignorant freedpeople who nursed and cared for them when their Slaves." He went on to describe how the control of land provided whites with an economic lever to coerce freedpeople's work, control their votes, and punish any resistance. This was "not the work of one or two evil disposed persons, but is a preconcerted plan, acted upon it seems by whole communities of persons lately in rebellion who too cowardly themselves openly to oppose the Laws of the Land, seek to incite riots and perhaps an insurrection." Liedtke closed his report by suggesting the need for some program by which the government might employ freedpeople for a year, a span that might break their dependence on white landowners and thus remove their economic leverage. Only such an action could "counteract these evil designs."[20]

Writing again to Governor Holden in August 1868, Stephens re-apprised him of the tense situation in Caswell. He opened the letter by describing two recent, violent episodes. In the first, an unruly crowd at a Conservative rally and barbecue turned on Jim Graves, a black farmer and Republican, beating him "very severley." In the second incident a young white farmer, Nathaniel Johnson, assaulted an unnamed freedman and then struck the man's brother with a stick. When the freedmen fought back, Johnson drew a pistol and shot one of them in the thigh. A race riot seemed a real possibility as a group of freedpeople gathered to capture Johnson, but Freedmen's Bureau officials managed to calm the crowd. Stephens tentatively concluded that outside troops were not needed in the county at that time. Perhaps wishfully he declared that "the old and most respectable citizens are opposed to the proceedings of the wild and reckless men and boyes, & that will be stoped." Showing that his trust in those "respectable citizens" only extended so far, he wrote that if the governor did decide troops were necessary, "send (Col) in preferance to white, if you can."[21]

Soon after, Stephens passed along the plea of freedman farmer Jacob Pass. Sheriff Griffith had seized Pass's crop of corn and tobacco as payment of a $15.90 fine owed for a misdemeanor. Pass pled poverty and noted—perhaps with Stephens's coaching—that subsistence farm products were supposed to be exempt from debt collection under the new state constitution. Stephens had also enlisted the support of the Freedmen's Bureau in this case, following a tactic that had ultimately been successful in his political battle with Brown. Despite his past disagreements with Stephens, Lieutenant Liedtke attached a note endorsed by his superior officer to the petition, pointing out that not only was Griffith wrong in this case but he should technically be barred from serving as Caswell's sheriff since he had served as "Sheriff before, during and since the Rebellion."[22]

Stephens had things to worry about in addition to a vengeful sheriff, labor disagreements, and interpersonal squabbles. He and Holden both believed that the violence across the state was increasingly being organized by a conspiracy in the form of the Ku Klux Klan and similar white supremacist secret societies. Founded in Tennessee by a group of Confederate veterans shortly after the end of the Civil War, the Ku Klux Klan spread across the South in 1868. It was not a unified organization, it replicated through emulation rather than central planning, and its chapters—sometimes styled "dens"—operated independently. Similar organizations intent on controlling freedpeople and resisting Republican governance sprang up in North Carolina as well under such names as the "White Brotherhood," the "Constitutional Union Guard," and the "Invisible Empire." The violent efforts of these secretive organizations emerged as a serious problem in Alamance County in 1869, and the troubles quickly bled over into Caswell the same year. Klansmen targeted both blacks and whites who supported the Republican Party, as well as individuals who seemed to defy what they saw as community norms, using terror for both political and social ends. Their actions often took place after sunset, when groups of night riders carried out threats, beatings, and even murder.[23]

Stephens did not know it, but the leader of Caswell's new Klan den was John G. Lea, a Confederate veteran then just in his mid-twenties. John was a member of the prominent Lea family that traced their residence in Caswell to the colonial era, and his relatives had been among the county's largest slaveholders. A number of Leas remained invested in bright tobacco after the war. John also seemed destined for prominence. His father, Thomas, had once served as a justice of the peace and was a well-respected tobacco

North Carolina night riders often wore elaborate or even farcical disguises to mask their identities and further terrorize their victims.
"The Masked Sentinel," from Albion W. Tourgée, *A Fool's Errand, by One of the Fools; the Famous Romance of American History* . . . (New York: Fords, Howard, and Hulbert, 1880).

planter who had owned fifty-eight slaves at the start of the war. The Leas' slaveholding and tobacco cultivation had produced great wealth: in 1860 the census taker estimated that Thomas owned $15,000 worth of real estate and $67,700 in personal property, making him one of the richest people in Caswell.[24] Although just seventeen at the start of the war, John served in the Confederate army like many other Leas, enlisting in Company C of the 41st North Carolina Cavalry Regiment as a corporal on May 6, 1862. He then took up tobacco farming after the war. In the 1870 census he was listed as well-to-do—worth a comfortable $8,500—but still single. He boarded in the household of his sister, Ann, and her husband, William Graves, near Milton in the northeast corner of the county.[25] Despite this relative prosperity, Lea's future, we might imagine, looked cloudier in the years after Appomattox than it had before the war. His family remained socially and economically prominent, but they could no longer rely on the prestige and forced labor that came with being slave owners. He found himself among those "downwardly mobile" planters' sons who, historian Michael Fitzgerald explains, feared "the war had wrecked their futures."[26] Perhaps he envisioned his leadership in the Klan as a step toward reestablishing the old community order that had long served his family well.

Lea's role in the Klan remained a secret, however, and Stephens himself took on surreptitious duties in 1869 when he added another job at the behest of the governor that would bring the two men into direct conflict. That year Holden established a statewide force of two dozen "detectives" charged with rooting out the secret societies like the Ku Klux Klan that he believed to be undermining Republican rule through violence and intimidation. The Republican General Assembly authorized the detective force, whose agents were instructed to operate with discretion, keeping their work secret if possible. The state would pay their expenses and furnish a small salary, and the detectives were expected to report to the governor's office on a weekly basis. As much as $500 was authorized for each arrest that came out of their investigations, and the detectives were granted broad power to collect information and evidence, deputize posses to make arrests, and detain suspected criminals if local law enforcement refused to do so. To draw modern analogies, the detectives were to be part undercover operatives and part US Marshals.[27]

Stephens's detective district encompassed the northern Piedmont, with Caswell County at its epicenter. In 1869 he drew a salary of $150 for the work, a not-inconsequential sum when accompanied by a state reimbursement for a claimed $272.20 worth of expenses in the line of duty. These payments comported with those to other detectives across the state.[28] Stephens's reports to the governor characterized his efforts as vigorous, involving multiple trips throughout Caswell and into Rockingham County to investigate outrages and abuses. The Rockingham situation seemed much the same as in Caswell. In December 1868, Rockingham citizens had petitioned Albion Tourgée to help them investigate a series of outrages that had occurred in the county, and in the summer of 1869 the *Greensboro Register* would record that Rockingham "men have been shot in their own houses; the houses burned down over their heads; men and women inhumanly whipped and beaten, by these armed night-marauders."[29] Stephens rather grandiosely promised Holden that his work would undermine the local Klan, or even put a dent in the statewide organization. In June 1869 he wrote the governor that "the information that I have recvd from [an informant in Rockingham] I am satisfied will lead to the detection of the entire organization of the state whitch is very formitable at presant." A little over a month later he reiterated that "the ifforts put forwith by the authoritys, I have good reason to believe will prove sucsessfull in restoring peace and quiet to the country."[30]

Stephens noted often in his reports that this was hazardous work and as such argued that it warranted greater financial support. He rarely included specific details of his efforts in the letters, usually alluding to incidents and promising more to come. As early as May 1869 he informed Abial W. Fisher, who supervised the detective force for the governor, that "I am watched and suspected," and he warned Fisher, *Do not trust anything to the mail.*"[31] Frequent mention of the dangers of the job served as support for Stephens's regular requests for additional funds. He pushed Fisher to send him money to supplement his detective's salary. At times these demands took an extortionate tone, as when Stephens mysteriously hinted that he had kept "my word as to certain matters" and therefore deserved the money. He also bypassed Fisher on occasion by sending regular letters to Holden outlining his expenses on the job and requested that the state furnish him a horse and additional funds to be used in organizing a posse to serve warrants.[32] Stephens appears only in the detective pay recorded for 1869, though he continued the work in 1870.[33]

Despite the intention that it remain secret, his position as one of Holden's detectives seems to have quickly become public knowledge. He spoke of his efforts to ferret out Klan members to two men in Rockingham County in 1869 and made an effort to recruit a potential detective in Greensboro, and word of these conversations made their way back to Caswell. There rumors began to circulate that Stephens received seven dollars a day for his work and was flush with cash despite recently complaining of destitution. Local

Conservatives were suspicious that he relayed their statements and actions directly to Governor Holden. He was, they came to believe, not just a political opponent but a spy.[34]

In 1869 a family tragedy further clouded Stephens's reputation with Caswell whites, receptive as always to news that cast the senator in a bad light. In June of that year, Yanceyville resident Jacob Doll recorded in his diary that Stephens's mother had died. In ill health, she had moved to town following John, and he had assumed some of the responsibility of caring for her. What seemed suspicious, Doll wrote, were the circumstances of her death. Mrs. Stephens's "throat was cut & she died almost immediately," he noted. The coroner's jury would conclude that she had died in a bizarre accident, cutting herself on the sharp edge of a broken chamber pot in a fall. Rumors immediately swirled that John had killed her in order to be done with the burden of her care and to obtain her house. Although few people seemed to seriously believe these accusations, the scurrilous gossip served as another weapon with which to assassinate Stephens's character.[35]

As sensational as the episode was, most of Stephens's enemies cared more about arson than matricide. Out of the swirling state violence a central theme emerged for white Conservatives by 1869: property destruction. They claimed that the greatest threat to safety and security was the black arsonist, often egged on to destroy property by the scalawags and carpetbaggers who manipulated their votes. As Republicans attempted to crack down on the Klan, Conservatives countered with the specter of the arsonist as the greater public enemy, and these opposing accusations are crucial for understanding Stephens's place in local struggles. Conservative newspapers across the state belabored the theme, calling attention to potential acts of arson and condemning what they saw as the Holden administration's willingness to look the other way when it came to the destruction of Conservatives' property. By late 1869, the northern Piedmont was beset with these fires, Conservatives claimed. In Caswell they pointed to the burning of some commercial buildings in Yanceyville and the destruction of the tobacco barns and crops of several prominent white Conservatives.[36] Josiah Turner, the state's most outspoken Conservative voice in his position as editor of the *Raleigh Sentinel*, portrayed Caswell and neighboring Alamance as the epicenter of a coordinated Republican campaign to control the state through intimidation. In May 1870 he noted "the repeated burning of tobacco barns, granaries, and mills, which have been going on in Caswell for the last twelve months," and blamed this campaign for the rise of the Klan.[37]

The situation in Caswell and Alamance was hardly unique. Accusations of rural arson had resonance throughout North Carolina during the late

1860s and early 1870s, with Conservatives blaming the fires on freedpeople in general and the Union League in particular. Barn burnings like those in Caswell, Turner wrote, "have shed their lurid glare on the bosom of night, in almost every county in the State, from one end of it to the other."[38] Turner and his allies argued that these fires were the epitome of community disorder created by the tumult of war, the upending of social and racial conventions, and debates over the ownership and use of agrarian landscapes. Elsewhere in the Piedmont, angry vigilantes would capture and lynch at least three freedmen accused of barn burning in Orange County, and papers blamed a series of barn burnings in Gaston County on the local Union League chapters.[39] In Mecklenburg County, Haywood Guion, accused of heading a local Klan den, defended himself by blaming Union League barn burners as the true instigators of the county's wave of violence. He believed the actions were directed from league headquarters in Raleigh and claimed that his and other Klan chapters organized as a defensive measure. To hear Guion tell it, his men were cultural and literal firefighters.[40]

The state's Republicans also occasionally mentioned arson, although their accounts expressed more uncertainty about where to place blame. The Republican *Raleigh Standard* reported on numerous cases of arson, sometimes accusing white night riders and on other occasions admitting that the culprits were unknown. The *Greensboro Register*, another Republican paper, noted the frequency of house fires and night riding in its 1869 summary of midsummer court proceedings and alluded to the terror wrought by burning and counter-burning. Fire could be a legitimate tool of self-defense, the paper asserted. If Klan depredations continued, editor A. B. Chapin advocated that Republicans retaliate "to put down these outrages and their perpetrators, by due course of law if possible—*by armed force and active retaliation, if they must*."[41] For the most part, however, the state's Republican leaders declared that they worked to prevent the use of fire as a political weapon.[42]

Arson was an issue of great concern for whites throughout the South during Reconstruction, as many landowners sought ways to retain control of farmland, attract or coerce black labor, and resume profitable production of commodity crops. Accusations of arson flared up in other districts, from the South Carolina Upcountry to northern Alabama.[43] But what was it that made the specter of arson so powerful, so terrifying? What made the burning barn seemingly as frightening as the knife or gun? The answer in the North Carolina Piedmont lay in society's material fabric. There fire had a particular power, a power rooted in the region's agrarian history and culture. Fire had long been a double-edged sword in Caswell, as in much of the rural South.

It was a management tool used in shifting cultivation, as farmers girdled trees and burned brush to clear fields and fertilize the soil. The region also had a long history of woods burning to open up the understory and create better range for semi-feral livestock, and much of the Piedmont remained open range through Reconstruction. These fires sometimes had a mind of their own; intentional woods and field fires could escape their bounds to consume valuable timber, claim wooden fences, and incinerate buildings. Nineteenth-century rural southerners thus had a healthy respect for both the utility and the danger of fire.[44]

In North Carolina, most Reconstruction accusations of arson dealt with the destruction of tobacco barns. The nature of tobacco barns provides understanding of farmers' paranoia. After harvest, tobacco was placed into log barns to dry, or "cure." Most farmers cured their crop with direct heat; some growers had begun to use sheet metal flues and fireboxes to convey heat through the barn, but the majority still used log or charcoal fires built inside the barn itself. For a week or more at a time they kept fires constantly burning on the floor of the barn, drying the tobacco leaves hanging on tiers of wooden sticks above. This was simultaneously tedious and nerve-racking work. One Piedmont newspaper described the condition of tobacco farmers during curing season in the following manner: "[Farmers] have to watch their barns day and night, and get pretty well smoked, so that from the loss of sleep and red eyes and hard work, some of them are nearly as crazy as bed bugs."[45] The barns themselves were made of pine logs, chinked tightly along their length but with openings along the base of the walls and at the ridge line of their A-framed roofs; the barns were essentially giant flues designed to promote steady-burning curing fires.[46]

Given these hazards, barns in the tobacco belt had long burned with some frequency. Farmers tending fires through the night fell asleep and failed to notice a fire escaping its proper bounds; a hard gust of wind just as a barn door opened blew embers into the rafters; a poorly tied bundle of dry leaves fell from the tiers and onto the fire, instantly igniting. These sorts of accidents happened regularly, and once in flames the logs of a curing barn, dried by countless past fires, were nearly impossible to extinguish. Farmers could only watch as a valuable structure and the tobacco that represented part or all of a year's work went up in flames. It must have been a bitter sight. Even after curing was complete, farmers frequently stored their tobacco in their barns for weeks or months at a time, waiting for good market conditions. During this time the dry and quite flammable crop represented both a source of stored wealth and a great vulnerability. It was a bank with no vault. Before the Civil

War, when slaves performed much regional tobacco work, a barn on fire often raised questions of sabotage. Was the fire a true accident, or the vandalism of a disgruntled slave? Masters were often unsure and were unsettled by the possibilities.[47] These questions and worries surely outlived the Civil War and emancipation, lurking behind the arson accusations of Reconstruction.

The war itself had given fire new and threatening implications. The last year of the conflict brought direct Union campaigns targeting southern agricultural systems in an effort to break southerners' will to continue fighting. These attacks often took the form of systematic burning of stored cotton, corn, and tobacco, along with barns, storehouses, fences, and cotton gins, and soldiers carried off or shot livestock in their path. The result was what historian Lisa Brady labels "war upon the land."[48] While the most notorious campaigns of destruction took place at the direction of Philip Sheridan in Virginia's Shenandoah Valley and William T. Sherman during his march through Georgia and the Carolinas, Union agricultural warfare became a widespread tool as the war progressed. North Carolina's Piedmont escaped the worst of this destruction but still saw its share of wartime fires. Sherman's troops visited the state in 1865, although they were gentler there than in South Carolina. Tellingly, Caswell Klansmen connected Albion Tourgée to this destruction, believing him to be "a bummer . . . from Sherman's army."[49] (They were only partially correct. Tourgée's unit, the 105th Ohio, had fought under Sherman in both the Atlanta Campaign and the March to the Sea, but only after he had left the service. Tourgée resigned in late 1863, nearly invalided by the chronic effects of a back injury suffered at the first battle of Bull Run.)[50] Connecting Tourgée to Sherman tied him to the man white southerners most associated with vengeful fire.

Parts of the state untrampled by Sherman's march still suffered the fires of war. Garrisoned and transient Confederate troops pillaged woodlots and burned fence rails in their campfires. Union cavalry general George Stoneman led one of the largest raids of the war through the western mountains and into the Piedmont during 1865, his soldiers fighting and burning as they went.[51] And North Carolina's divided civilians engaged in violence that often included arson. Along the coast, partially occupied by the Union military from early in the war, citizens and irregular combatants found themselves in a shifting mosaic of localized violence and burning buildings.[52] In the western mountains, arson also became one weapon in the struggle between mountaineers who supported the Union and those with Confederate sympathies. One Confederate lieutenant colonel promised that such Unionist actions would be met with home and barn burning in an "eye for an eye" campaign.[53] Many North Carolinians during Reconstruction must have retained memories of these wartime acts of arson—real or feared—that coupled with the constant threat of farm fires to make arson a truly potent psychological weapon.

More than worry and memory made arson a devastating practice. Fire was so effective a tool during and after the war because arsonists targeted the weak points in the rural countryside, the built environment of the rural landscape centered on farm technology. In some ways farms were hard targets to significantly damage. Night riders could "scrape" a plant bed in the spring, destroying a year's seedlings, or a crop could be trampled or burned in the field.[54] These acts of "eco-terror" imposed great financial harm on a farmer, meaning the loss of part or all of a year's income, but they were relatively temporary forms of destruction. For all the talk of landscapes destroyed or ravaged, this sort of ultimate devastation was easier said than done. The soil remained, ready to produce a crop the following year. But agrarian landscapes did have their weak links: the technology—whether rudimentary or complex—created by farmers to make the land more productive and manageable. Barns stood at the center of these built environments, as places where crops and livestock were stored. This is the reason, perhaps, that William Faulkner made the disreputable character Ab Snopes in *The Hamlet* a barn burner, in so doing defining him as a serious threat to the stability and prosperity of his agrarian community.[55] Similar foci of the rural built environment included gristmills and milldams, cotton gins, fences, sugar mills, and agricultural implements. Although these too could be rebuilt or replaced, to do so involved more effort and greater cost than replanting a burned field or scraped plant bed. In the parlance of modern irregular military operations, the destruction of agricultural technology was a "force multiplier," amplifying the power of the arsonist through striking at the spots where southern people and environments intersected.[56]

Despite their fears of arson perpetrated by freedpeople and white Republicans, or maybe because of them, Conservatives were quite willing to use organized violence to further their own aims. An Alamance lynching in February 1870—the same month that the Fifteenth Amendment's ratification promised to secure black men's voting rights—made this abundantly clear. The target of the violence was Wyatt Outlaw, a prominent African American businessman and Union League leader, and almost certainly one of Stephens's acquaintances. Outlaw's likely father, Chesley Faucette, had been a prominent white planter before the war, his mother a slave. Faucette was a strong Unionist, participating as a leader in the Alamance Red Strings during the war, and his unacknowledged son took up similar work in the years after the war. Outlaw served in the Union army, and upon his return to the county he opened a carpentry shop and unlicensed bar in the town of Graham. There he helped establish an African Methodist Episcopal church as well as the Alamance Loyal League, as the county's Union League chapter was known. Governor Holden named Outlaw one of Graham's town commissioners in 1868, as part of his effort to consolidate Republican political power through the appointment of local officials across the state.[57]

Outlaw's growing prominence grated on Alamance Conservatives. As town commissioner he worked to combat Klan activities, even as his critics accused him of immorality and theft. They also accused him of barn burning, a claim pregnant with the fears noted above.[58] On the evening of February 26, 1870, a group of as many as 100 Klansmen rode into Graham, seized Outlaw from his home in the presence of his family, carried him to the town square, and hung him in front of the courthouse. According to some accounts the mob then mutilated his body with knives. The killers left a note pinned to Outlaw's corpse that read, "Beware, you guilty, both white and black," a clear effort at political and social intimidation. To hide their identities, the Klansmen soon afterward killed William Puryear, a mentally disabled freedman, who purportedly had recognized some of the killers.[59] The county's Klan also targeted Alamance senator T. M. Shoffner, who had angered them as the author of a bill authorizing the governor to use the militia in any county deemed in insurrection and to call for federal troops if necessary. Conservatives heaped abuse on Shoffner's character, and he fled Alamance for Indiana after receiving death threats, although his bill would prove important in the months to come.[60]

Governor Holden saw these events in Alamance County as definitive proof that secret societies had moved from resistance to open rebellion. The Freedmen's Bureau could be of little use in quelling the violence—always understaffed, by the spring of 1870 it was largely unfunded, most agents were laid off, and even the bureau schools had closed their doors—and so Holden turned to Washington for help.[61] Within days of Outlaw's lynching he petitioned President Grant to send troops to quell the insurrection in the county. Federal officials expressed some doubt that there was a general rebellion afoot in the northern Piedmont but ultimately approved dispatching a few companies of soldiers to assess the situation on the ground. The first troops arrived on March 4, and Holden clamored for reinforcements in the days that followed, arguing that perhaps 900 Klansmen were at work in the county. The governor made clear what he wanted from US soldiers: a suspension of habeas corpus and military trials of rebels. He mused that "if criminals could be arrested and tried before military tribunals and shot, we should soon have peace and order throughout all this country. The remedy would be a sharp and bloody one, but it is indispensable as was the suppression of the rebellion."[62] Holden hardly had half measures in mind.

New Martial law.

In Yanceyville John Stephens was equally concerned. Like Holden, he sensed that the murders in Alamance marked an escalation of Conservatives' efforts to seize control of political processes and the economic structures of the countryside. Across Caswell, incidents of intimidation against the county's African Americans were on the rise, and he grew increasingly concerned that he too would be a target. Stephens took to carrying two or three pistols on his person when in public and made it well known that he would use them if threatened. Fearful that these prophylactic measures would not protect him, he took out a $10,000 life insurance policy to provide for his family in case of his death.[63] In late April he wrote Tourgée to confide that Klansmen in Caswell seemed primed to replicate the actions of their allies in Alamance. They had continued "committing their helish deeds," including the recent beating of a white Republican and the castration of a freedman. Mixing politics with personal business, as was his fashion, Stephens then asked Tourgée to vouch for him in his effort to secure a loan for $1,500.[64]

Despite these concerns, there is some evidence that Stephens soon increased the pace of his Union League work as well as resorted to more militant measures himself. Josiah Turner's *Raleigh Sentinel* complained mid-May of a rash of barn burnings and assaults in the Piedmont and singled out the targeting of Conservatives in Caswell. In that county, he wrote, "this week, we hear of the burning of the barns of Mr. Lea and Mr. Hinton, together with all their tobacco."[65] Elsewhere in the county, the paper asserted in another edition, mills and granaries had burned in recent months under suspicious circumstances.[66] Caswell's Conservatives must act, Turner declaimed, and if such action was violent then he understood the impulse. "We can well conceive, that the most bitter feeling must be engendered in a community, when, almost every week, the property of the most estimable citizens of the county is consumed by the incendiary's torch, and by parties supposed to belong to the Union Leagues."[67] The Republican press also admitted there had been a rash of arson attacks in Caswell that spring and did not deny the possibility that the local Union League was involved. The *Raleigh Standard*, edited by Joseph Holden, the governor's son, noted that the burning of barns and other property destruction had set the community on edge by May.[68] Several historians of varied political leanings would concur in the years that

followed that Stephens likely played a hand in organizing this arson campaign, even as they differed on whether the fires were primarily self-defense
in the face of Klan night riding.[69]

Given the violence and uncertainty blanketing Caswell in the spring of
1870, Stephens made a surprising decision on May 21. That Saturday afternoon the county's Conservatives held a political meeting in the Yanceyville
courthouse, and Stephens decided to attend. Although it was geared toward
party activities, especially determining a slate of candidates for the coming
elections, the meeting was open to the public. Open or not, the appearance
of the county's most prominent "scalawag" was sure to draw notice if not outright hostility. Perhaps Stephens thought it his duty as a Republican senator
(and as a secret detective for the governor) to keep tabs on local Conservative plans. Maybe he even envisioned bridging the divide between parties. A
relative asserted years later that he had attended "to show them that he was
not afraid to go, and also to see what tactics the Democrats would use in the
campaign."[70] He most likely assumed that a very public meeting in broad daylight at the heart of the county seat was one of the safest places he could be.
Both his wife, Fannie, and brother William (who lived with him at the time)
suggested that Stephens anticipated some trouble, as he made sure to arm
himself with a revolver and two derringers before leaving for the meeting.[71]

The Democratic meeting that day focused on the coming elections, strat-
egizing how best to regain control of the county from Republican influence.
Stephens sat among the crowd, slouched at the end of a bench in a black felt
hat yet making no real effort to hide himself as he scribbled notes throughout the proceedings. Midday he walked home—his house was located just
a quarter mile from the courthouse—for a bite to eat and then returned for
the resumption of the meeting at 2:00 p.m. Throughout the day Conservatives cast glares his way from time to time, and one speaker, Phillip "Squire"
Hodnett, pointed Stephens out and denounced his presence for the audience.
Hodnett heatedly proclaimed that the senator was in attendance as a spy
to report the proceedings back to the governor and president. (Although
Hodnett had too much confidence in Stephens's political connections, he
was essentially correct regarding the work of the governor's detective.) Then,
midafternoon, when Stephens's old opponent for the state Senate, Bedford
Brown, rose to speak, a former county sheriff, Frank Wiley, tapped Stephens
on the shoulder and chatted quietly with him for a minute before leaving the
courtroom. Shortly thereafter Stephens followed, heading down the stairs to
the basement level of the building. He never came back to the meeting, nor
did he return home when it broke up.[72]

The main entrance to the Caswell County Courthouse.
Jack E. Boucher, *Exterior, Entrance Detail*, Historic American
Buildings Survey, 1962, Library of Congress.

By late afternoon Stephens's friends and family noted his absence and began to grow concerned, fearing foul play. His wife, brothers, and several black townspeople organized a search and began combing the courthouse square, concentrating on the courthouse itself, the last place Stephens had been seen. The search extended into the darkness but turned up no sign of the missing senator.[73]

Yanceyville resident Jacob Doll wrote in his diary that evening about the buzz and consternation in town as the sun went down. He recorded that Stephens had last been spotted near the old clerk's room in the courthouse basement, and "about 6 O clock he was missed by his family & they began to look for him. . . . After dark the search became general." Doll wrote that the town's black citizens organized a party to guard the courthouse throughout the night, suspicious that Conservative machinations were afoot. Their fears seemed confirmed the following morning, when one of Stephens's brothers gave a shout after peering through a window on the ground level of the building. There, as daybreak lightened the sky, he could see something lying on a pile of wood in the old clerk's office. Was it a body? When they broke into the locked room the men found Stephens's corpse with "a rope looped & drawn tight around his neck. He was stabbed twice in the neck & once in the heart."[74]

Stephens opponents in the conservatives kill him brutely in the Courthouse, A place of law & justice

Four

PURGATORY

Whether they were from Texas or h[el]l, they were Kuklux, and
they were aided in their diabolical schemes by the Kuklux of Caswell,
who are equally guilty and equally deserving of the halter.

JOSEPH HOLDEN, *Raleigh Standard* (1870)

[handwritten marginalia: Continued plus for brutal justice.]

ho did it? The question raged across the state in the days
and weeks following the discovery of John Walter Stephens's
corpse on the woodpile in the basement of the Caswell
County Courthouse. Most Republicans and more than a few Conservatives
believed that local Klansmen were to blame, in light of the night riding that
had taken place in Caswell and the actions in Alamance in the preceding
weeks. The first step in investigating the killing was a coroner's inquest,
held in the immediate aftermath of the killing. (These inquests were preliminary investigations designed to establish the cause of death and, when
foul play was suspected, to collect evidence.)[1] County coroner A. G. Yancey
and twelve jurymen inspected the scene and body. Certain that a crime had
taken place based on the evidence, they proceeded to investigate; over the
course of five days they conducted interviews of thirty-five witnesses who
had been in or around the courthouse on the day of the murder. Stephens
had obviously been the victim of homicide, the jury concluded, meeting his
death through a combination of strangulation and stabbing, but they could

make no immediate determination as to who committed the deed. The jury left the scene with more questions than answers.[2]

Just as important as finding the culprits, maybe more so, were questions concerning what might come from the crime. What would Governor Holden do about the killing, especially in light of the similar targeting of Wyatt Outlaw? Would Holden act directly, using state militia even without federal military backing, which he had been unable to secure in the months leading up to the assassination, or would he persist in the search for political solutions and rely on county officials to keep the peace? Put another way, would the state's response be civil, or military? The decision hinged on his determination that either the North Carolina Piedmont was plagued by criminals using violence to advance their political and economic ambitions, or the region was the site of an organized insurrection. Complicating matters, exactly what had happened in Yanceyville remained uncertain in the days following the murder.

The running newspaper war that had attempted to define Stephens's political life immediately shifted to giving meaning to his death, with editors and correspondents working to shape the case and its outcomes. Who committed the crime was the first question in contention. Initial reports coming from Yanceyville were often garbled. Four days after the killing a Raleigh paper reported that the senator had been "taken by a band of masked persons from his house, and shot, his body being pierced by 40 balls, and then hung up in the Court H[o]use at Yanceyville." This report perhaps confused the details of the Caswell crime with those of Outlaw's lynching.[3] Republicans suspected the Klan from the start, linking Stephens's murder to Outlaw's killing and the threats directed at T. M. Shoffner. In the *Raleigh Standard*, editor Joseph Holden, the governor's son, baldly stated of the killers, "Whether they were from Texas or h———l, they were Kuklux."[4]

Albion Tourgée tried to draw national attention to the crime and the conspiracy he thought was behind it. On May 24 he sent a letter to US senator Joseph Abbott describing the murder, listing numerous other Piedmont outrages, and pinning blame for them all on a Klan intent on overthrowing Republican governance and subjugating freedpeople. The letter eventually found its way to the *New York Tribune*, which published it in August, prompting an uproar back in North Carolina.[5]

Conservative papers countered Republican claims with their own theories. While they rarely denied the possibility of Klan violence, they worked to muddy the waters. Josiah Turner at the *Raleigh Sentinel* observed that Stephens had accumulated plenty of enemies: his various duties as detective for Holden (an open secret by this time), senator, Freedmen's Bureau agent, and justice of the peace had generated numerous grudges.[6] Other articles suggested that the killing quite possibly stemmed from internal Republican political squabbling. "A Citizen of Caswell," in correspondence to the *Sentinel*, claimed that "Stephens had become odious with many of his own party" and had last been seen speaking with two African American men on the day of his murder. The room in which his body had been discovered had last served as an office for an agent of the Freedmen's Bureau, the writer also noted, and a black janitor supposedly held the only key. Building on these statements, within a few days of the assassination the *Sentinel* had outlined a "false flag" conspiracy theory that entailed North Carolina Republicans doing away with Stephens to drum up outrage against Conservatives and sway the coming elections. Deftly weaving together these suppositions, Turner mused, "Was he [Stephens] in the way or was he the *sorriest* sheep in the *flock*, and must he be slaughtered for political purposes[?]"[7] Here was the darkest and most twisted of conspiracies, one in which Stephens was more sacrificial lamb than sheep.

Another Caswell correspondent assured *Sentinel* readers that whatever the case, "it is beyond question that he was not murdered by disguised men or participants in the Conservative meeting."[8] To emphasize the claims that Conservatives frowned upon such extralegal actions, Yanceyville's leading white citizens gathered on May 23 to denounce the killing and call for peace. The group was careful to not point any fingers at potential culprits.[9] Facing tremendous community pressure, on June 2 Stephens's brothers copublished a statement exonerating "certain prominent individuals" who had been suspected of involvement in the murder. Despite the failure to that point to identify likely suspects, in print the brothers claimed to be "fully satisfied that the investigation had been thorough, full and satisfactory."[10]

Equally important to the newspaper and community debates was the issue of Stephens's character. Whoever murdered him, did Stephens deserve his fate? Unsurprisingly the arguments quickly firmed up along party lines and again found voice in regional papers. The *Raleigh Standard* printed a version of the "chicken" story that had long plagued Stephens, only in its recounting the senator had killed his own birds in preparation for crossing to Union lines to avoid conscription for Confederate service. A neighbor falsely claimed the chickens as his, took Stephens to court over the matter in a vindictive attack, and "a prejudiced jury found him guilty." In this telling the temperamental shirker became a persecuted loyalist, a man who was too principled for his own good rather than one lacking in principles.[11]

Conservative papers countered, making Stephens out as a clear villain. He was a "notorious character" who cheated his political allies out of money, an arsonist, a thief, an opportunist, and an all-around scalawag.[12] The same day that it carried the news of Stephens's death, the *Greensboro Patriot* ran two separate articles intimating that the senator had gotten what he bargained for. The murder was simply the law of lex talionis (an eye for an eye), one suggested, while the other smugly asserted that "carpet-baggers, that foul scum of creation, that have dipped so deep into the dregs of political infamy and corruption, that have well-nigh plunged the nation into the abyss of social disorder, bankruptcy, and despotism, are beginning to receive their reward of contempt from all honest people."[13] A polarizing figure in life, Stephens was becoming even more divisive in death.

A booklet describing the killing and speculating about suspects and motive quickly capitalized on the sensational event. Andrew Jackson Stedman, a newspaper editor from the small town of Danbury to the west, released *Murder and Mystery*, which claimed to outline the facts of the matter.[14] The pamphlet was detailed and, in some respects, relatively nonpartisan: Stedman claimed no personal relationship with Stephens, no definitive knowledge of his killers, and no political motivation. However, its printing by the *Greensboro Patriot*, a voice of the Conservative Party (and a thorn in Albion Tourgée's side), perhaps indicated Stedman's sympathies.[15] Whatever his personal politics, Stedman ultimately concluded that Stephens was indeed a bad character, carefully documenting several stories that framed the senator as greedy and cunning. In addition to the now familiar and much contested chicken-stealing tale, Stedman described Stephens's deceptions in business dealings, an effort to shirk his duty to care for his ill mother, and an enthusiasm for bribery and graft that resulted in his expulsion from the congregation of his Methodist church. The pamphlet also noted the suspicious circumstances of his mother's death and labeled him abusive and arbitrary in execution of his duties as a magistrate.[16]

Reprinting the coroner's inquest, Stedman provided readers with details about the investigation into Stephens's demise. Turning to the question of the likely culprits—the coroner had declared the murder "done by the hands of some unknown person, or persons"—Stedman admitted that he was unsure, yet he cast the preponderance of suspicion on Republicans. The booklet included anonymous statements by members of that party that Republicans were "tired of" him "and that he must be gotten rid of on some terms." The concluding summary conveyed the impression that a falling-out in the party was the most likely impetus for the murder. Overall, Stedman's pamphlet suggested that Stephens was something of a villain, at the very least represen-tative of the bad qualities of local Republican Reconstruction, and muddied the waters regarding likely culprits.[17] Stedman both mirrored and helped reinforce the Conservative sentiment concerning the assassination, and the arguments in *Murder and Mystery* remained standard Conservative opinion in the following years.

The public may have received divided messages about the assassination, but Governor Holden was convinced that he knew the truth of the matter. He believed that the Klan was acting as a secretive but semiofficial army of the Conservative Party and was targeting Republican officials. Klansmen had killed Stephens just as they had killed Outlaw and driven Wilson Carey and T. M. Shoffner from the upper Piedmont, all in a concerted effort to over-throw Republican authority and carry the coming August elections through brute force and intimidation. The Klan, Holden wrote, held "absolute control, for the last twelve months, of the counties of Alamance and Caswell." This was an insurrection; it was "new treason" just a few years after a cataclysmic war to stamp out the old treason. It was, in fact, exactly the sort of circum-stance for which the Shoffner Act was designed.[18]

Holden's first action was to offer a $500 reward for information about Klan activities in Caswell, in particular Stephens's murder; the death of a freedman named Robin Jacobs, who had been killed near Leasburg; and the whippings of twenty-one other Caswell citizens said to have taken place in April and May.[19] When this reward offer generated no arrests, Holden's next step was to issue a declaration on July 8 that Caswell was in insurrection.[20] Holden believed that the few federal troops on the ground in Alamance were not a sufficient force to address the expanded declaration of insurrection, and he used the Shoffner Act's provisions to create state militia units to dispatch to Alamance and Caswell, as well as to guard key state offices in Raleigh and monitor the coming elections. Some regional Republicans praised the decision as long overdue. The *Greensboro Republican* thought martial law necessary, since "the poor hard working people out in the fields from morn to night are toiling and groaning and praying for better times amongst us, for peace, for a cessation of kuklux and league horrors, for northern gentlemen with capital to come among them, for no more strife, for peace officers to do their duty, for the screws to be put on no tighter, (and God knows Congress has nearly screwed us to death now!)."[21] Local recruits were insufficient to the task, Holden believed, and perhaps untrustworthy in their allegiances, so he turned to troops from outside of the Piedmont. He placed George Kirk, who had been a Union colonel during the Civil War, in charge of the force of six-month volunteers. Some members of the militia were African American men from eastern North Carolina, and the others Kirk recruited from the state's western mountains.[22]

Like so many of his political maneuvers, Holden's decision to use black and mountain troops under the leadership of Kirk was at once calculating and foolish. Appalachian troops and freedmen did hold the promise of reliable loyalty in the tumult of North Carolina's Reconstruction. The western part of the state had long resented the planter power of the Tidewater and Piedmont sections, and Unionists had composed a significant percentage of the population in most mountain counties, questioning secession before the war and then sometimes openly opposing the Confederacy after North Carolina joined the rebellion. Many of Kirk's troops had remained staunch Unionists during the war and had been tested in the guerrilla violence that had plagued certain corners of the mountains. Holden no doubt assumed they would be loyal and more than willing to police Piedmont Conservatives and former rebels who had brought about the late war. It also seemed politically expeditious to reinforce ties to the white mountaineers who formed an important arm of Republicanism in the state.[23]

The decision may have seemed wise for these reasons, but it also opened Holden up to accusations of placing politics and party before the state's interests. The choice of Kirk as commander was particularly controversial. The colonel had made a name for himself during the war by leading Union raids from East Tennessee into North Carolina, and many people in the state associated his name with invasion, fear, and pillage. He was the sort of figure whom parents might have used to frighten unruly children, not one who leaped to mind for calming a brewing insurrection in Alamance and Caswell Counties. Instead, Kirk's selection seemed an indication that Holden planned on fighting fire with fire. Most of Kirk's white soldiers may have hailed from North Carolina's western counties—he posted his call for volunteers in the state's western towns, requesting the service of men who had fought under him in the war—but Kirk also apparently recruited a few men from East Tennessee, a region where guerrilla war had raged to an even greater degree than in western North Carolina.[24] Conservatives quickly seized upon this to label Kirk's force a horde of angry and vindictive Tennessee Unionists intent on extracting vengeance from their Tar Heel neighbors. The *Greensboro Patriot* labeled him "Ku Klux Kirk," arguing that his soldiers dealt in terror to a greater extent than did Piedmont night riders. At the same time, Democrats made fun of the militia as comprising ignorant backwoods rubes, in contrast to the men of community prominence they often arrested. Even some federal soldiers stationed in the Piedmont questioned the militia's legitimacy as a force of law and order, perhaps looking down their professional noses at temporary soldiers. Captain George Rodney, in command of federal troops stationed in Yanceyville, labeled the militia "nothing more than an armed mob" intent on stirring up the sort of trouble it claimed to be suppressing. Collectively, the decision to use mountain soldiers headed by a notorious Union officer exposed Governor Holden to claims that he cared more for personal victory and maintaining his office than he did for peace or defending the state's sovereignty.[25]

Whatever the composition and motivations of the militia, once they reached the Piedmont Kirk's troops moved quickly to stamp out night riding in the two counties by arresting all of the men whom Republicans believed to be Klan members. In Caswell this included most of the individuals whom community gossip had connected to Stephens's killing, including Frank Wiley, James T. Mitchell (captain of a local Confederate unit during the war), and Joseph Fowler. The arrest list also included a large percentage of citizens interviewed in the initial coroner's investigation. But other prominent local figures were also swept up in the raids, simply for being influential Conservative leaders, Holden's opponents suggested. John Kerr was one example. There was little to suggest the former state legislator, congressional representative, and superior court judge was involved in a Klan conspiracy, but he was arrested by Kirk's men just the same. The soldiers even detained and questioned A. G. Yancey, the county coroner who had conducted the initial investigation in the aftermath of the senator's murder, before releasing him for lack of evidence.[26] While Kirk's men attempted to round up additional suspects, the bulk of the prisoners awaiting transport to Raleigh were held in the very courthouse in Yanceyville in which Stephens had been murdered.[27]

The capture of Frank Wiley, a prime suspect in the killing, proved especially polarizing. Kirk's men apprehended Wiley as he was working in his tobacco field: like so many county residents, the former sheriff relied on the crop for at least part of his income. He was seemingly unconcerned with the countywide manhunt for murder suspects, since he had neither fled nor altered his daily routines. Stephens's allies believed the former sheriff was an active member of the Klan and involved in the murder plot, and they celebrated his arrest as a step toward justice. Conservatives offered a different narrative, portraying Wiley's capture as the epitome of Holden's tyranny.

As with everything to do with the assassination and the following events, there are varying accounts of how Wiley's arrest took place. The standard Republican description portrayed the event as anticlimactic, although it did mention that Wiley had to be bound when transported on horseback to Yanceyville.[28] Klan leader John G. Lea painted a much different picture in an account decades after the fact, limning Wiley as a heroic figure. According to Lea, "Lt. Col. Burgin with eight men went down after ex-sheriff Wiley, nine miles from Yanceyville; went in his tobacco field where he was standing and told him they had come to arrest him." Wiley refused to acknowledge the soldiers' legitimacy or to submit to the arrest, at which point the troops "rushed on Wiley, who knocked down seven of them, but one slipped up behind him with a fence rail and knocked him down; they then put Wiley on a horse, bare back, tied his feet to the horse and whipped him nearly all the way to Yanceyville. The blood flowed freely, he being in his shirt sleeves. Burgin told me that Wiley was the bravest man he ever saw." To cap this story of defiance in the face of daunting odds, Lea claimed that once the party reached Yanceyville, Kirk's soldiers threatened to shoot Wiley unless he provided the names of other Caswell Klan members. "With his head straight as could be," Lea remembered, "he opened his coat, slapped his chest and dared them to shoot."[29]

It is easy to see the mythologizing of a martyr in Lea's story of Wiley's defiance. In a community centered on agricultural labor, a man working in his field was a powerfully symbolic figure. Wiley might be portrayed as an independent Jeffersonian yeoman beset by an abusive Republican government that did not reflect the local will. There is another analogy Lea might have wished to invoke in his description of the arrest: that of the story of Cincinnatus, a popular figure in antebellum American political rhetoric. In Lea's tale, Wiley, like the Roman leader, had left his work in the fields to lead his community in a time of trouble and then beat his sword into a plowshare and returned to his agrarian labors. Lea's testimony implied that Wiley's arrest, complete with Christlike torture, was a mockery of both justice and community ideals. It also neatly transformed what might be seen as a cowardly act—secretly conspiring to surprise and kill the senator—into the behavior of a brave man.

Conservative community outrage could not immediately halt Kirk's and Holden's actions, but two events did start to unravel what was coming to be known as the "Kirk-Holden War." The first was the arrest of the most outspoken Conservative voice in the state: Josiah Turner. Turner had served as a state senator during the Civil War and had been director of the North Carolina Railroad, and he then became the vocal and acerbic editor of the Raleigh Sentinel. In the latter position he devoted a great deal of copy to a long-running feud with Governor Holden. (The previous year Turner had gone so far as to claim that Holden's allies had orchestrated an attempt on his life in order to silence his criticisms.)[30] Republicans liked to insinuate that Turner secretly headed the Ku Klux Klan in the state, although there is no real evidence to support the contention. Turner did, however, seem to cheer on vigilante violence in print. A passage from the *Sentinel* in the days leading up to Stephens's assassination gives the flavor of Turner's inflammatory attacks on Holden, the Union League, and Republican political rule in the state:

> The secret society [Union League] of which the Governor is, or has been, President, has had as complete control in North Carolina and the South, as the old Jacobin clubs had of France. Eighty thousand negroes, lead [*sic*] by five hundred carpet baggers and one hundred educated office holding natives, made up the clubs or leagues in North Carolina.
>
> The work must be now to dissolve them.
>
> Every day they are fast crumbling to pieces. We heard a prominent Republican declare, and repeat it, that his party could carry the election in August by intimidating the white men with the military.[31]

For Holden and his allies, Turner's words seemed to be coded instructions to Klan chapters rather than mere rhetorical attacks. In the editor's claims of Republican voting intimidation, Holden's allies saw instead a blueprint for Conservative-organized violence at the polls.

Goaded by the *Sentinel*'s constant criticism of the militia and its actions, Kirk's men, perhaps misunderstanding Holden's desires, arrested Turner at his home in Hillsborough. This action exceeded their authority, however, as Hillsborough was located in Orange County, which had not been declared in insurrection. Kirk's men carried the indignant editor to Yanceyville, where, in an act fraught with symbolism, they imprisoned him in the very room in which searchers had discovered Stephens's body. Conservatives seized upon Turner's arrest as proof that the declaration of martial law had become a witch hunt of the governor's political opponents rather than legitimate suppression of a rebellion.[32]

The Yanceyville prisoners did not bear confinement in silence. Turner and his fellow detainees complained of harsh treatment at the hands of Kirk's militiamen, but their protests gained more traction when they focused on the legal issue of habeas corpus. Eighteen of the suspects held at the courthouse (including Wiley) petitioned for their release to the civil courts, as outlined in state law. They noted that the 1868 constitution drafted by Republicans had stripped the governor of the power to suspend habeas corpus, even under a declaration of martial law. Convention delegates had considered a situation very like that in Caswell when crafting the law, and when the habeas protection came up for debate, a move to either suspend it in instances of insurrection or delete it altogether lost in a resounding defeat, seventy-two votes to just six. The resulting constitutional language was straightforward, instructing that "the privilege of the writ of habeas corpus shall not be suspended in this State."[33] Additionally, in debate leading to passage of the Shoffner Act in early 1870, permitting the governor to suspend habeas corpus in cases of insurrection had again been considered and rejected, with some Republicans still joining Conservatives in opposition to the provision.[34] Together these actions made the legislature's stance on habeas hard to ignore.

Holden's plans for the prisoners were unclear—perhaps in his angriest moments he contemplated following through on his threat to conduct military tribunals and shoot traitors—but, whatever his intentions, for several weeks he had Kirk detain the suspected Klansmen without surrendering them to the judicial system. (In the meantime, Kirk himself was quite uncertain of the situation on the ground. He awaited instruction from Holden and worried that his position was exposed, convinced on several occasions that he was surrounded by a virtual army of Klansmen who might attack his troops at any moment.) The detainees' habeas petition found a sympathetic ear in Richard Pearson, chief justice of the North Carolina Supreme Court. Pearson enjoyed bipartisan support, having managed to carefully dance through the political minefield of the Civil War years. He served as the state's chief justice during the rebellion and on the bench lent some support to North Carolina's Unionists while avoiding alienation of the state's diehard rebels. Pearson's politic behavior continued during Reconstruction, with the result that he had appeared on both the Republican and the Conservative tickets in the 1868 election. Pearson personally and professionally disliked the vigilantism of the Klan, but he also frowned upon efforts to circumvent the legal system upon which he sat at the pinnacle.[35]

Presented with the detainees' petition, Pearson issued a writ of habeas corpus that directed Kirk to deliver the prisoners to Raleigh for trial. Kirk refused on the grounds that he was acting under Holden's direct command, with instructions that he not surrender the prisoners without an order from the governor's office. In communication with the chief justice, Holden refused to give such an order, arguing that his actions were necessary to forestall rebellion and the situation was thus a military rather than a civilian matter. Holden promised that he would deliver the men to the courts once the insurrection was suppressed, but to do so any earlier was to risk letting the Klan conspiracy subvert the legal process. Given their freedom, men like Kerr and Turner might influence the courts and incite additional violence. Pearson was frustrated with Holden's stalling tactics and insulted by the intimation that state courts were vulnerable to political influence, but he resisted instructing state marshals to take the men by force, writing that he "was unwilling to plunge the State into a civil war, upon a mere question of time."[36]

With their petition to Pearson stymied, the prisoners then appealed to federal district court judge George Brooks. Brooks concurred with Pearson on the illegality of Kirk's actions and ordered that the colonel produce the prisoners, observing that due process and state law demanded it. In a last-ditch effort to salvage the situation, Holden sent an appeal for support to President Grant in Washington. He was disappointed. Grant refused to intervene and the attorney general replied on the president's behalf, advising Holden to remand the prisoners since the state law seemed so clear on the subject of habeas corpus. The White House likely viewed the events unfolding in the North Carolina Piedmont as a potential embarrassment for Congressional Reconstruction efforts and hoped they could be resolved quickly and quietly. From the perspective of the Oval Office, Holden's administration was beginning to look more like a liability than an asset. With his appeals exhausted and in hopes of staying in Washington's good graces, Holden yielded to Brooks's instructions and ordered Kirk to deliver the prisoners to Judge Pearson in Raleigh.[37]

This was a political blow for Holden, but it remained unclear whether the end result would be a victory for the prisoners. When Kirk and Holden relinquished control of the men to the civil courts, they did so with the expectation that trials would follow. In Raleigh, Chief Justice Pearson also intended to see that North Carolina's courts had their say. He was troubled by how the prisoners had been arrested and detained, but the state's attorney general had taken out a bench warrant on the suspects after their arrival in Raleigh, and thus Pearson believed proceeding with prosecution was justified.[38] Now that they were within the legitimate court system of the state, it would proceed to dispense justice, with the North Carolina Supreme Court overseeing the preliminary hearing due to its politically charged nature. Confident in his authority, Pearson declared, "Now we have plain sailing; if there be 'probable cause' against the prisoner, let the State prove it." In late August six of the chief suspects in Stephens's murder—Frank Wiley, Felix Roan, Joseph Fowler, James T. Mitchell, and two other men described just as "Hill" and "Roan"—faced Pearson in a preliminary hearing to determine whether they should be remanded to Caswell County for trial. Twenty-two other men from Caswell

Raleigh was a small but growing Piedmont city at the time of the Stephens murder hearing. C. N. Drie, *Bird's Eye View of the City of Raleigh, North Carolina, 1872* (Raleigh, NC: C. Drie, 1872), Library of Congress.

and Alamance whom Kirk had arrested, among them former state and US representative John Kerr and Caswell County's sheriff, the much-maligned Jesse Griffith, were released for "want of evidence."[39]

The state sought to prove two fundamental details: first, that the defendants had reasons to wish Stephens dead, and second, that they had the opportunity to kill him. Strong evidence on both questions would warrant prosecution. For its part the defense aimed to cast doubt on one or both issues. If there was no motive or no clear opportunity, then Wiley and the others should not be charged. The resulting Raleigh inquest was much more elaborate than that of a typical case, stretching over several days as both sides called dozens of witnesses. Thirty-eight people took the stand in the Wiley portion of the hearing alone. Many of the deponents who testified, including three of the four defendants (charges against the aforementioned "Hill" and "Roan" were dropped without proceedings), had previously testified to the coroner's jury in the immediate aftermath of the killing, but now the stakes were higher.[40]

Chapter Four

Proceedings began on the morning of Monday, August 22, in the supreme court chamber. It was a full room. Interested spectators were in attendance, and numerous lawyers gathered at the prosecution and defense tables: five for the state and seven speaking for the defendants. (One of the prosecution's team, Attorney General Lewis Olds, happened to be Governor Holden's son-in-law.)[41] The swearing-in of a long list of witnesses was the first item on the agenda, notable among them Fannie Stephens, widow of the deceased, as well as one of his brothers, William. Several of the witnesses were African American, which highlighted the changes that had occurred in the five years of Reconstruction, since black testimony had not been permitted under state law just a few years prior. (Throughout the trial the reporter taking notes for the *Raleigh Standard* was careful to denote the race of each witness, consistently referring to black witnesses as "colored." This may have been to call into question their trustworthiness, to imply inherent politicized viewpoints, or simply force of habit in a society in which race was always considered important.) With the witnesses finally sworn in and midday approaching, Judge Pearson adjourned for the morning, sending Mrs. Stephens to her hotel and the other witnesses into the care of court officers. Scanning the crowded room, Pearson then announced that the afternoon's proceedings would move to the Wake County Courthouse to better accommodate the "large and interested audience" that had gathered to witness the trial. Upon resumption, Wiley's examination would be first, followed individually by those of the other accused men.

The hearing began in earnest in the roomier surroundings at three in the afternoon. One of Wiley's lawyers immediately fired a shot across the state's bow, moving that one of Kirk's officers be placed under arrest for threatening to kill some of the prisoners if they were released. Justice Pearson said he would take the motion "into consideration" and then steered the hearing back on course, with a Caswell doctor named "P. Roan" taking the stand to establish the fact that Stephens had indeed been killed and the nature of his death. Coroner Yancey had called Roan, a local physician, once the body was found on the morning after Stephens went missing. In Roan's opinion it was clear that Stephens had been killed in the courthouse storage room, which had once been the Freedmen's Bureau office, and that the method of murder had been a combination of strangulation and stabbing. He also noted that search parties had attempted to check the room the evening before, but the door was locked, the key was missing, and nothing could be seen in the darkness by looking through the room's small window. Other witnesses followed on Monday afternoon and Tuesday morning, establishing the chronology of

Stephens's presence at the Conservative political meeting, his disappearance at some point in the afternoon, the search for his body throughout the night, and its discovery the next morning.

In this section of the testimony, freedman Lewis Hill's deposition brought up what became an important point of contention throughout the hearing: Was it Stephens or Wiley who had initiated the conversation between the two men on the day of the killing? If Wiley made first contact, that might be seen as evidence that he intended to lure the senator someplace where conspirators could attack him. If Stephens had initiated discussion instead, it made the conversation with Wiley look more benign and undermined the state's case. Wiley had claimed that Stephens approached him, but several black witnesses for the state, Hill among them, maintained that they saw Wiley touch Stephens on the arm or shoulder and initiate the conversation during the Democratic meeting.

On Tuesday morning the courtroom had a few empty seats, but they quickly filled up until it was again standing room only to view the proceedings. The crowd expressed a "most lively interest" as William Stephens, John's brother, took the stand. William described his brother's worries for his personal safety—he told the crowd that John had developed the habit of carrying three pistols on his person in public—yet he had persisted in his political work even when it took him to dangerous places like the Democratic Party meeting that day in Yanceyville. William had been in attendance at the meeting as well, and he noted that one speaker had personally targeted John in his comments. Pointing to the senator, Squire Hodnett had declared Stephens to be a spy for Governor Holden, sitting in the meeting to take notes and report on its proceedings. It was shortly after Hodnett's denunciation, William added, that he saw Wiley approach his brother and thought he heard the former sheriff invite him to discuss something downstairs. The two men then left the room, followed a few minutes later by defendant Joe Fowler and another man, Thomas Hubbard.

Even more damning was the testimony of freedman Joseph Womack that followed. He had been in Yanceyville on the day of the murder to speak to Stephens; Womack had been whipped by a group of Klansmen, and he had hoped the justice of the peace could do something about it. Womack told the court that he had witnessed Wiley, Jim Mitchell, Logan Totten, and three men he did not know slipping out of the lower level of the courthouse a short time after Stephens had gone downstairs. Wiley, he remembered, "looked as if he had been exerting himself, for he was sweating." Black witnesses who followed Womack that afternoon confirmed that Wiley's actions and appearance on the afternoon of the killing seemed odd, and several also recalled seeing Joe Fowler, John Lea, and Tucker Bennett in the lower level of the courthouse that afternoon. The state, having presented an argument that Stephens was murdered and placed Wiley in close proximity to the victim and the crime through numerous witnesses, then paused its case. To this point it had made little effort to establish Wiley's motive for killing Stephens, reserving witnesses to that effect for later in the hearing. This first round of testimony concluded, court adjourned for the day with the defense to outline its argument upon reconvening the next day.

Wednesday morning began with Frank Wiley on the stand, laying out his version of what transpired in Yanceyville on May 21. His testimony differed in some important respects from that of the state's witnesses. Stephens had approached him early that morning, he stated, with a proposal that Wiley run for county sheriff as a moderate. If he did so, Stephens promised that no Republican candidate would oppose him in the interest of generating a fusion ticket to "help harmonize the people." If it appeared to others that Wiley initiated contact during the political meeting in the courthouse that afternoon, he explained, it was only because he was following up on the earlier conversation. And he insisted that it was Stephens who motioned for him to go downstairs, where Wiley declined to run for sheriff and then exited the courthouse, leaving Stephens in good health. He then proceeded to furnish a long list of people he had spoken to or who saw him that afternoon as he engaged in sundry business. As an aside, he also added that he and J. C. Wilkerson had seen Stephens in the assessor's office later in the day, hale and hearty. Besides, he concluded, he had no motive. He bore Stephens no ill will, since as magistrate the senator had once settled a labor dispute between Wiley and a freedman in a fair manner. Sowing a final seed of doubt, Wiley happened to remember seeing Stephens speaking with an unknown black man in the courthouse that afternoon. Although his testimony conflicted with other witnesses in spots, all of the details Wiley provided were consistent with his statements to the coroner's jury three months prior.[42]

Wiley then stepped down, and the defense witnesses who followed attested to a general hard feeling among many county whites against Stephens but denied that there was any local secret society or Klan conspiracy afoot. The murder must have been personal and not political, they collectively asserted. One witness, Colonel Withers, even denied that any whippings whatsoever had taken place in the county and said that no murders had been committed besides that of Stephens and, bringing up a bit of old gossip, that of the senator's mother "in her son's house." (Oh, and maybe "one instance of a colored man near Prospect Hill," he added, as if it hardly warranted mention.) Others testified that Stephens had indeed been seeking to convince Wiley to run for sheriff and was eager to initiate a conversation with him that day.

On Wednesday afternoon, seemingly fed up with the growing circus surrounding the hearing, Chief Justice Pearson moved the proceedings back to the supreme court chamber. He notified the lawyers that they might invite observers, "provided it was not too much crowded." The defense spent the rest of the day's session in the smaller venue producing more witnesses willing to testify that Wiley could not possibly have killed Stephens and casting suspicion on other parties. For example, J. C. Wilkerson, Wiley's primary alibi for the time immediately following his meeting with Stephens, also testified that he saw the senator in conversation in the basement with an unknown freedman. Both A. J. Hooker and A. J. Kimborough swore that they had seen Stephens after Wiley rode out of town that afternoon and that the senator was in the company of black men at the time. The theme continued the following morning, with character witnesses attesting that Wiley's community standing was "above reproach." Summarizing the testimony through Wednesday, the *Greensboro Patriot* crowed that there was "no evidence against [Wiley] as yet."[43]

Midmorning the defense rested, and the state countered by producing more witnesses to complete its case for charges. The drama reached its highest pitch when Fannie Stephens took the stand. She provided little new evidence as to who might have killed her husband or how they accomplished it, but she did speak to his state of mind on the day of the crime. John had left the house fearing trouble and armed with three guns, and she was immediately concerned when he did not return after the Conservative meeting wrapped up. Having been placed on the stand largely for pathos, the widow then stepped down. Most of the state witnesses who followed were African American, attesting to Stephens's importance to Caswell's black community and making a case that his murder must have been motivated by Conservatives' political or racial animus. The most significant testimony came from Calvin Bigelow, who swore that he saw Wiley and Stephens enter a basement room together that afternoon. He confessed that he had told no one this crucial detail before this hearing, including Kirk's soldiers, because he was afraid of what might happen to him. Perhaps Bigelow had heard of William Puryear's fate following Outlaw's lynching. Collectively the witnesses reinforced the case that Stephens had made dangerous political and social enemies among county Conservatives in his varied positions.

On Friday the court was ready to hear closing remarks in Wiley's hearing. The *Weekly Standard*'s reporter noted of the prosecution's remarks only that Mr. Badger's forty-minute speech was "forcible." Defense counsel R. H. Battle responded with his own two-hour presentation, decrying the Ku Klux Klan and similar violent organizations but arguing that the accused was not party to them. "If Mr. Stephens could speak from his grave," Battle melodramatically opined, "Mr. Wiley would be the last man he would accuse of his murder, and he (Stephens), would say, let not Wiley be prosecuted." After a midday break, another lawyer for each side weighed in, each speech coming in at two or more hours and each seeming determined to win the hearing based on the sheer energy and volume of oration.

At the conclusion of this full day of solicitation, Chief Justice Pearson announced that he would need a few days to contemplate a decision in Wiley's case. The court proceeded to take up the accompanying cases on Saturday, August 27. The hearings for Felix Roan, Joseph Fowler, and James T. Mitchell were much shorter than that of Wiley and mainly focused on the likelihood that the men had been near the courthouse basement at the time of the killing. A few new claims stood out. Black witnesses testified that Roan made statements about Stephens's impending death prior to the assassination and that Roan was convinced that Stephens had orchestrated the recent barn burnings in the county. Henry Stephens, another of John's brothers, attested that there had been bad blood between John and Fowler, the latter once throwing a rock at the Republican, and that Fowler publicly called John a "rascal" on the day of the murder. Another witness described seeing Wiley, Mitchell, and John Lea together in the courthouse basement shortly after Stephens disappeared. Altogether the evidence against Roan, Fowler, and Mitchell was much thinner than that facing Wiley, but their fate was almost certain to be tied to the decision in the ex-sheriff's case. Following this testimony, Pearson formally dismissed charges against Hill and the other Roan, against whom the state failed to bring evidence, and adjourned.

As he retreated to his chambers, Pearson's decision seemed less than certain. The state and the defense witnesses, regardless of race or political affiliation, actually agreed on most of the details of the day of the killing. To wit: many Caswell whites had harbored hard feelings against Stephens; the senator was in attendance at the Conservative meeting in the courthouse, where speakers singled him out for verbal abuse; and he did leave the meeting room in order to speak with Frank Wiley in the basement sometime prior to his death. The few issues on which they differed were significant, however, leaving crucial questions. Was there an active chapter of the Ku Klux Klan in the county carrying out night riding against white Republicans and African Americans? Did Stephens initiate the courthouse conversation on the day of the murder, or did Wiley? Was Stephens seen alive after he met with Wiley? Neither side absolutely proved its case, in large part because so much relied on hearsay and eyewitnesses, and each furnished so many witnesses willing to testify to contradictory things. Some of them must have been lying, but how to be certain who was dishonest? So much depended on the reputations and respectability of the witnesses. Indeed, on its surface the defense's argument seemed stronger: the state's case was built on Wiley's proximity to Stephens and his likely animosity. No one claimed to have seen the killing, much less witnessed Wiley or his accused accomplices engaged in the attack. There were no confessions, no conclusive physical evidence, and little likelihood that such were forthcoming. The defense had produced numerous witnesses, however, who claimed to have seen a hale and hearty Stephens in Yanceyville after Wiley had left town, which, if true, absolved him of any direct involvement. The question, of course, was whose testimony Pearson would choose to believe.

On Monday, August 29, Pearson rendered his decision. The judge found sufficient evidence to send the cases of Wiley, Mitchell, and Roan to trial in Caswell's superior court (Fowler is strangely absent in extant accounts of the hearing, likely indicating that his case was dismissed). Wiley and Mitchell were to be remanded for murder and Roan as an accessory to murder. Their bonds were a steep $5,000. Summarizing his decision, Pearson noted that the facts were slim—a murder had taken place in the courthouse and the accused had the opportunity to commit it—but the large body of testimony did, he believed, raise legitimate suspicions of the men's guilt. Pearson was uncertain of the eventual prosecutorial outcome, however. As the cases went forward, he wondered "how much reliance can be put in the testimony of reluctant white witnesses, and of persons who have been slaves, and are now citizens? This is a practical question and the learning of the law does not aid much in its solution." This question did not, it might be noted, speak to what actually occurred in the basement of the courthouse that day. Instead, it was indicative of how much had changed in North Carolina in the five years following the war and how contested and tenuous those transformations were. Whatever the ultimate verdict, Pearson glumly noted, it could not erase "a foul mark on the reputation of the County of Caswell."[44]

On its face, Pearson's decision seemed at least a partial victory for Republicans and Holden. True, the court had dismissed the charges against a

Chapter Four

majority of those men whom Kirk had arrested, but Wiley and two other central suspects were to stand trial for the killing at the heart of the insurrection. Conservatives saw it as a clear-cut win, however, believing that Caswell's county court would never find the men guilty. To remand the prisoners to Yanceyville was simply to delay their freedom and in the process gave county Conservatives a chance to openly vote against Holden's course of action. Conservatives displayed this belief by celebrating the decision in Raleigh's streets, firing cannons, burning barrels of tar, and listening to congratulatory speeches as the prisoners left town.[45] The crowd's optimism was well-founded. Back in Caswell the cases against Wiley, Mitchell, and Roan were soon dropped for lack of evidence. No one would ever be prosecuted for the murder of John Stephens.[46]

No suspects available too little evidence

Even as the prime suspects in Stephens's murder slipped away into the shadows, two events initiated in the closing month of 1870 kept the assassination and its aftermath in the state and national spotlights. That December, largely at the urging of North Carolina Republicans, including Holden and Tourgée, a special committee of the US Senate heard testimony on the situation in North Carolina. President Grant may have ignored Holden's pleas for federal reinforcements on the ground, but some congressional Republicans were interested in learning more about the state's Klan outrages. These collected interviews were then published in two Senate reports, giving official, federal form to contested arguments concerning Stephens, Holden, and the Klan and shaping public perception. The reports also provided fodder for generations of historians to come.[47] Although other states were experiencing their share of violence driven by the Ku Klux Klan and similar secret societies—the situation was particularly bad in South Carolina and Louisiana—the committee's attention to North Carolina made the state symbolic of extreme resistance to Congressional Reconstruction. The report's main focus was on the events that led to the declaration of martial law in Alamance and Caswell Counties, including Stephens's murder, as well as on the prosecution of Holden's and Kirk's campaign to stamp out the Klan. Two questions were central to these depositions: Had there in fact been an insurrection taking place in the state's Piedmont in 1869 and 1870, and was the governor's response necessary, just, and legal?

To the first question, the committee examined documents from the months in question, focusing on material produced by Holden's office and interviews with federal soldiers who had been stationed in the region at the time. Most sources agreed that there had been a good deal of racially and politically motivated violence in Alamance and Caswell leading up to the declaration of martial law. Holden himself had written Washington that masked groups were targeting Republicans in an organized fashion and that a full accounting of Klan actions in North Carolina "would be a tale of terror and woe that the people of this country have never heard before."[48] Federal soldiers agreed with this assessment, at least to an extent. Henry Hunt, a colonel in the 5th Artillery, noted that "the ill-treatment of colored people was alleged" throughout the state. And Lt. Paul Hambrick, who investigated the situation in Alamance in March 1870 for Maj. Gen. Edward R. S. Canby, wrote that the Klan's "object appears to be to drive the *colored* and *Union* men of said county from the said *county* and State. This they accomplish by *murder* and *corporal punishment*."[49]

Still stronger evidence came in the form of testimony forwarded by Holden from a group of sixteen Alamance men who claimed to have once been Klansmen (or members of similar groups called the White Brotherhood and Constitutional Union Guard). William Quakenbush, for example, admitted to having participated in a nighttime raid that administered thirty lashes to a man whose crime had been to boast that he would shoot any Klansmen so bold as to threaten him. Quakenbush held the whip handle for ten of the blows himself, but only, he pled, because he "was compelled to do it."[50] The confessions continued. F. U. Blanchard and J. J. Younger described leaving a coffin at a door as an intimidation tactic, J. C. Whitesell was party to three nighttime floggings, and J. F. Hopkins stated that the Klan had "intended to carry the next election, if they had to kill or run off all the negroes" to do so.[51]

More moving was the testimony of a number of victims of night riding, with the committee focusing in particular on accounts from Alamance. The killings of Outlaw and Stephens were recounted, of course, along with the murder of Puryear to eliminate him as a potential witness to Outlaw's killing. Added to these incidents were less "infamous outrages." The senators learned that raids often took a similar form: "From eight to twenty persons in disguise would go to the house of the intended victim in the night, and before any one was aware of their presence they would break into the house, drag out the party to be punished. In the meantime they would gag, and by other means stop any alarm by the other inmates." One by one, witnesses and victims testified to the sort of abuse that followed. One black man had "his back flayed with a stick," while a woman was choked "in a most inhumane manner." Freedman Caswell Holt had been attacked twice. In one incident he was shot in the shoulder and through a lung, and on another occasion he was whipped and beaten with a stick.[52]

Not all of the raids targeted African Americans. White Republicans like Stephens were also persecuted. Klansmen killed two white scalawags in Alamance, brothers Daniel and Jefferson Morrow, presumably for being active members of the Republican Party. A disguised party shaved half of Alonzo Corliss's hair and beard and whipped him because the northern man taught at a school for black children. They also painted him black and left him with "his head and face cut and disfigured in a most cruel manner." Two white men who worked at a cotton mill, one as a superintendent, were also beaten, presumably for their political leanings. Witnesses testified to the congressmen that these attacks often sought to embarrass, shame, or dehumanize victims through some form of sexual abuse, especially when they targeted freedpeople. One young freedwoman was "made to exhibit her person, while the fiends proceeded to inflict blows upon her private parts." Klansmen seized Nathan Trolinger and forced him "to mutilate his own private parts with his pocket-knife," and another group "potterized" (castrated) John Bass.[53] Kidada Williams and other historians have shown that such sexual violence was common across the postwar South, as control of bodies often served as brutal shorthand for control of social and political processes.[54]

Collectively these deponents made it clear that beatings and bloodshed were frequent in the region prior to Holden's declaration of martial law, but they were more divided on exactly what the violence signified. Holden's communication made it evident that he believed the actions were nothing less than an insurrection that aimed to put former Confederates in control of the state. It was the Civil War continuing in the form of guerrilla violence. In a direct plea to President Grant, Holden described the Klan's intentions "to obtain the control of the government. It is believed that its leaders now direct the movement of the present [state] legislature."[55] He furthermore repeated wild rumors that Nathan Bedford Forrest himself was somehow involved and that former president Andrew Johnson was secretly head of the national Klan. Turning from conspiracy theories to local numbers, Holden pointed to Alamance as an example of the odds he faced. There he claimed the county's Klan held some 900 active members, a figure that would have done the county proud had it been wartime enlistment.[56]

The papers and testimony of federal troops dispatched to the Piedmont in response to Holden's various pleas for aid were dubious of the governor's claims that a general insurrection was afoot. Captain G. B. Rodney, who was in Yanceyville to observe and assist Kirk's militia, reported that even though "Colonel Kirk feared an attack and barricaded the court-house," he believed the whole scare could be chalked up to "foolish reports of negroes."

He "knew and saw nothing of any 'Ku-Kluxism.'" Captain Royal Frank, of the 8th Infantry, also believed Holden's claims to be inflated and that there was no general insurrection underway. Even if the violence was politically motivated, he concluded, it was the product of internal state squabbles rather than an expression of dissatisfaction with the nation's leadership. Henry Hunt concurred. The Klan was not overtly political, he believed. Instead, it largely enforced community mores, as its "machinery was used to punish theft, burglaries, insults to women, and other offenses in no way connected with politics. In fine, their principal business seemed to be to do the work usually performed by 'regulators' and 'vigilance committees.'" Stephens's murder was an exception, in that it had certainly been politically motivated, but Hunt saw no evidence that the Klan had been involved. Looking on from his post in Raleigh, Captain Frank believed the Klan had some political aims but also thought the organization had come about in response to Union League violence against white Conservatives. He threw up his hands at the issue as too tangled to sort out.[57]

The real trouble in Alamance and Caswell, some federal observers argued in correspondence presented to the committee, came from the schemes and actions of Holden and Kirk. In August, Hunt had worried that Kirk's arrests and his failure to yield prisoners to civil authorities might be the spark that kindled rebellion where there was none before. He found that local African Americans were nervous and fearful, circulating rumors that re-enslavement would follow the coming election; that Holden's press was stirring up those fears; and that Kirk's worries about the Klan were trumped up to justify his actions. In Yanceyville, Rodney likewise put the finger of blame on Kirk in a missive drafted at the end of July, noting the officer's various conspiracy theories and concluding that "there is no fear of any disturbance between the citizens and military unless Kirk provokes them to it, and it seems to me he has been endeavoring to do so ever since he has been here." Two weeks later he was even more convinced that Kirk was to blame. His militia was "nothing more than an armed mob," led by a man intent on manufacturing unrest *after* he made arrests in order to justify them. "His men roam around the country, and pillage and insult the people with impunity." The result of these suspicions was tension between federal soldiers and the state militia. Captain Rodney recorded Kirk's militia hurling insults—and on at least one occasion, a stone—at his soldiers stationed in Caswell. "The militia threaten to burn the town of Yanceyville when they leave, and unless there is a strong force of United States troops there when they are disbanded nothing will prevent them."[58] On one occasion one of Kirk's militiamen even fired at and wounded a federal soldier, Private James Bradley. The militiamen argued that Bradley was drunk and wandering past the state encampment late at night when a jumpy watchman shot him, "acting in accordance with orders received from his superiors." Federal commanders predictably blamed the state troops and recommended they be disbanded or removed from Caswell.[59]

Although the committee's report aired a good deal of the doubts circulating around Holden's decisions, it gave the final word to the testimony of Lieutenant Hambrick. He concluded that there was much truth to the Klan rumors: "There is one fact clearly established: that is, that there is such an organization in said county [Alamance]; that it is composed in part of men who have heretofore stood high in the county; that they are completely organized, and that they have murdered innocent citizens and mutilated others too numerous to mention."[60] The committee seemed uncertain about the aims and means of Holden's actions—perhaps the state had countered wrong with wrong—but members largely agreed with Hambrick's assessment of the Klan and similar Conservative secret societies. These congressional hearings would do much to shape national understandings of the Klan as a threat to the rule of law in the South, but they did less to shed light on the convoluted events taking place in North Carolina.

The impeachment trial of Governor Holden, beginning in Raleigh about the same time that Congress took testimony on North Carolina's Klan, made a much clearer public statement. A political sea change made Holden vulnerable. State Republicans' failure to retain control of the insurrection and assassination trials had foretold the outcome of the August elections. With Wiley, Roan, and Mitchell free and Holden's course rejected by Washington, Conservatives were poised to flex their muscles in Raleigh. They won significant gains at the polls, almost certainly because violence had suppressed the Republican vote. The result of the elections was "almost a two-to-one majority in the state legislature" for Conservatives, including an edge in the Senate. Locally, Caswell County moved from the Republican into the Conservative column and Wilson Carey, who initially seemed the victor in his race, was removed and replaced by Democrat Livingston Brown over accusations that Kirk's men had manipulated the ballot box while they occupied Yanceyville. Fourteen other counties that were home to active Klan chapters also moved from Republican to Conservative control in the 1870 election.[61]

Although it was not a gubernatorial election, with control of the legislature North Carolina Conservatives moved to end Holden's political power once and for all. In December the General Assembly began impeachment proceedings against the governor, a trial that would span the first three months of the new year. Holden was charged with a total of eight offenses, ranging from an illegal declaration of martial law in Alamance and Caswell Counties to violation of the state's habeas corpus statutes. The governor's son Joseph was still serving as a representative from Wake County, but he could exert no leverage as the North Carolina Senate served as the court of impeachment. (Joseph had also resigned the Speaker's chair in March 1870 to focus on the statewide Republican campaign and his resumption of the editorship of the *Raleigh Standard*.) Lengthening the odds against Holden, Chief Justice Pearson presided over the impeachment trial, just a few months following his clash with the governor over Kirk's denial of the judge's writ of habeas corpus. On that charge, at least, Pearson had already issued public statements that Holden had violated the state constitution.[62]

Holden's defense team, William N. H. Smith and Edward Conigland, faced an estimable set of prosecutors who were well-recognized names in state politics. William A. Graham and Thomas Bragg were both former North Carolina governors, and they were joined at the bench by Augustus Merrimon, who had served in the state House of Commons and was soon to lose a tight governor's race himself before winning election to the US Senate in 1872. Bragg had also helped defend the Caswell conspirators in their preliminary hearing in front of the state supreme court.[63] (Highlighting how North Carolina's convoluted politics made strange bedfellows, Merrimon had been an outspoken critic of the Confederate government, only to adopt a Conservative stance after the war, and Hinton Rowan Helper—once an ardent Republican—had dedicated his rabidly racist anthology *The Negroes in Negroland* to Merrimon in an endorsement of his Senate campaign.)[64]

Holden's lawyers put up a stiff fight despite the odds. The governor had acted upon necessity, they explained, since Alamance and Caswell had truly been in rebellion. Paralleling the Klan testimony before Congress, they listed more than sixty outrages that had occurred in the two counties, "and not a solitary man in Caswell or Alamance has been punished for it." Wyatt Outlaw's death at the hands of a large mob of disguised men had demonstrated the widespread and organized nature of the violence, and John Stephens's carefully planned assassination was its denouement. Surely such events implied more than impromptu or individual criminal acts. One of Holden's solicitors attempted to transport the legislators back to that fateful day in Caswell.

And now, senators, go with me for a moment to the town of Yanceyville. The court house there, in the bright month of May, under the full glare of an afternoon sun, is filled with the citizens of the county and listening to harangues of political orators. Stephens, a state senator from that district, is present in the meeting taking notes of the speeches, he being a republican and the speakers his political opponents. At four o'clock he is enticed from the meeting by Wyley [sic] and in company with him he leaves the room and is never again, so far as human testimony has divulged, seen alive. At daylight the next morning his body is found with a rope almost buried in the muscles of his neck, and fatal stabs in his breast and neck.[65]

Stephens had clearly been killed at "the command of some secret oath-bound association," the defense continued. As evidence of this they offered a new accusation that two African American men, Tilman Brown and Archibald Doll, swore that they had overheard several white men discussing a plan to kill Stephens on the day of the murder. A cover-up followed the carefully orchestrated political murder: the defense argued that Conservatives had hidden away the accused conspirators, including Wiley, so that they were not available for testifying at the impeachment trial, and that they had forced Yanceyville residents, including Stephens's brothers, to sign a letter declaring that they believed the killers had not come from the local community. If this campaign of secrecy and intimidation was not proof of conspiracy and insurrection, what was? The assassination had been the culminating blow in a campaign of terror designed to overthrow the state's Republican government, and hence Holden was justified in his vigorous efforts to stamp out Ku Kluxism.[66]

At the core of the defense was thus an effort to focus the impeachment trial on Stephens's killing as much as on Holden's subsequent actions. Holden himself issued a public statement in defense against the articles of impeachment that followed the same tactic. In it he stressed the ways in which he had sought to eradicate the Klan through cautious and measured methods—such as offering a reward for information on Stephens's and other murders—and only when this proved fruitless did he then draw on the authority granted by the Shoffner Act to declare insurrection. He had followed the law, he summarized, while Conservatives had counseled lawlessness, and the real crimes took place before the Kirk-Holden War rather than during it.[67]

Prosecutors countered detail for detail, willing to engage in debates over community violence as well as Holden's responses. Stephens was murdered, yes, but there was no proof that Klansmen had killed him. And yes, there had been violence in Alamance and Caswell in the months leading up to the murder. But these actions were tit for tat, they argued, since it was black arsonists' attacks on Conservatives' property at the instigation of Republican leaders like Stephens that triggered county night riding. This vigilantism was thus community policing necessitated by the state's inability to uphold and enforce the law, they argued, and therefore Holden's claims to be suppressing disorder were mere farce. Holden himself had promoted lawlessness as head of the state's Union League, they continued, and later used the consequences as an excuse to consolidate power. Prosecutors also inverted the defense's claim of a conspiracy. That no one had been found guilty of outrages, including Stephens's killing, was not evidence of a concerted cover-up by secret societies; it was instead proof that a declaration of martial law and Kirk's arrests were unfounded. It was no conspiracy when innocent people were found innocent: it was simply justice. When men like Wiley were captured, imprisoned, and denied the protection of the civil court system, "was there any probable cause existing, any evidence then or thereafter produced against these gentlemen, some twenty or more in number? None whatever." The prosecution concluded that the real criminal was thus Holden, intent on clinging to his ill-gotten office by flouting the very laws he had sworn to uphold.[68]

Unsurprisingly, given Conservatives' new control of the Senate, the body would agree with the prosecution on most counts. Holden was found guilty by the required two-thirds majority on six of the eight charges laid against him. The legislature upheld the declaration of martial law in Alamance and Caswell as within the governor's authority, thanks to the Shoffner Act, but found him guilty of abusing his power in deploying the militia and in selecting Kirk as its leader, of ignoring writs of habeas corpus, and of sanctioning Josiah Turner's arrest in Orange County, outside of the bounds of the area declared in insurrection. A few Republicans voted with the Conservative majority on some of the charges, perhaps believing Holden had become a party liability. The Senate's formal decision ruled "that the said W. W. Holden, governor, be deposed from office and forever disqualified from holding any office of profit or trust in this state." He was the first governor in the history of the United States to be successfully impeached. In the end, Stephens's killers had a hand in stripping power from Holden almost as thoroughly as they eliminated the meddlesome state senator a few months earlier.[69]

One detail remained. Lest some future state government try to renew the prosecution of Conservatives implicated in the violence of the time, in 1873 the legislature passed "An Act for Amnesty and Pardon" covering any past crimes committed by members of secret societies. The only exceptions were "rape, deliberate and wilful murder, arson and burglary." The state's Union League, Red Strings, and Heroes of America were included in the list of applicable secret societies so as to lend the act a bipartisan appearance, but its intended beneficiaries were citizens who had been involved in Klan chapters and similar Conservative bodies.[70] This built upon a Grant administration pardon of suspected Klansmen who had been held by the federal government. The following year the state exemptions were removed: even murder was forgiven. Wilson Carey, who voters had returned to a seat in Raleigh, was among the representatives who entered a formal protest against the legislation, arguing that it "encourages the tendency of bad men to commit crime by organizing secret societies . . . hoping by this means to escape the punishment due and demanded in such cases." Carey was right, in that North Carolina would be unable to ever prosecute anyone for Stephens's murder.[71] The killers were forgiven under the law, but forgiven did not mean forgotten.

Handwritten annotations:

↳ State Leg instituted a pardon that applied to all crimes, essentially → burying the Stephens case

Clear act of foolishness
↓
Just because they are secret doesn't mean they can't be detected and punished.

Holden's actions burn him

Five

PRETEXT

The scallawags, carpet-baggers and negroes who composed the large
majority were wholly irresponsible, and launched upon a course of
wild extravagance in order to feather their nests at the public expense.
The work of this mongrel body could not be checked by the few
brave spirits, who fought day and night with desperate persistence,
to stem the tide of reckless extravagance and corruption.

MARY WOODSON JARVIS, "The Ku-Klux Klans" (1902)

[handwritten margin note: Wrong attitude + cause.]

ric Foner, the nation's preeminent historian of Reconstruction, has written that "Republican control unraveled" in North Carolina with the impeachment of Governor William Woods Holden, but the political path was a bit more circuitous than that.[1] The brief period of Republican political dominance between 1868 and 1870 had been incomplete and more fragile than it appeared on the surface, yet the party was surprisingly difficult for Conservatives to stamp out even after Holden's fall because it offered legitimate attractions to some white Tar Heels as well as the majority of the state's black residents.

[handwritten margin note: Republicans still very important]

Conservatives had gained a legislative majority in the state elections of 1870 and then thrown off the hated leadership of Holden, but they hardly held complete sway in the years that followed. The 1868 state constitution that Republicans had crafted proved too popular to immediately overturn;

initial attempts by Conservatives to call a new constitutional convention failed. Republican Tod Caldwell, made governor by Holden's impeachment, also proved willing to cooperate with federal efforts to eradicate the Klan and managed to win the office in his own right in 1872 (and when he died in office in 1874, Republican Curtis Brogden finished the term). In the 1874 elections the Republican candidates still polled well, and African American voters remained confident enough in Wilmington to take to the streets in defense of their voting rights. Not until the 1876 election cycle did Conservatives—by then openly calling themselves Democrats again—gain control of the legislature and the governor's office at the same time. That year they reelected wartime governor Zebulon Vance to the executive position and were able to craft a new constitution and return control of county governance to the older antebellum system of appointed officials. Even then, there remained white Republicans in significant numbers in the state, especially in the mountains, in addition to the African American party backbone. In Caswell County, Wilson Carey, whose first term was so embattled and who was forced to temporarily flee the county out of fear for his life, won reelection to the state House of Representatives as late as 1889.[2] As one historian of the era notes, in the last decades of the nineteenth century, North Carolina "party allegiance was in some measure dependent upon local issues, habits, and loyalties as opposed to the greater questions of state and national concern."[3]

A similar situation existed in Virginia's southern Piedmont, just across Caswell's northern border. Democrats had maintained the helm there during Reconstruction, but a biracial political coalition known as the Readjusters threatened Democratic hegemony into the 1880s, and it was not until a race "riot" in Danville, Caswell farmers' main tobacco market, which left four African Americans dead leading into the state election of 1883, that the issue of race began to tear that coalition apart.[4] Even after Democrats seized the reins of power in the Piedmont of both states, the possibility of an interracial political alliance steadily bubbled under the surface, as evidenced in the region's dalliances with a politicized Farmers' Alliance and populism late in the century and an interest in liquor prohibition campaigns that bridged racial divides. Neither John Walter Stephens's death nor Holden's impeachment had completely killed North Carolina Republicanism, but together they would eventually prove mortal wounds.[5]

A crucial step in establishing and then solidifying Democratic power was recasting North Carolina's experience in the Civil War and Reconstruction. Memory, ever malleable, had to be remade. Although the state had been a somewhat reluctant member of the Confederacy with a durable and multifaceted peace movement and a body of soldiers who deserted at high rates, postwar Democrats rewrote North Carolina's wartime role as that of a southern stalwart betrayed by a few duplicitous scoundrels like Holden. Republican control of the state for a few years during Reconstruction—with significant internal support from both freedpeople and white Republicans found in every part of the state—was similarly transformed into an oppressive exercise in military and political occupation, guided by Washington and executed by traitorous scalawags and carpetbaggers on the ground, again epitomized by Holden and a supporting cast of characters that included Albion Tourgée and Stephens. African Americans became ignorant pawns rather than political actors in their own right. With this new historiography, Conservatives' Reconstruction rhetoric eventually became the state's public memory.

Although Stephens was never as crucial to the state's remembrance of Reconstruction as was Holden, efforts to shape the memory of Stephens's character—and hence the meaning of his death—began immediately and gained steam after Holden's removal. Newspapers from time to time rehashed the assassination and the resulting martial law and impeachment of the governor, although without the furious back-and-forth that had characterized the exchanges in the summer and fall of 1870. The federal government also kept the violence in the national conscience for a time, permitting a public re-airing of events when it held a second set of Klan hearings. Inspired by the claims of North Carolina Klan outrages collected in testimony before Congress in 1870, the US House and Senate formed a joint committee to investigate secret society violence across the entire South. North Carolina's hearings thus became a template for trying to root out the broader southern secret society problem. To that end, the committee collected testimony in Washington and also sent subcommittees into the field across the South during the summer of 1871 and then published its findings in a massive thirteen-volume report in 1872.[6] The committee's investigation led to the second Ku Klux Klan Act—in the judgment of historian Heather Cox Richardson, "the last firm Northern Republican defense of African-Americans"—which made federal crimes of acts of terror committed in disguise.[7]

The first volume of testimony collected by the committee again focused on North Carolina, bringing attention to many of the same issues highlighted in the previous year's Senate investigation. Stephens's assassination remained a touchstone, as witnesses—including those from other sections of the state—frequently noted the importance of the senator's death and the unrest in Caswell and Alamance Counties. The violence in the northern

Piedmont had reverberated among Conservatives and Republicans in the rest of North Carolina, shaping their perceptions of the state's Reconstruction efforts.[8] This investigation was less interested in exploring Holden's and George Kirk's actions during the martial law declaration and more focused on compiling a list of Klan crimes in the state, in line with the testimony collected from the other southern states. Some Democratic talking points appeared in the record, however. For example, Haywood W. Guion, accused of heading a Klan chapter near Charlotte, argued that it had been the Union League that had initiated hostilities in the Piedmont region through a concerted campaign of arson targeting the barns and other property of white Conservatives. The Klan was, he argued, simply a defensive organization that formed in response to these criminal actions when the state proved unable or unwilling to maintain order.[9] And James Justice, a Republican member of the state's House of Representatives, agreed that Holden had made mistakes in his handling of the Klan, especially in his faith in Kirk, who alienated many of the whites in the state of all political persuasions when he arrested "the innocent with the guilty."[10]

Despite these continued rumblings about where to lay blame for the origins of the state's terrorism and the Holden administration's response, the committee's reports did much to cement for a national audience the notion that the Klan had derailed Reconstruction through a concerted and coordinated campaign of terror, intimidating, whipping, and killing black and white Republicans like Stephens who dared attempt to have a say in southern politics. The senator became symbolic of all the Republican politicians murdered in this violence, which included assassinations of state legislators in South Carolina, Arkansas, and Georgia.[11] North Carolina thus served as a poster child of the ongoing failures in rehabilitating the rebel South.

This legal testimony on Capitol Hill furnished one vision of North Carolina's Reconstruction, but popular fiction would provide an even more influential take a few years later. Stephens's old friend Albion Tourgée did more than any other person to define the senator as a martyred patriot. Tourgée had been one of the most vocal critics of the Piedmont Klan, both from the bench and, briefly, as co-owner and editor of a Republican newspaper in Greensboro.[12] Frustrated with the effectiveness of Conservatives' violence and North Carolina's Redemption, he turned to fiction to publicize the tragic collapse of Reconstruction. Tourgée's literary defense of southern Republicanism was more successful—at least for a time—than his actions on the ground had been in North Carolina, but it was slow to gain momentum. His first effort to explore the region's politics and racial issues through fiction came in 1874, when he published *Toinette: A Novel*, under the pen name Henry Churton.[13] In this book Tourgée wrote through an accusation that had shadowed his recent career: that he had cheated on his wife by engaging in an interracial relationship with an underage girl. Sometime in 1869 Tourgée and his wife adopted Adaline Patillo, a thirteen-year-old girl of mixed race, into their household. Adaline had been born into slavery, the property of Albert A. Patillo of Yanceyville, who was a prominent judge as well as a slave trader at the start of the Civil War. (One legal historian has suggested that it is likely that Adaline was Albert's illegitimate daughter.) Tourgée almost certainly met Adaline and her mother when his judicial work, including meetings with Stephens, took him to Yanceyville.[14]

Indeed, Stephens seemed to have been intimately involved in the adoption arrangement. In May 1869 he had instigated proceedings against Albert Patillo for fraud, and in a letter describing the suit to Tourgée he rather cryptically asked the judge to provide him with information about the law as it concerned illegitimate children, although he did not explicitly link the question to the Patillo case. Four months later it was Stephens who coordinated transportation for Adaline to travel to Tourgée's house in Guilford County.[15]

Adoption into the Tourgée household helped Adaline escape poverty and provided her with educational opportunities. It was thus a case of Christian kindness and charity, the judge argued, but his critics were quick to see more lascivious motives. In the face of Conservative suggestions that miscegenation was one of the true aims and great evils of Reconstruction campaigns for racial equality, Tourgée's adoption of Adaline proved powerful fodder for the opposition press. The *Raleigh Sentinel*, a Conservative organ, noted the arrangement and suggestively commented, "This is generous of the Judge—very generous! Is Tourgée a married man?" His wife, Emma, eventually questioned the adoption decision as well, perhaps because it provoked so much scurrilous gossip.[16]

Although Tourgée denied any impropriety in his real family affairs, *Toinette* openly embraced the theme of intimacy across racial lines and revealed Tourgée grappling with the proper nature of black and white relationships now that slavery was dead. What system would rise in its place? In the novel a southern planter named Geoffrey Hunter falls for a light-skinned enslaved girl, the titular Toinette. The couple's love affair produces a child, and just before the outbreak of the Civil War Hunter sends Toinette to freedom in Ohio, where she attempts to pass as white. The war reunites the couple when Hunter is wounded in service to the Confederate army, captured by the enemy, and is placed under the care of Toinette, who is now a Union

Albion W. Tourgée as he appeared at the height of his literary career in the 1890s. "Albion W. Tourg[é]e," from Albion W. Tourgée, *The Story of a Thousand* (Buffalo, NY: S. McGerald and Son, 1896).

nurse. Even as the war is dismantling the old barrier to their love posed by slavery, Hunter is unable to see past Toinette's former status as a slave, and she is unwilling to be less than a true wife. As a result of these irreconcilable perspectives, the relationship falls apart. The couple had defied southern norms until the war but were unable to transcend racial mores after Toinette's emancipation. In this tragedy, Tourgée seemed to be grappling with the North's unease with the social changes wrought by the end of bondage. The war had dismantled slavery, but the northern commitment to freedpeople had steadily eroded as Reconstruction grew longer. Had emancipation ultimately been for naught?[17]

Toinette went largely unremarked, in no small part because Tourgée did not immediately reveal himself as the author. Although it may have been rooted in elements of Tourgée's real-life relationship with Adaline Patillo, with the authorship hidden readers received it as a maudlin, if titillating, work of fiction. The judge's next attempt at writing about Reconstruction would make a much bigger splash. In 1879, *A Fool's Errand* appeared on booksellers' shelves. Although it was also a novel, this time Tourgée adhered much more closely to the real details of North Carolina's Reconstruction experience, making it immediately clear to readers that the writer had an inside perspective on the effort, even though, as with *Toinette*, Tourgée first published the book under a pen name. *A Fool's Errand* proved wildly popular. Booksellers struggled to keep it in stock in the months following its release, the volume sold 150,000 copies during the first year, and it drew international interest as it was reprinted in several languages. Critics hailed it as "the *Uncle Tom's Cabin* of Reconstruction."[18] The protagonist was Comfort Servosse, modeled on Tourgée himself (the unlikely name perhaps something of a hint as to the author). Another central character was John Walters, a thinly veiled evocation of John Walter Stephens. Like Tourgée, Servosse was a Union veteran who moved to North Carolina shortly after the war in pursuit of economic and political opportunity. Faced with social hostility from his new neighbors and then with outright violence, Servosse's faith in the northern support for Reconstruction falls apart in a chapter describing Walters's assassination in details that mirrored the contemporary accounts of Stephens's killing. Tourgée portrays the northern failure to act in the aftermath of the murder as more crushing than the killing itself, leaving Walters-cum-Stephens a martyr on the altar of a lost cause.[19]

Tourgée depicted Walters as pure of heart and motives, honorable in every respect. He was rough-hewn but noble, and self-conscious about his lack of education, which he attributed to the system of slavery that had also oppressed poor whites. Overcoming these disadvantages himself, Walters was determined to provide the state's whites and blacks with better opportunities through his political actions. Tourgée crafted a character that was nothing less than an improbable composite of Hinton Rowan Helper and Frederick Douglass. A version of the infamous "chicken" story appeared in the novel, only without any poultry: in *A Fool's Errand* Walters faced wartime troubles not over accusations of petty thievery but instead for his devout Unionism, which culminated in facing down an armed conscription officer and posse. In a like manner, when surrounded by Klansmen in the courthouse basement who demanded that he renounce his work for freedpeople and the Republican Party or be killed, Walters proudly embraced death before dishonor. (Wyatt Outlaw's lynching also appeared in the novel, portrayed by the murder of the character "Uncle Jerry.")[20] Historian David Blight observes that Tourgée "dared to say, in season and out, that the war and its aftermath were all about race," and Stephens's death became an important event in his account of the fall of Reconstruction.[21] Stephens had been killed by Klansmen, but he had also been betrayed by the cowardice of a nation unwilling to follow through on the promises of Reconstruction.

Tourgée was able to furnish such a detailed account of Stephens's murder because he claimed to have insider knowledge of the killing in real life. In the months immediately following the assassination, Tourgée worked to gather evidence regarding the culprits in both Stephens's and Outlaw's murders. His interest was both professional and personal. (Reflecting his friendship with Stephens, he kept in touch with the senator's family in Caswell, counseling his widow, Fannie, and offering political advice to his brother William, who was himself active for a time in the county's Republican Party.)[22] In December 1872 a man named J. G. Hester brought Tourgée a sworn statement from Patsie Burton, an African American woman who worked as a servant in the house of Iverson Oliver. In the paper Burton claimed to have overheard a conspirator discussing Stephens's death. In her sworn testimony to Hester, she described Frank Wiley's arrival at Oliver's house on the evening of May 21, 1870, the day of the murder. Curious, she listened at a closed door as the two men conversed, and Burton overheard Wiley confess to having a part in the killing. The former sheriff then named ten other men involved, including Joe Fowler and "Jerry" Lea. Wiley seemed to relish being a participant in the deed, or at least he thought it had been necessary, at one point telling Oliver that it had been "the best days work of my life."[23]

"Excited" by overhearing the revelation, Burton let slip an exclamation, which the two men heard, and Wiley quickly left the house. In the days that followed, Iverson Oliver indirectly questioned Burton about that evening, trying to ascertain what she might have heard. To cover for her eavesdropping she claimed she had burned herself drinking hot coffee, resulting in a yelp of pain. Still suspicious, another Oliver relative mentioned in passing conversation with Burton that anyone who knew anything about the events in the courthouse and spoke to anyone about them might end up dead themselves. Despite this clumsy threat, some two and a half years later she was apparently ready and willing to discuss the furtive conversation she overheard that night. Conservatives would shrug off Burton's claims as fantastical, but they informed the account of the killing in *A Fool's Errand*, and Tourgée's fiction would in turn embed many of the affidavit's details into the popular narrative of the event for years to come.[24]

In an effort to further assure the public of the truth of the details in *A Fool's Errand*, Tourgée revealed himself as the book's author within the year. He also appended a supplement titled *The Invisible Empire* to an 1880 edition of the work, in it reprinting testimony gleaned from the congressional reports on Klan activity in 1871 to demonstrate that *A Fool's Errand* was indeed more fact than fiction. Tourgée was hardly above a little literary embellishment in his interpretation of the Ku Klux Klan's activities in this appendix, however. In it he argued that the secret white supremacist organizations like the Klan were a greater threat to the nation than the Confederacy had been. He believed that across the South their members numbered "in all an army greater than the Rebellion, from the moldering remains of which it sprung, could ever put into the field!" Their victims—Stephens among them—were also legion, as numerous as the war dead. "Ah! the wounded in this silent warfare were more thousands than those who groaned upon the slopes of Gettysburg!"[25]

The same year as the publication of the enlarged edition of *A Fool's Errand*, Tourgée also released a sequel of sorts. This novel, *Bricks without Straw*, attempted to focus on Reconstruction from an African American point of view, in some respects returning to questions and techniques he had first explored in *Toinette*. It also sold well, although the book failed to make the same lasting impact as *A Fool's Errand*, perhaps because its narrative veered a bit further from reality.[26] The public read *A Fool's Errand* as reporting from the field, whereas *Bricks without Straw* had to stand more firmly on its literary merits. Taken as a whole, Tourgée's early body of work attempted to craft a national interpretation of Reconstruction and race using his own experiences in North Carolina as a lens into the complex and often tragic events of the age. He clearly saw himself—the "fool"—as one victim of the times, with southern African Americans collectively forming another. Stephens was also a victim. He stood in for all white southern Union men who suffered for their loyalty, another category of "forgotten" Americans sacrificed to the practical politics of reconciliation.

Seeing the writing on the wall, Tourgée left North Carolina and returned to the North in 1879, motivated by financial misfortune, his wife Emma's complaints about their circumstances, and continued hostility from Democrats, who increasingly operated the levers of state power.[27] The most important factor in the decision may have been the obvious collapse by that time of Republican prospects for control of the state. The state's "Redemption" looked impossible to roll back at the decade's end, and Tourgée no longer had the stomach for a hopeless fight. Although North Carolina seemed temporarily lost, he would not give up on the vision of a more equitable United States. Throughout the 1880s he remained a prolific author, publishing numerous books tackling questions of race and the nation's Reconstruction experience, although none would achieve the popularity of A Fool's Errand.[28] In 1896 he served as chief counsel for Homer Plessy in Plessy v. Ferguson, the seminal Supreme Court test of Jim Crow segregation, and in that work his hopes were also thwarted. In 1905 the Niagara movement, a precursor to the National Association for the Advancement of Colored People, named Tourgée a "Friend of Freedom," along with Frederick Douglass and William Lloyd Garrison.[29]

Just as the newspaper war that raged in the months after Stephens's murder offered conflicting takes on events, Tourgée's literary efforts met their own rebuttals. William Royall, a Confederate veteran turned New York lawyer, furnished one. In a "reply" to A Fool's Errand printed by a New York publisher, Royall argued that Tourgée had the crucial details backwards. The real problem in North Carolina (and the South more broadly) had not been conspiratorial whites pursuing violence against freedpeople but abusive Republican governance headed by carpetbaggers. Men like Tourgée had created the sorry situation and then sought sympathy when the defeated South resisted. Royall twisted the knife a little by noting that a Reconstruction fraud investigation in North Carolina had unearthed accusations that Tourgée had accepted thousands of dollars of bribes from railroad hustlers George Swepson and Milton S. Littlefield. Royall judged A Fool's Errand to be "a wilful, deliberate, and malicious libel upon a noble and generous people" and its author "one of the most contemptible fellows of those who have libelled them."[30]

One more literary rejection of Tourgée's most famous work came from another southern expatriate, in this case college student Charles Oscar

Beasley. Beasley was born in 1860 on the western edge of North Carolina's Piedmont in Salem, an up-and-coming tobacco town, and grew up in the state before attending college at the University of Pennsylvania. He would remain in Philadelphia after graduation, like Tourgée working as a lawyer and editor. Although Beasley would eventually become an active figure in Republican politics, in 1882 he still remained a rebel at heart. That year he released a novel titled *Those American R's: Rule, Ruin, Restoration*, which expressed a good deal of sympathy for North Carolina's Conservatives in the wake of the Civil War. Beasley took umbrage at Tourgée's portrayal of the period: it was too simplistic, too much a stark tale of good and evil, when the reality on the ground was much more complicated. In some respects, however, Beasley agreed with Tourgée, blaming much of the troubles of the time on opportunistic politicians and the lack of both a coherent national plan for how Reconstruction should proceed and a clear set of aims.[31]

Like *A Fool's Errand* (upon which it was clearly modeled), *Those American R's* somewhat awkwardly welded a love story to commentary on Reconstruction politics. Also set in North Carolina's Piedmont, Beasley's lightly fictionalized take on the period followed quite a different story arc than did Tourgée's tale. The important real-life players in the state appeared under fictional names, including Governor Holden, George Kirk, Milton S. Littlefield, John Stephens, and Josiah Turner. In Beasley's telling, Klansmen were wrong to pursue their extralegal methods, but their violence was directed at an equally mercenary set of carpetbaggers. Like competing flocks of buzzards, the two factions picked at the prostrate state. The real villains of Beasley's story were the duplicitous and self-serving Holden, willing to cast aside the people's rights and liberties to maintain his office, and the mercenary and unscrupulous Kirk, portrayed as little more than a brute. Littlefield's character danced around the edges, influencing state politics with well-placed bribes. Stephens appeared as the character Stephen Floyd, whom Beasley painted in a comparatively balanced light. Floyd was a true believer in his cause, even if his political power came almost exclusively from a calculated exploitation of black voters and the patronage of the state's corrupt Republican leadership. The Castleton family, the book's protagonists, bore a grudging admiration for Floyd, and they were shocked when he was murdered in circumstances that mirrored Stephens's real assassination. His killing along with the subsequent Kirk-Holden War encouraged their removal to the North, where they hoped to find better and more peaceful prospects.

Beasley's sympathies for the white South and its racial mores grew more evident as his story followed the Castletons to their new northern home, the city of "Philopolis." There the hero of the second half of the book, Jenkins Castleton, almost certainly intended to represent Beasley himself, noted that while he regretted the violence and sloth that was characteristic of southern elites, he was even more troubled by the northern obsession with labor and profit. He complained that Philopolis rang with the grasping cries of "Lucre, lucre, give me lucre!"[32] He also observed northern hypocrisy concerning race, as in many places above the Mason-Dixon Line laws limited black suffrage or imposed racial segregation, even as a northern-dominated Congress sought to advance racial equality in the former Confederacy. Beasley had Castleton's character assert the naturalness of segregation. In an extended argument for the intrinsic freedom of Americans to discriminate against one another, Castleton pled, "If it be a warm day and the [street]car is crowded with colored dames, do not prevent me from going out and standing on the platform for 'fresh air.'" Furthermore, he wrote, "if I happen to remove to some State where there is no law against miscegenation, do not count me cruel if I forbid the colored gallant (as I do some white ones) from calling upon my daughter with matrimonial intent." Discrimination was only natural, he concluded, for "'Civil Rights' and 'Social Rights' do not flow the one from the other."[33] Emancipation was one thing, Beasley wrote, but social equality quite another.

Here was a North Carolinian vision of race relations firmly in the vein of Hinton Rowan Helper. The real challenge for white Americans, as Beasley envisioned it, was not to produce a more equitable society. Instead, it was to build up new economic and political systems in the place of those torn down by the war, and he hypothesized that the path to do so ultimately lay through a white rejection of blind allegiance to political parties. Beasley clearly hoped that African Americans were to be discarded from the body politic and that the labors of men like Stephens, whose appeal had crossed racial lines, would come to naught.

North Carolina's Democrats were even more unambiguous in their rejection of Tourgée's conclusions in the years spanning the publication of his books. As the balance of state political power steadily shifted toward Democrats in the aftermath of Holden's impeachment, they worked to shape memories of Holden, Stephens, the Klan, and Reconstruction. The end results may have been questionable as history, but they made good politics. One particularly outspoken voice was that of Randolph Shotwell, who, like Josiah Turner, had been a Conservative newspaperman during Reconstruction, in his case editing the *Rutherfordton Western Vindicator*, the *Asheville Citizen*, and then Raleigh's *Farmer and Mechanic*. And like John Lea, Shotwell had participated in the early Klan, taking a hand in efforts to drive Republicans out of politics in the state's western mountains. In the 1880s, after the state's "Redemption," he briefly became a state legislator, and in 1885 he was appointed the state librarian. In an autobiographical manuscript drafted in the late 1870s or early 1880s, Shotwell named Stephens "a Radical Senator and a tool of Holden's," given to making "midnight raids of an amatory, and predatory nature." Stephens was a boil on the body politic, yet just a symptom of the rot that underlay the Republican Reconstruction effort. In one breathless sentence of Faulknerian length and complexity, Shotwell summed up Democrats' stance on the postwar landscape and how those years ought to be remembered:

> Ninety thousand negroes, brutal by nature, debased by habit, and inflamed to arrogant swaggering by the scheming tricksters both State and National, who had vested them with the full privileges of citizenship and cold-blooded design to use them for purposes of robbery and oppression, constituted the "Party of Progress, and Moral Ideas"—so-called; though the real control of this formidable body of men—oath bound in secret Leagues, and still more firmly shackled by race-prejudices—was in the hands of a small number of shrewd demagogues and Place-men, under the leadership of Holden and [state senator] John Pool, and composed chiefly of Carpetbaggers, who had followed the "Bummer" Sherman into the State, and were left here as driftwood after the army disbanded in 1865, or had drifted down from the North, on the principle of buzzards congregating at a carcass.

In light of these sorts of Republican oppressions, Shotwell concluded, the emergence of the Klan was a natural response. White Conservatives had sought to defend their freedom and liberty, not to mention their natural leadership of state society.[34]

John H. Wheeler, a prominent antebellum politician who turned to writing state history after the war, shared Shotwell's opinion. The events of 1870, he wrote, took place during "a fearful epoch in our history when the lives and liberties of innocent and worthy citizens were exposed to the tender mercies of lawless power." The oppression came not from the Klan, Wheeler continued, but from Governor Holden and Colonel Kirk's campaign against North Carolina's Conservatives. Stephens sat at the center of the maelstrom, "one of the disreputable waifs of circumstance whom the troubled waves of civil war brought to the surface. He was of low origin, of dissolute habits

and disreputable character." Wheeler repeated some of the most slander-
ous accusations of the time in his rambling history of the state published in
1884, writing that Stephens "had been arraigned for petit larceny and other
offenses. His mother was found murdered in his house in broad daylight, with
her throat cut from ear to ear, and no one ever knew, nor did the coroner's
jury decide, by whom or how the murder was done."[35] The message was
clear: the sort of man who could slay his own mother would certainly have
few scruples about abusing political office for personal gain.

Other state documentarians took a different approach, editing the Reconstruction era to omit discussion of prominent Republicans, whether scalawag
or carpetbagger. Popular biographical reference works paid scant attention to
men like Stephens and Tourgée. Jerome Dowd's *Sketches of Prominent Living
North Carolinians* (1888), for example, heaped praise upon Democrats but
said relatively little about their opponents. And the *Cyclopedia of Eminent and
Representative Men of the Carolinas of the Nineteenth Century* (1892) contained
entries for Bedford Brown and Jonathan Worth but none for Carey, Outlaw,
Tourgée, Stephens, or even Holden.[36] Still, most late nineteenth-century
Democrats were more than willing to name the figures they saw as villains
of past decades.

Democrats like Shotwell and Wheeler became mainstream white voices
in the state after Reconstruction closed, but a few white Republicans in the
mold of Tourgée remained in the final years of the nineteenth century to
defend Stephens's memory. One example was lawyer Luther Carlton, a relative of the senator. In essays in publications of Wake Forest and Trinity (later
Duke University) Colleges, Carlton praised Stephens as a martyr to a cause
in which he truly believed. In the Trinity article, he described his relative
as "known by all as an honest, fair-dealing, christian man. He was a most
loving husband and kind father, and an energetic worker in the Methodist
church."[37] Stephens had shifted his allegiance to the Republican Party after
the war from principle rather than opportunism, Carlton argued, assuming
great danger in the process. "His position was a trying one, but he bore it
heroically."[38] Caswell's African American population mourned his death,
recognizing the loss of a true friend, Carlton wrote, and even the assassins
eventually felt remorse for their terrible crime. He asserted in summary that
the senator "was unswerving in his brave adherence to the principals [*sic*]
he professed. He crowned a worthy life by a martyr's death; he was pursued
with fearful malice and bigoted hate to the very portals of the tomb." But
Carlton was confident that the passage of time would redeem Stephens in
public memory.[39]

As these various accounts suggest, arguments about the assassination were more abundant than new facts in the two decades following Stephens's death. But what had been a knotty mystery for more than twenty years—who had in fact killed the senator?—suddenly seemed on the brink of unraveling in the 1890s. Carlton named two suspects in his description of the crime: Frank Wiley and Felix Roan. By now they were familiar names. Both had fallen under suspicion in the days after the killing, were among the pool of men swept up in Kirk's arrests, and had defended themselves in Judge Richard Pearson's court, and Patsie Burton had named them both in Tourgée's investigation. Wiley had remained in Caswell for a few years after his case was dropped. In 1876 he ended up in court again, this time facing suit for embezzling a portion of an estate for which he served as executor. He was perhaps fortunate that the case was tried before Judge John Kerr, one of the other men suspected of involvement in Stephens's death and arrested during the Kirk-Holden War. Kerr found in the former sheriff's favor.[40] Sometime thereafter Wiley moved to Catawba County in the western part of the state, perhaps fleeing his association with Stephens's death or his other legal troubles for a clean slate. He passed away shortly thereafter, and, according to some accounts, in his final hours he raved about his complicity in the assassination and the resulting guilt he felt for his part. The claim was not widely circulated at the time and seems not to have made much of a public impression.[41]

Felix Roan's dying confession generated a much bigger sensation. Roan passed away in his Caswell home late in 1891. Claiming that he wanted to make a clean breast of his affairs, he had invited the editor of the *Orange County Observer* to the room where he lay and proceeded to give a deathbed confession to the slaying of Senator Stephens. In this testimony Roan named three accomplices: Wiley, James T. Mitchell, and Steve Richmond, who had not featured prominently in earlier speculations about the killing. All four men had been swept up in the Kirk arrests and were freed as the prosecution fell apart, and with Roan's passing all four would be dead.[42]

Roan provided plenty of details in support of his claims. In his tale he described how the county's Klan chapter had passed a verdict of death on Stephens in a secret meeting and that Wiley was indeed charged with luring the group's target down to the courthouse basement under false pretenses. Roan noted that Klansmen in the Conservative meeting underway on the main level of the courthouse had known of the plan and kept up "much cheering and stamping of feet—the intention being to drown any noise that might proceed from" the room where the killing was taking place. In the basement with the condemned man, the ceiling thumping with the covering noises taking place above their heads, Roan and his allies had ordered Stephens to leave the state or renounce the Republican Party if he wanted to avoid death. Stephens refused, and at that moment one of the conspirators, presumably Wiley, wrapped a cord around his neck and drew it tight. Roan and Richmond—who were both physicians—then sliced the captive's jugular veins with the lancets they carried, and Roan proceeded to stab the senator in his heart for good measure. Further demonstrating their careful premeditation, the conspirators had brought along a bucket to catch the blood spilling from the dying man, so that it might not run under the door and reveal the location of the killing. Their grim work done, Roan's party left the body in the old Freedmen's Bureau office, locked the door, and fled Yanceyville before Stephens's absence could be noticed.

In almost every respect this confession neatly matched the account of the killing that Tourgée had related in *A Fool's Errand*.[43] The *Raleigh Signal* carried the extended confession and reprinted it on several occasions, but despite its political leanings toward the Republican Party and its steady defense of the legacy of Holden's administration, its coverage conveyed some ambivalence about the victim as an individual. By the 1890s the frequent portrayals of Stephens as an ignorant scalawag proved too entrenched to be entirely shaken off. In laying out the backstory, the paper chalked up the senator's political success to Caswell's "large negro majority" during Reconstruction, a portion of the population that held "absolute confidence" in Stephens even though he "was not a man of particular ability." If Stephens was poorly qualified as a politician, the paper still attempted to redeem his bravery and integrity in its descriptions of the killing itself. In recounting Roan's confession, the article noted Stephens's steadfast refusal to abandon his party and Caswell's African American voters, even on threat of death. Faced with the Klan's demands, Stephens "told them that they might kill him, but that he would not leave the State nor desert his principles as a Republican."

Furthermore, Stephens remained a religious family man to the end. Blurring the *Signal*'s interpretation with Roan's words, the article's narrative continued. After the senator refused to abandon his political principles, Roan informed Stephens of his impending doom. Upon this news the senator pled to be allowed to look out the room's sole window at his home one last time. The article, striking a maudlin tone, described that "as he gazed out of the window, he saw two of his little children playing in the yard in front of his door. He looked at them for a minute or two and then his wife passed through the yard. This was the only time that Stephens showed signs of emotion." He then knelt to pray for himself and his killers before facing death. If the political actions of men like Stephens who tried to enact Reconstruction had often gone awry, the *Signal* implied, they were undertaken in good faith on genuine principles.

Roan's confession rather conveniently named only dead men as co-conspirators. And all of the accused had already been connected to the crime by the state's aborted prosecution and then again in Tourgée's campaign. Much of what Roan confessed had thus become common in state gossip. It was, in short, a list of the usual suspects. A cynical reader might surmise that Roan's motive with his deathbed testament was to place other living Klansmen arrested by the state in 1870 in the clear. The dead could thereby absolve the living of any shadow of guilt. The *Signal* accepted the confession uncritically, however, and noted that it made quite a splash: "Raleigh and the State have been all agog during the past week over the confession of Dr. Felix Roan." But this state of astonishment did not last long. Roan's confession seemed to clear up any remaining mystery surrounding the notorious murder, yet the admission mysteriously all but disappeared from popular memory in a span of a few years, so much so that numerous early twentieth-century North Carolinians could continue to wonder aloud and in print, "Who killed John Stephens?"

Why was this the case? Perhaps Roan's confession did not "stick" because it was overwhelmed by a building consensus among North Carolina whites concerning the meaning and legacy of the Reconstruction period, a consensus in which Roan's details did not neatly fit. According to this coalescing public memory, Reconstruction had been a mistake on the state and national levels, the misguided work of politicians like Holden and Stephens who sought to gain personal advantage from tragedy. Little room was left for dissenting voices like those of Tourgée or Carlton, or even space for Klansmen's regrets like those Roan expressed. In particular the racial massacre that took place in November 1898 in Wilmington marked the end of an era for North Carolina. On the tenth of that month violence exploded in the port city as white Democrats sought to destroy their "fusion" political opponents who were attempting to unite the interests of the state's white Populists and black Republicans. The result was dozens of African Americans dead in the streets and the final step in North Carolina's Redemption.[44] What had begun with the killings of Outlaw and Stephens was completed with murder in the streets of Wilmington.

Indicative of this rising tide of sentiment, the Tar Heel State produced a wave of writers whose ink blotted out Tourgée's portrayal of Reconstruction and the Ku Klux Klan at the start of the twentieth century, even as Roan's testimony seemed to confirm it. Some of them wrote the authorized version of events. One of the state's official secondary school history textbooks symbolized just how hostile the mainstream white take on the period had become by the start of the twentieth century. John W. Moore's *School History of North Carolina* first appeared in 1879, when Reconstruction and Stephens's fate were fresh memories. The book was soon adopted by the North Carolina Board of Education for use in public schools. Moore was from a prominent planter family in the eastern part of the state and had served as a Confederate officer in the Civil War. Nonetheless, in the first edition of his textbook he had covered the Stephens murder and its aftermath in neutral, straightforward terms. He wrote simply that "unknown persons most foully and mysteriously murdered" the senator and then proceeded to recount the Kirk-Holden War and the governor's impeachment in a dispassionate sketch.[45]

By 1901 Moore's textbook was in its fourteenth edition, much revised and enlarged. He now devoted a whole chapter to the murder and the subsequent political turmoil. Stephens's death remained a "mystery" in the expanded textbook, but Moore now cast strong doubt on Holden's belief that the Klan was responsible. The schoolbook repeated a Conservative claim that among the county's whites, "Stephens was an object of derision and contempt rather than hatred, there was neither desire nor cause to put him to death."[46] Students also learned that George Kirk was "a brutal ruffian of infamous character, and known to be such"; that Caswell and Alamance Counties had been peaceful, not in need of martial law; and that their citizens—including men "known and honored in every portion of the State"—had been much abused by Kirk's soldiers.[47] In this revised edition, Holden was a villain intent on making a mockery of state law. Moore described how "the Chief Executive of the State was daily making his preparations for holding a drum head court-martial to try the best men in all the land, tie them to stakes and shoot them like dogs, while the judiciary, standing in sight and in hearing, declared itself helpless!"[48] North Carolina's hero in the new story was federal justice George Brooks, who forced Holden to turn over the prisoners to the state courts, for "it was he that saved her Constitution and her laws and the liberties of her people." To hammer the chapter's lesson home, Moore capped it with a set of didactic questions for students. Among them, he asked, "Who were accused as the murderers of Stephens? Upon what ground was this denied?" and "What man was put in charge of the State troops? Where was Kirke [sic] from, and what was his character?"[49] Even the least attentive students must have left the chapter sure of Moore's take on events.

No less official were the words of Senator Zebulon Vance. In 1890 the former governor set down his thoughts on Reconstruction as a chapter in a defense of the coalescing "solid South" penned by fourteen prominent southern politicians. Vance dwelled longest on the railroad scandals that plagued Holden's term and sprinkled in stories derogating the corruption and ignorance of state Republicans, paying special attention to black legislators. Martial law had been a crude power play, Vance concluded, and he was relieved that "the state was redeemed amidst the thankful prayers of all honest men." Still, he worried that it would take a number of years for the state to finish correcting the harmful actions of the era.[50]

Extracurricular readers found their own North Carolina writers busily shaping the public memory of the state's Reconstruction and the violence that played such an important part in it. Thomas Dixon, a minister turned novelist, embraced white supremacy and portrayals of Republican Reconstruction as thoroughly corrupt in an authorial voice that resonated far beyond the boundaries of the Tar Heel State. First in *The Leopard's Spots* (1902), which he conceptualized as a corrective reimagining of Harriet Beecher Stowe's *Uncle Tom's Cabin*, and then in the even more popular *The Clansman* (1905), Dixon framed slavery as good, the Civil War as a noble if doomed crusade, and Reconstruction as an unadulterated bastardization of American democracy. In the aftermath of war, Dixon wrote, only the chivalric Ku Klux Klan had saved the South from political corruption, miscegenation, and bloody racial conflict.[51]

Dixon was born in Cleveland County in the Piedmont and was familiar from birth with the political strife and violence that swept the region in the years after the Civil War. In his autobiographical account (published posthumously), Dixon lauded members of his own family who had participated in the Ku Klux Klan, including tales of his mother sewing robes for the local den and his uncle's service in his county's Klan chapter. Dixon had been raised on stories of Holden's misrule and the noble struggle to cleanse the state of Republican influence. He recounted a boyhood brawl with a friend over the question of whether the governor had a right to call out the militia in 1870 to keep order, and he held particular contempt for Tourgée, whom he thought a craven carpetbagger unqualified in the law.[52] Memories of those early days stuck with him, later serving as fodder for his fiction. Dixon modeled Amos Hogg, the corrupt scalawag governor in *The Leopard's Spots*, on Holden, and he dedicated his most popular work, *The Clansman*, to his uncle LeRoy McAfee, informing readers that he had been a "Grand Titan of the Invisible Empire Ku Klux Klan."[53]

Dixon's flattering portrayal of the Klan found a new and even larger audience when *The Clansman* was made into a major motion picture in 1915: *The Birth of a Nation*. Directed by D. W. Griffith, *The Birth of a Nation* became Hollywood's first "blockbuster," a success driven both by its innovative cinematography and how it captured the zeitgeist of many white Americans grown comfortable with the racial vision of the Jim Crow system. Although the film drew some protest for its fawning portrayal of the Klan and its demonization of African American men as slavering rapists, the critical reviewers were overwhelmingly impressed by Griffith and Dixon's cinematic version of history. Among the movie's fans were several members of the Supreme Court as well as President Woodrow Wilson—trained at Johns Hopkins as a historian and political scientist and author of his own account of Reconstruction—who enjoyed a private screening at the White House. The historian-in-chief praised the film for its accuracy.[54]

Although it is less well known today than Dixon's enormously popular portrayals of the Klan, Myrta Lockett Avary's 1906 history of Reconstruction also found a general audience receptive to the messages of the Lost Cause and white supremacy. Avary too was a product of the southern Piedmont; in her case she was born in Virginia's Halifax County, which adjoins Caswell's northeastern corner and shared a history of reliance on bright tobacco. Her tome, *Dixie after the War* (printed by Doubleday, Page, which also served as Dixon's publisher), described the rise and actions of the Klan, and, like Dixon, Avary believed the North was to blame for the missteps of the age. She argued that regional violence began with the work of the Union League. Its chapters were the first postwar secret societies, Avary wrote, "where mystic initiation rites, inflammatory speeches, [and] military drills, were in order." Under the guiding hands of carpetbaggers and scalawags, the Union League shaped the South's African American population into "a terror and forced whites into the formation of counter secret societies for the protection of their firesides." The Klan was successful in its efforts, she thankfully concluded, as it ultimately "restored peace by parade and sometimes by sterner measures."[55]

Well-versed in the lore of the Piedmont, Avary included Stephens's assassination in her account of the peak of Klan violence. Despite misspelling the Republican's name as "Stevens," she assured readers that his killers were on the right side of history and the murdered man in the wrong. Whatever they may have read, the episode had been "misused by Tourgée in 'A Fool's Errand.'" She also hinted at insider knowledge of the event, even as she ignored, or was unaware of, Felix Roan's confession. Avary rather cryptically recorded that "I have been told that one of the slayers is living and that at his death, a true statement will be published showing who killed Stevens and how."[56] In case her allegiance remained uncertain, she wrote in summary, "For my part, I believe that this country owes a heavy debt to its noiseless white horsemen, shades of its troubled past."[57]

A chorus of North Carolina voices joined Dixon's and Avary's portrayals of Reconstruction in the state. For example, Mary Woodson Jarvis published an account of North Carolina's Klan in 1902 in the *North Carolina Booklet*, a state history magazine published by the Daughters of the American Revolution. Jarvis's voice carried a certain official imprimatur since her husband, Thomas Jarvis, had served as the state's governor from 1879 to 1885 and was an important architect of white supremacy in the Tar Heel State.[58] In Mary Jarvis's explanation of North Carolina's Reconstruction, the state's Republican "leaders were vultures, who considered the State as their prey. The scallawags, carpet-baggers and negroes who composed the large majority were wholly irresponsible, and launched upon a course of wild extravagance in order to feather their nests at the public expense." And what of the Klan? Jarvis continued, "The work of this mongrel body [Republicans] could not be checked by the few brave spirits, who fought day and night with desperate persistence, to stem the tide of reckless extravagance and corruption." She agreed with Avary that it had been the Union League that initiated violence through arson attacks and that the Klan organized as a response and was composed of society's best men. Although the secret society came to commit some questionable transgressions, she confessed, they were only the result of the perversion of its means and methods by a few low individuals undeserving of the robes. Writing of the violence and state response in Alamance and Caswell, she pointed the finger of blame at George Kirk's "cutthroats," who arrested prominent county men who "had never been members of the Ku Klux; and who knew nothing of its operations." Frank Wiley and his allies were the real victims of events in 1870, according to Jarvis.[59]

Frank Nash, an attorney who would go on to become a state senator and North Carolina's assistant attorney general, framed the story in much the same way when he wrote a biographical entry for Stephens that appeared in Samuel Ashe's compendious *Biographical History of North Carolina* in 1906. (Mary Jarvis's husband, the former governor, served on the collection's advisory board, reflecting the rather incestuous nature of North Carolina's historical memorialization at the time.) Nash also believed that Republican Reconstruction was thoroughly corrupt and the Klan a natural outgrowth of the situation. He too thought the Union League was North Carolina's most dangerous organization, and it was black barn burners who had escalated Piedmont violence. Lynchings were simply private policing.[60] Stephens was an instrumental figure in the state's turbulent Reconstruction, Nash argued. His short biography portrayed Stephens as a political opportunist and master manipulator of the era's racial tensions; altogether he was "one of the shrewdest and boldest and most vindictive of the negro leaders." The essay also blamed Stephens for instigating the local episodes of arson. Nash did point the finger at the Klan for the assassination but absolved Caswell County residents of any involvement in the killing. He believed that the attack had been conducted by Klansmen from other counties (as was supposedly common practice to obscure the identities of Klansmen engaged in vigilantism). Nash concluded that Stephens may not have been "a criminal in a legal sense, deserving death," but he thoroughly damned him anyway: "He was only a self-seeker, without the excuse even of fanaticism."[61] Better to be a criminal, Nash implied, than to engage in interracial cooperation for the sake of personal ambition.

Academic historians would also enter the fray, as they began to produce the first generation of scholarly accounts of Reconstruction. The initial extended "professional" treatment of the era in North Carolina came from Joseph Grégoire de Roulhac Hamilton, soon to be hailed as one of the state's preeminent historians. Born into a prominent slaveholding family of Alamance County, his father served alongside many Caswell soldiers as a major in the 13th North Carolina Regiment during the Civil War. Hamilton attended the University of the South in Tennessee before moving to New York to train at Columbia as a graduate student under the eminent historian of Reconstruction William Dunning. By the 1910s Hamilton was a professor of history at the University of North Carolina at Chapel Hill, where he would go on to found and then direct the university's Southern Historical Collection for several decades.[62]

In 1914, Hamilton published *Reconstruction in North Carolina*, which, in its characterization of the era as an exercise in folly, corruption, and racial pandering, was the epitome of the body of Reconstruction history produced by Dunning's students (often labeled the "Dunning School" of historiography). The central villains in Hamilton's tale were Governor Holden, Senator John Pool, and Colonel Kirk, together intent on keeping the state's rightful leaders from power and furthering its economic woes to feather their own nests. Although Stephens was a bit player in this larger drama, Hamilton also sought to define him as thoroughly corrupt and dangerous. He was venal, abusing his connections to Holden, and opportunistic, taking advantage of the political

Perhaps no historian did more to define John Stephens as a villainous politician than J. G. de Roulhac Hamilton. "Hamilton, Joseph Gr[é]goire deRhoulac [*sic*]," in Portrait Collection #P0002, North Carolina Collection Photographic Archives, Wilson Library, University of North Carolina at Chapel Hill.

influence he held with freedpeople. Hamilton also stated as fact that Stephens had been involved in the county arsons in the months leading up to the spring of 1870. In sum, he was vile: "a man of bad reputation and of evil political life." If his killing was dirty business, it seemed necessary nonetheless, for "if there be such a thing as the sacred right of revolution, then the Ku Klux movement as planned and carried out at first was justifiable. No free people ever labored under more galling oppression or more grievous misrule."[63]

W. E. B. Du Bois, as he worked on writing a rebuttal to the Dunning School's Reconstruction narrative, singled out Hamilton's study of North Carolina as a particularly egregious example of revisionist history. The book was "the climax" of the Dunning School, Du Bois wrote, and Hamilton the sort of white supremacist who could celebrate the Black Codes that sought to virtually re-enslave freedpeople as "'on the whole reasonable, temperate and kindly.'"[64] Hamilton's assessment of Stephens was just as harsh.

As Du Bois noted, Dunning and his students were busily and successfully revising the nation's understanding of Reconstruction in the early years of the twentieth century. Dunning's *Reconstruction, Political and Economic, 1865–1877* (1907) framed the period in general as a political and economic disaster, defined by corruption at the ballot boxes and in statehouses across the South. Under his guidance, Dunning's Columbia students and other historians influenced by their interpretations set about creating case studies that applied Dunning's narrative to each southern state. Dunning provided the interpretive framework and his students filled in the local details. Like Hamilton's account of North Carolina, many of these works became the standard texts on the subject for a generation or more in their respective states. Only with the civil rights movement would the Dunning School's interpretive framework gradually be supplanted.[65]

Hamilton's portrayal of Union League chapters as the most dangerous secret societies of the period and his interest in arson, and especially barn burning, were reflective of patterns in other Dunning School works. Walter Fleming, for example, declared that in Alabama the Union League epitomized "the absolute control exercised over the blacks by the alien adventurers [carpetbaggers]." In league meetings, he continued, leaders preached murder and arson as tools to obtaining and holding state power.[66] Other state studies were replete with claims that southern Republicans assaulted Democrats' property with the torch and thus brought night riding upon themselves. James Garner placed an incident of arson at the start of an infamous episode of racial violence at Meridian, Mississippi, in 1871 that claimed the lives of approximately thirty African Americans.[67] In South Carolina, John Reynolds wrote, it was black "violence and incendiarism" that had spurred the forma-tion of the state's Klan chapters.[68] And in her study of Georgia, Clara Mildred Thompson declared that Klan night riding and Union League arson were two sides of the same coin.[69] In these seemingly authoritative tomes, Hamilton and his Columbia cohort lent full credence to Conservatives' Reconstruction claims, dusting off and breathing new life into the figure of the black arsonist and a militant Union League for a new generation of Americans.

Hamilton's monograph became the standard scholarly treatment of the period in North Carolina for several decades. (Indeed, although today's his-torians have largely rejected Hamilton's conclusions, his book remains an often-cited reference thanks to its compendious details.) Even more import-ant for North Carolinians' general understandings of the era was a popular state textbook that Hamilton published five years later. It reiterated his take on Reconstruction and Stephens's murder. In *North Carolina since 1860*, Ham-ilton again emphasized that the Caswell senator was "a man of bad reputation and notoriously evil political life" who led and inflamed the local Union League, with the result that "barn-burning was seemingly the purpose of its existence."[70] Likewise, prolific state historian Samuel Ashe drew heavily on Hamilton's Reconstruction and Stephens summaries for his own two-volume history textbook, completed in 1925.[71] In a similar effort to ensure that the state's students learned the Conservative portrayal of Reconstruction, Ham-ilton prepared a state history syllabus with William Boyd, a fellow Columbia graduate and professor at Trinity College (soon to be Duke University). Drawn from their own teaching notes, the syllabus included a section on the Republican governance of the state and the Kirk-Holden War, complete with a unit on the "Political effects of Radical dishonesty and misrule" and a list of reading materials related to Stephens's assassination.[72]

In Caswell, a Dunning-esque interpretation of the killing had taken firm hold, at least among the county's elites. George Anderson, onetime clerk of court as well as an amateur local historian, summarized the local perception of the murder as it had become rooted in county lore. The months of martial law in the summer of 1870 had been "Caswell's darkest hour in the period of Reconstruction," a time when its people had been oppressed by Kirk's militia, men "of the lowest order, the dregs of society, cut-throats, thieves and convicts."[73] In public reminiscences, Anderson (who had been born just a year prior to the assassination, and thus had no personal recollection of the events) persisted in using the "chicken" epithet, placing the blame for the violence squarely on the Republican senator. He explained that Stephens was "a native who turned against his people for place and pay after the Civil

War and joined the Republican Party. He was put to death for what many believed were his crimes and follies."[74] In his selection of language—"put to death" and "crimes"—Anderson implied that the murder had been a just, even quasi-legal, action.

In a private letter written in 1914, Anderson's take was much the same. He wrote of Stephens as a politician who "had a complete mastery over the negroes in the County & they were ready to follow his lead." And he repeated tales of barn and house burnings in the days leading up to the assassination. The letter was in fact remarkably detailed, describing Wiley's effort to lure Stephens to the courthouse basement and the killers' use of both a cord and knives, along with other details that revealed Anderson's close study of accounts of the murder. The letter also included an intriguing detail seemingly not present in any published sources or court proceedings to that point in time. Anderson wrote that the assassins had taken with them the key to the storeroom holding Stephens's body as they rode out of town, casting it in Country Line Creek as their horses galloped east. Roan's confession more than two decades prior had mentioned disposal of the key but did not name the location. This knowledge suggests the possibility that Anderson had either conversed with one of the assassins or that certain unpublished elements of the killing had become a part of community lore. Despite this seemingly intimate knowledge and Felix Roan's frank admission that the Klan had planned and executed the killing, Anderson concluded his discussion of the assassination with a disavowal: "This was not a perpetration of the 'Klan.'" He also declared that "Stephens' murder was brought about, in my opinion, purely as a means of self preservation of our County."[75]

As the martial clouds over Europe promised to pull the United States into a war to end all wars, John Stephens's assassination remained a mystery. Nearly half a century earlier, the Klan conspiracy trial had fallen apart, pulling down Governor Holden's administration and eventually North Carolina Republicans' political power with it. A pair of confessions in subsequent years had promised some illumination and closure, but each had been muddied by denials and counterclaims, leaving some people convinced that the killers had been known all along and others sure only of their uncertainty. Almost fifty years after the event, it seemed likely that the killers would never be revealed with any surety and that the perpetrators were long buried.

If who had murdered Stephens was still clouded in the public mind, a sense of what the killing meant seemed to be firming up, at least for white North Carolinians. Albion Tourgée had produced the most articulate and widespread early framing with his best-selling books, taking a stab at reconstructing North Carolina memory even as the physical efforts to remake state politics and society fell apart on the ground. The "fool" did his best to accomplish his "errand" after the fact. But as Jim Crow and the Lost Cause cemented black disenfranchisement and white supremacy across the South, a new generation of white North Carolinians rediscovered Stephens's killing and reframed the story to suit their visions of past, present, and future. Popular writers like Thomas Dixon and Myrta Avary portrayed Reconstruction as a tragic, corrupt mistake, its villains opportunistic carpetbaggers and scalawags like Tourgée, Holden, and Stephens. Scholars gave this message a veneer of legitimacy, their footnotes and syllabi reinforcing the tragedy of the era and, by extension, justifying Jim Crow and Democratic rule in the present. Even the gloss of patriotism generated by the United States' entry into World War I—in Caswell, as across North Carolina, men registered for the draft at high rates, and the state's women were active in a range of volunteer causes in support of the conflict—failed to detract from the momentum of the Lost Cause Reconstruction narrative.[76] In the Tar Heel State, white supremacy and renewed nationalism proved comfortable bedfellows.

On the local level, some Caswell residents found the messages of Dixon, Hamilton, and like-minded authors appealing. Their Lost Cause interpretation redefined the Piedmont's Reconstruction violence as a struggle for freedom and redemption rather than a rearguard action following a lost war or a brutal campaign to suppress black liberty and make hollow the promise of emancipation. That men like Stephens and Outlaw were also residents of the Piedmont, with their own visions of a just future, seems not to have entered into the equation for many whites in power by the early twentieth century. For their part, black county residents struggled for opportunity against stiff odds, trying to make good on the Reconstruction promises that had crumbled in the intervening years. One example came in the form of the Yanceyville Colored School, in operation by 1907. The school opened in what had once been John Stephens's house. His widow and children had left Yanceyville a few months after the assassination and the house sat unoccupied for more than three decades, racial mores and its troubled past keeping both white and black tenants away. The senator's old home would serve as the county's first publicly supported black school until replaced by a more modern structure in 1925.[77]

The regional economic situation also provided fodder for memory's mill. The county's prospects seemed dimmed by the year the Great War began, at least for its rural residents. The 1850s had seemed an agricultural golden age, with bright tobacco at its peak of prosperity, but a set of circumstances had

By the early twentieth century, the tasks of tobacco work dominated the daily lives of many Caswell residents. Marion Post Wolcott, *Mr. W. H. Willis, a FSA (Farm Security Administration) Borrower and His Helper Grading Stripping Tobacco in Pack House on His Farm near Yanceyville, Caswell County, North Carolina*, Farm Security Administration—Office of War Information, 1940, Library of Congress.

eroded that promise as the nineteenth century gave way to the twentieth. Bright leaf remained in demand. Caswell tobacco production had fallen in the unrest of 1870 to about half of what it had been in the last census before emancipation (although it was still the highest total of any county in the state), but by 1880 it had bounced back to roughly 1860 levels.[78] And bright leaf was becoming the staple ingredient in cigarettes, which themselves became increasingly popular after the 1880s. On the eve of the Great War, cigarettes were, in fact, poised to replace chewing tobacco as the most common form of tobacco consumed in the nation. But the prices that farmers received for their bright tobacco had fallen, as growing competition from other regions intersected with a collusive buyers' market, culminating in the American Tobacco Company, a monopoly organized in 1890 by North Carolina's own James Buchanan Duke.[79] Marketing outlets seemed so restricted by the turn

Chapter Five

of the century that Caswell's farmers lamented about being "oppressed and in bondage to the tobacco combine" (Duke's American Tobacco Company).[80]

Additionally, erosion and soil exhaustion had taken their toll on county fields, stripping away the soil wealth that had once made Caswell a land of agrarian promise. Food crops proved poor alternatives to tobacco, as local farmland often produced but weak stands of corn and wheat, lackluster productivity that reflected years of heavy cultivation with little fertility returned to the soil.[81] The timber needed for constructing and fueling tobacco barns was increasingly in short supply as well.[82] And the center of bright tobacco cultivation had shifted south and eastward into the state's coastal plain.[83]

On the eve of the First World War, an out-of-state doctor assigned to Caswell as part of the Rockefeller Foundation Sanitary Commission's hookworm eradication campaign characterized the county as poor and backward. He described Milton as depressing and full of vacant houses. Yanceyville was home to a "very impressive" but "not well kept" courthouse, but in his opinion the county's most distinctive feature was its lamentable roads.[84] By the 1930s, an economist asserted that the wastage was complete, writing that "in those parts of North Carolina where tobacco is grown almost exclusively, there is the most apparent poverty, not poverty of money alone, but poverty of culture, poverty of soil; poverty of good homes and social environment; poverty of health and of everything that goes to make rural life that ideal mode of living."[85] The cumulative result of these forces was a general sense that Caswell's golden age had been wasted, wrecked by war and then Reconstruction at the very moment the future had seemed blindingly bright.

Duke and other tobacco magnates were not solely responsible for the regional agricultural decline. Caswell farmers contributed to the troubles through cultivation that was sometimes abusive and through their own willingness to rely on a single staple crop. Caswell residents and not James B. Duke plowed their own fields up and down the slopes and cut their forests to cure barns of tobacco, and sometimes they recognized their own culpability. But such introspection was rare. Who was to blame for the county's drift into somnolence seemed clear to those who shaped an embittered regional memory: the North and northerners' Republican allies in the state, both black and white. They had enslaved North Carolina's prospects to speculators, freedpeople, and greedy politicians, frittering the future away for worthless railroad bonds and the black ballot. Who was to credit for the death of the county's most prominent scalawag seemed to forever remain a mystery, however. At least until one July day in 1919 began to unravel the tangled stories of the past.

Six

PRIOR
APPROPRIATION

[Q.] Were the people of the South punished for engaging in the war?

[A.] Yes; by losing nearly all that they possessed, and further by having a horde of men called "carpet-baggers" sent down South to rule over them and rob them of the little left to them by the ruins of war.

CORNELIA BRANCH STONE, *U.D.C. Catechism for Children* (1904)

The year 1919 was a bloody one. US servicemen were back from the murderous fields of Europe, in many cases bringing with them the Spanish flu that would kill hundreds of thousands of Americans in the following months. They arrived on a home front that was far from peaceful. That year the nation's racial violence reached a level not seen since the darkest days of Reconstruction. Americans' paranoia about communism and Jim Crow's violent enforcement of white supremacy through lynching often intersected during the hot months of "red summer." Contributing to the violence was the Ku Klux Klan, which had been reborn a few years prior in Georgia, on the granitic dome of Stone Mountain, outside of Atlanta, the brainchild of William Joseph Simmons. By 1919 this new version of the "Invisible Empire" counted approximately 3,000 members in Georgia and Alabama and stood poised to add thousands more the following year. Attempts to organize a black sharecroppers' union in the delta of eastern Arkansas led to a violent white backlash that left 200 or more African Americans dead in the countryside surrounding the farming town of Elaine. Across the South at least 63 other people were lynched that year—most of them African American—a number significantly higher than in 1918 or 1920, and the highest total of such murders since 1903. Thomas Dixon's novels remained popular reading, and *The Birth of a Nation* still played in the country's theaters. In schools across the nation, Dunning School textbooks defining Reconstruction as a period of farcical corruption and black misrule held pride of place in curricula. It was an age, historian David Blight summarizes, "when the American apartheid had become fully entrenched."[1]

North Carolina was no exception to these national trends. In recent years it had also experienced bloody moments of racial violence, epitomized by the Wilmington riot that left perhaps as many as 30 African Americans dead in the city's streets.[2] In Caswell County, a mob of more than 150 people had hung and then shot Bud Mebane to death near Yanceyville in 1885, after the black man was accused of raping and murdering a white woman. Just across the state line in Danville, in 1917 an enraged posse shot to death Walter Clark, a black man who was also accused of murder.[3] And, like Hinton Rowan Helper of the previous generation, some white Tar Heels in the early twentieth century envisioned an expansion of segregation in the state's rural countryside as well as in its cities. Wilmington industrialist and developer Hugh MacRae (who had been an instrumental figure in instigating Wilmington's racial massacre) organized planned agriculture communities in the state's coastal plain that encouraged settlement by European immigrants while banning African American residents. Clarence Poe, editor of the influential Raleigh-based periodical *Progressive Farmer*, likewise lobbied for state legislation that might create all-white rural districts, since Poe believed that competition with black farmers increased land prices and drove down the standards of living for white yeomen. Like Helper, MacRae and Poe focused their attentions on the fate of the state's white citizens; in their visions of the future, black farmers were at best an obstacle to the state's prosperity.[4]

For one of the final living conspirators involved in John Walter Stephens's assassination, the moment must have thus seemed ripe for a revelation. John G. Lea decided that the time had come to tell of his part in killing Stephens. To that end he visited Raleigh on the second of July, 1919, to record his story for the North Carolina Historical Commission. On a personal level, perhaps his body warned him that he could expect only so many more years in which to tell his tale. He had never achieved the economic or political power of antebellum Leas, like his father, but he had built a respectable career in Danville, Virginia, as a tobacco trader. Now, however, he had grown old. He was in his late seventies, and all but one of his fellow Caswell Klansmen were dead of age or illness. And the nation seemed receptive at that moment to celebrating the South's rearguard action in defense of white supremacy and states' rights in the aftermath of the Civil War. What better time for an old man to claim an important role in the first Klan than when its second iteration was on the rise?

It also seems as if Lea's involvement in the killing was suspected by certain figures interested in state history, and thus the secret might escape with or without him. In his voluminous new history of the state's Reconstruction, Joseph Grégoire de Roulhac Hamilton had mentioned in passing that the leader of Caswell's Klan was believed to have been "John G. Lee [sic]."[5] Perhaps the professor steered the Historical Commission to reach out to Lea. In a cover sheet that accompanied his testimony, Lea furnished a hint in that direction, noting that he provided the account "at the request of the North Carolina Historical Commission." After a half century the shadowy conspiracy no longer seemed very secret.[6]

Whatever motivated it, Lea's confession, so casual in language, seems also to have been carefully crafted. He had, after all, virtually half a century to think about it. Whereas Frank Wiley and Felix Roan had approached their deaths bearing guilt for their part in the murder, Lea seemed to retain nothing but pride. As he unfolded his tale in the commission's office, he explained that he was the hero of the story—not a vain, glory-seeking hero but the sort of man whom communities hope to produce in moments of grave crisis. Faced with "the stirring events of that time," he did what any community-minded man of the place and age would do: he organized a secret society intent on overthrowing the county's government, with fire and sword if necessary. He was the one who had put together the county's Klan chapter, he had presided over a secret trial of Klansmen that determined Stephens must die, and he had kept the secret to protect other participants. His lips had remained sealed throughout his 1870 arrest, the subsequent conspiracy trial in Raleigh, and during all the years that followed. Left unsaid was that other participants—namely Wiley and Roan—had broken that trust.

Other than revealing his leading role in the events, the details that Lea furnished that day largely matched popular understandings of the assassination put together in past courtrooms and in the pages of works like those of Albion Tourgée and Hamilton. He confirmed that Wiley had indeed baited Stephens to the courthouse basement by promising to discuss the sheriff's election that fateful May afternoon so long ago. Some of the county's leading

Conservatives were indeed privy to the killing, Lea revealed, and a few had even participated. And there had been a concerted effort to provide alibis to those involved in the months that followed and to cast blame on other people. On their way out of Yanceyville, Lea mentioned, the killers tossed the basement room key into Country Line Creek in the hopes of delaying discovery of the body, thereby confirming a detail that at least a few community whites apparently already knew.[7]

It is interesting to note that although he named numerous parties to the murder—including Wiley, James T. Mitchell, James Denny, Joe Fowler, Tom Oliver, Pink Morgan, and Steve Richmond—he failed to mention Felix Roan. In Lea's recollection, Mitchell strangled Stephens and it was Oliver who stabbed him, not Richmond and Roan. It is unclear whether Roan overstated his own role in the killing, Roan omitted some of the conspirators like Oliver in order to avoid implicating them, or Lea fostered some resentment toward Roan for his dying declaration. One or the other of the men provided false details, but no clear evidence points to which one told the truth.

The bulk of Lea's testimony served to justify the murder rather than to furnish dramatic new details. As he spoke to the state officials, he described a widespread white resentment in Caswell of the political and social changes of the time and accused Republicans of corruption and arson. Lea also framed the Klan's action as brave rather than cowardly. They may have used deception and numbers to surprise and overpower Stephens, but he noted in particular that he and Wiley had stoically endured threats and deprivations when arrested by Col. George Kirk's soldiers in the aftermath of the killing. And he recalled with satisfaction the crowds in Raleigh that had celebrated the prisoners' release, judging this public approval to be a statement in support of Klan actions and in condemnation of Governor William Woods Holden's political course. He had been right in 1870, Lea believed, and the many intervening years had only reinforced his certainty.

Now that most of the other Klansmen and assassins were dead, Lea was free to tell the tale and take the credit.[8] Or at least to record his story, for with the agreement of the Historical Commission, his testimony was to be sealed and locked away from public access. It would be revealed only when he died. Exactly why the confession remained secret is not clear. Presumably Lea was the one who insisted on the stipulation. There seemed little danger of his prosecution fifty years removed from the crime, especially given that North Carolina had granted clear amnesty for any crimes committed by Klansmen during Reconstruction, up to and including murder. A set of US Supreme Court decisions in the 1870s had also placed tight limits on the federal power to enforce the Fourteenth Amendment, guidelines that would not begin to break down until the civil rights era. Together these legal precedents promised to insulate the killer from any judicial consequences. Still, Lea may not have fully trusted these decisions and viewed a posthumous revelation as the safest route, or at least an avenue that prevented any direct questions or recriminations.[9]

Whatever Lea's personal motivations for providing the sealed confession, the men in the room that day tasked with keeping North Carolina's records believed that Lea's story was worth collecting, even if it meant keeping the account secret until his death. (It was a death that would not come until 1935, when Lea reached the age of ninety-two.) Fred A. Olds, a figure of great importance in shaping North Carolina's early twentieth-century public history, was one of the attendees. A longtime Raleigh newspaperman, Olds was also bitten by the antiquarian bug. As something of a hobby, he began collecting state historical objects and documents in 1885. As his collection grew, he spent years lobbying for the creation of a state museum or archive to safeguard and display the materials. The legislature finally agreed and in 1902 opened a Hall of History, which was attached to the capital's Agricultural Building and was later absorbed by the Historical Commission. Named the hall's first director, Olds would have a vital hand in creating and codifying North Carolina's historical memory in the early twentieth century.[10] Olds remains a visible presence to this day: his likeness is one of three statues that greet visitors to the North Carolina Museum of History, where the institution lauds him as "the father of this museum" who "collected many genuine historical treasures and interested hundreds of people in the state's history."[11] Olds seems to have been the official who solicited Lea's testimony, an action that demonstrated his belief that the assassination story was one such "treasure" of North Carolina's past.

Also present in the room as Lea spoke were the secretary of the Historical Commission, Robert D. W. Connor, and the commission's president, John Bryan Grimes. Both men were prominent state leaders whose public profiles only increased after 1919. Grimes served as North Carolina's secretary of state for more than twenty years, spanning the day of Lea's confession. He also held a number of other important leadership positions, from membership on the board of the State Literary and Historical Association and the State Board of Agriculture to the presidency of the Tobacco Growers Association, and he published state history pamphlets as a hobby.[12]

Connor was perhaps even more influential. He was the son of a prominent family from Wilson, North Carolina, another Piedmont tobacco town. Ever conscious of the ties between his family's prestige and the state's history, Connor was an active member of the Historical Commission from its 1903 founding and was instrumental in making it the state's de facto historical repository.[13] He would become the first archivist of North Carolina, then held a Kenan Professorship in history and government at the University of North Carolina at Chapel Hill, and finally was the first archivist of the United States. Along the way he also worked for the state's Department of Education, wrote an authoritative history of colonial North Carolina, and sat on the editorial board of a state history magazine. Connor held a special intellectual interest in the confession: as an undergraduate at the University of North Carolina, he had written a prize-winning senior history essay on the Ku Klux Klan.[14]

Like so many white southerners of the age, Connor was also fixated on race. Among his varied publications was a discourse on the "race elements" of North Carolina's white population.[15] Perhaps with ideas about racial hierarchy in mind, as an archivist and historian, Connor had done no favors for the memory of Reconstruction Republicans. In 1913 he had compiled an almanac of state government as a reference for North Carolina lawmakers, which included an exhaustive list of past officeholders. This *Manual of North Carolina*—to be reissued for many years—entirely omitted John Stephens, instead listing Bedford Brown as Caswell's senator from 1868 to 1870, despite the fact that he never sat in Raleigh. Caswell's representative Wilson Carey made the manual, but so did his 1868 opponent William Long, who, like Brown, Republicans refused to seat, and Connor included a note by Carey's name to make readers aware that he was a "Negro."[16] Connor's almanac was yet another official condemnation of Republican governance during Reconstruction. Indeed, Connor's life seemingly threaded through all of the corners where history making and white supremacy intersected in the state. He briefly attended Columbia, where he studied under William Dunning; was a friend and confidant of many Dunning School historians, including Hamilton; and even found time to coauthor a book with *Progressive Farmer* editor and rural segregationist Clarence Poe. Together they published a flattering biography of Charles Aycock, one of the instigators of the Wilmington massacre and, as governor, an architect of Jim Crow in the state.[17]

The institution that collected and secreted Lea's confession was as invested in its interpretation as were Olds, Grimes, and Connor. The North Carolina Historical Commission was part of a region-wide expansion of state archives in the very early twentieth century, institutions made possible by the entrenchment of Jim Crow. With the Democratic Party seemingly in firm control of the present, state officials could afford to devote attention to securing the past. As historian W. Fitzhugh Brundage has observed, southern agencies like the Historical Commission provided "a patina of professionalism and 'science' to a narrative of southern history already familiar to and embraced by many white southerners."[18] Together the commission and the men in the room as Lea confessed did perhaps more than any other body to define what North Carolinians learned about the past.

In all their august record keeping and documentary positions, Olds, Grimes, and Connor held their silence concerning the confession sitting in storage in Raleigh. In the commission's biennial report covering 1919, there was no mention of the Stephens document in an otherwise exhaustive account of institutional accessions, nor did Olds's appended report from the Hall of History mention the confession.[19] Connor proved especially disciplined in keeping the secret. Drawing on his extensive knowledge of North Carolina's records, he wrote a new, sprawling history of the state in the late 1920s, in it covering Stephens's assassination and the resulting state turmoil in some detail. Despite knowing full well the perpetrators of the crime, in his book he simply wrote that the murder had been "charged to the Ku Klux" but remained a mystery. He was careful to make no mention of Lea but was less reticent when it came to judging Stephens, writing matter-of-factly that he was "a corrupt Republican leader."[20]

By 1919 Lea had outlived the man he helped kill by almost half a century, and he would outlast Olds and Grimes as well. He remained in Danville, renting a house and engaging in a little farming into his eighties after his career in the tobacco business was over. In 1930 he filed for a veteran's pension from the state of Virginia for his service in the Confederate cavalry nearly seventy years earlier, claiming "old age" as his disability.[21] When the former Klansman finally passed away in 1935, to be laid to rest in a cemetery on a hill overlooking Danville's tobacco factories, only Connor remained alive of the men who had sat in that Raleigh room sixteen years earlier. When word of Lea's death finally reached Connor's office in Washington DC, the nation's chief archivist contacted the North Carolina Historical Commission to let staffers know of the record secreted in their files.[22]

Regional papers had a field day with the confession's unveiling. More newsprint was devoted to Stephens's assassination in 1935 than at any point since 1870. The stories tended to be of a particular bent. There was no grim satisfaction that the chief suspects had in fact been the assassins, no lament that justice had gone unserved for two-thirds of a century. Instead, the papers collectively demonstrated the complete entrenchment of the Dunning School's version of Reconstruction and Stephens's life and death. The confession had not been hidden like a dirty secret; it had instead been protected from "nosy historians," the *Raleigh News and Observer* declared. The *Danville Bee*—the paper in Lea's adoptive hometown—agreed, admiring "the integrity with which the secret was kept." In a *Bee* editorial in the same issue that covered the confession's revelation, the editor praised the assassination as a brave act that had helped right the wrongs of Reconstruction governance. The hero of the story was Lea, he unabashedly wrote, for his action "shows that the same indomitable spirit that enabled the forces of [Robert E.] Lee to fight against such odds for so long a time persisted in the more serious battle for the supremacy of the white people in the war's aftermath."[23] From Alamance County, Burlington's *Daily Times-News* jumbled important details as it added to the cacophony. Its editor labeled Stephens a carpetbagger rather than a scalawag four separate times and recorded that he was killed "while a rally of negro Republicans was under way in the courthouse." The report was more accurate when it claimed that Lea was part of a concerted effort "to maintain the hold of white democracy in North Carolina."[24] General Lee's fight may have been a Lost Cause, but Lea had fared better in his contest.

Distant newspapers toed the line, even when their facts were equally scrambled. The *Washington Post*'s headline declared that "Now It Can Be Told" (as if an 1870 or 1919 revelation had been off the table), while the cross-town *Star* labeled Stephens a carpetbagger in its article title.[25] Efforts to further authenticate the details of Lea's confession made clear where authority for the story's public lessons lay. The Historical Commission called in Hamilton from his office at the University of North Carolina to examine the document. The historian declared it completely trustworthy and only regretted that his old friend Connor had not made the confession available to him as he worked on various accounts of the state's history.[26]

In the years that followed 1919, the Lost Cause version of Reconstruction continued to be fleshed out, further preparing white audiences to accept Lea's arguments about the era. For example, Claude Bowers's influential *The Tragic Era* (1929) attracted wide readership, and in many respects Bowers seemed determined to "out-Dunning" the Dunning School. Reconstruction in Bowers's portrayal was not just a tragedy but a farce, one that mercifully ended only after more than a decade of debacle. Stephens made an appearance in this book, too. Bowers imagined the senator as one of North Carolina's most radical politicians who pushed a malleable Governor Holden into indefensible positions.[27] And just after the Lea revelation, Margaret Mitchell's *Gone with the Wind* (1936) appeared. The enormously popular Pulitzer

Prize–winning novel and the 1939 film adaption that followed did much to cement in national memory that white southerners were the real victims of the Civil War and that their opposition to federal Reconstruction in the years that followed was a heroic struggle.[28] Bowers and Mitchell hammered home the notion that men like Lea had been on the right side of history.

There were dissenting voices, of course. Historians like Francis Simkins and Robert Woody slowly pulled back from the old Conservative arguments that Reconstruction was rotten to the core, noting the real progress made during the period on certain fronts, even as they repeated old stories about Republican graft.[29] And the way that Bowers's *The Tragic Era* so thoroughly and uncritically repeated old Conservative tropes angered W. E. B. Du Bois, proving to be one motivating factor that led him to draft his own study of the period, a rebuttal that became *Black Reconstruction in America*.[30] Du Bois's book, which reframed the real shortcoming of Reconstruction as its inability to follow through on promises of political, social, and economic equality for African Americans, appeared in 1935, the same year that Lea finally passed away. This work, along with Reconstruction accounts by other black writers like John Lynch and Carter Woodson, marked the beginnings of a historiographical shift on Reconstruction, as academics began to rethink the aims, successes, and failures of the period.[31] Although revision would take place slowly and somewhat hesitantly, periodically goaded along by calls for more inclusive work by historians such as Simkins, Howard Beale, and John Hope Franklin, it finally bloomed in the 1950s and 1960s in parallel with the civil rights movement.[32]

The work of framing the past also took place locally. Caswell's white residents (and they dominated the making of public memory in the county for much of the twentieth century) added their own layers of meaning to slavery, the Civil War, and Reconstruction during the interwar period. Much of this local memorializing involved forgetting the county's wartime divisions in favor of celebrating the Confederacy and the postwar Conservative "Redemption." A Yanceyville chapter of the United Daughters of the Confederacy, headed by George Anderson's wife, had an important role in this memorialization. In a 1917 report to the state office, chapter members asserted that "we shall continue to strive to keep alive, with our best interest, all that relates to the Confederate soldier." Their work included organizing a Confederate Memorial Day celebration, holding an annual veterans' picnic, sending Christmas cards to surviving soldiers, and soliciting donations for state and local memorials.[33] In September 1921 the county chapter erected a monument in honor of local Confederate soldiers like Lea on Yanceyville's

In an effort to shape local memory of Caswell's Civil War experience, the county's chapter of the United Daughters of the Confederacy erected a monument to Confederate soldiers in 1921. Marion Post Wolcott, *Confederate Monument and Cannon [machine gun] on Square in Yanceyville, Caswell County, North Carolina*, Farm Security Administration—Office of War Information, 1940, Library of Congress.

courthouse square, just a few feet in front of the building in which Stephens was murdered. Like United Daughters of the Confederacy chapters across the South, through the erection of public memorials these Caswell women were invested in sacralizing what had once been a secular struggle.[34] Thirty-four Confederate veterans attended the monument's unveiling ceremony. Their names were not recorded, but it is possible, perhaps even likely given his local importance, that Lea was in the crowd. In 1937 the same group dedicated a Confederate Memorial Library a few blocks away, and its members also operated a chapter of the Children of the Confederacy, which taught youth the virtues of the Lost Cause and the tragedy that had been Reconstruction and Republican misrule.[35]

One eccentric yet telling tribute to the Stephens drama was penned by local newspaper reporter Tom Henderson. Described by one acquaintance as "a strange fellow who had made a brilliant record at the state university and was a recognized Greek scholar," Henderson wrote a short, fictionalized, romantic treatment of the murder and Klan night riding titled *Ann of the Ku Klux Klan*, most likely sometime in the 1940s.[36] The heroine of the tale was

Ann Lea, sister of John G. Lea, a "lovely bud of blossoming womanhood" with "an athletic body." Masked violence was a family affair in the tale—six of Ann's brothers rode with the Klan—and although Ann longed to be directly involved in this vigilantism, she resigned herself to sewing and hiding the den's costumes. Henderson explained that the local Klan chapter was organized at Ann's family seat, Leahurst, the "colonial home of the Leas under grant of King George of England," as if to trace the Klan's lineage to the very founding of county society and an older form of chivalry.[37]

One evening Ann stumbled into a Klan meeting led by her brother, the very gathering in which they made the decision to assassinate Stephens. Their secret out, she was sworn into the chapter so as to keep its confidence. In that same meeting, Henderson wrote of John Lea squarely laying blame for the troubled times on Stephens and the Union League, which Lea believed burned farmers' barns, upset the county's social order, and threatened the virtue of white women. The fictional Lea swore that "this is the white man's country, and by the eternal gods it shall remain so."[38] At the conclusion of the harangue the Klansmen drew names to determine who would participate in the killing and took a blood oath to secrecy, an oath ironic in light of the contested confessions in the decades following Stephens's murder. "Never a klansman would betray the trust of their secret and . . . never a klansman should die, until the last one had passed away, but that another klansman would be there at his deathside, to hold his hand and to seal his lips if, in subconscious delirium, he should start to tell his secret or to name a name of a brother klansman."[39] Here Henderson—like so many other chroniclers—seemed oblivious to Wiley's and Roan's attempted confessions, which fell far short of his romanticized and unrepentant Klansmen.

Henderson claimed factual accuracy for his novella, but certain details were demonstrably false. For example, he labeled the Democratic political meeting in the courthouse a Republican gathering and had Stephens leading it. In an effort to establish his credibility, however, Henderson appended certain historical documents to the end of the story. These included the recollection of a former Caswell sheriff, "Baz" Graves, who condemned vigilante violence but defined Stephens as an agitator, and testimony from George Anderson, who had once served as clerk of court and who was more concerned about the actions of Governor Holden and Colonel Kirk's militiamen than those of the Klan. Claiming to have authored a balanced account, in a postscript Henderson declared that he wrote the story "without prejudice and without intention of offending or injuring." And he gave Stephens a speaking role—of sorts—in *Ann of the Ku Klux Klan*. "The ghost of John

Walter Stephens" made an appearance to plead on his own behalf. Spectral Stephens's defense was thin and rather apologetic, distilled to the mistakes of a man who failed to grasp the desires of Caswell's white populace. His ghostly form regretted that "'I was a Republican leader at a time when it was unpopular to be a Republican.'" Lest readers develop too much sympathy for Stephens, Henderson also included Graves's much blunter assertion that Stephens had courted his fate: He "was a n—— leader, and undoubtedly he inspired n—— to unlawful deeds." Good riddance, Henderson and Graves seemed to say in unison.[40]

If its details were debatable, portions of *Ann of the Ku Klux Klan* echoed fellow North Carolinian Thomas Dixon's old work. The racial tropes of the time were abundant. Black men were "foul beast[s], fresh from the jungles of Africa," and Ann is assisted in her work by a faithful mammy, Liney, whose speech Henderson represents with heavy dialect, and who is "really one of us [the Leas] and just as loyal."[41] Henderson made his didactic purpose clear in a breathless jeremiad of a sentence at the start of the work. In it he explained that the Klan was "organized to safeguard property and save southern womanhood from the loot and lust of those who, just one generation removed from the wild savagery of Africa, were exulting in the exotic and voluptuous freedoms of Abraham Lincoln's emancipation proclamation—freedoms for which they were unfitted and unprepared, in the enjoyment of which they were being encouraged and spurred on by unscrupulous white men, both northern 'carpetbaggers' and southern 'scalawags,' the riffraff of ... the Union and Confederate armies, who were using them for their own political, financial, social and personal aggrandizement."[42]

It is worth noting that Henderson's portrayal of Stephens was more moderate, or at least more ambivalent, in another venue. In a 1939 article in *The State* (a North Carolina general interest magazine), Henderson used the "chicken" sobriquet to describe the senator yet put a more positive spin on the scalawag's character. There too he jumbled many of the historical details: Stephens was a Confederate veteran in this telling, mistakenly killing his neighbor's poultry while on a furlough from the front, and he was nearly the victim in the resulting shooting, with no mention of the men he shot. But Henderson also described the senator as largely a victim of the times rather than a criminal warranting vigilante justice. It was his naive interest in forging a multiracial political coalition rather than any particular personal malfeasance that led to his death. And in this version of events, the story's ghosts were the assassins rather than the murdered politician. Henderson related rumors that "most of those who participated in that ghastly deed have died horrible and tragic deaths. I knew that one, who had fled to a distant state, had draped himself in a Confederate flag and ended his own life with a gun in his own hands."[43]

Henderson may have played fast and loose with both historical details and interpretation in *Ann of the Ku Klux Klan*, but, like Bowers's much better-known history, his novella did capture the dominant white vision of North Carolina's Reconstruction that had coalesced by World War II. Following the national implementation of Jim Crow, the interpretations of Dunning School historians like Hamilton, the rise of a second Klan that mythologized the first one, and Lea's confession that provided a sort of "final word," most Caswell whites imagined that Reconstruction had been a misguided effort at best, an act of cultural, economic, and race war at worst. Contesting voices like those of Tourgée and Du Bois made little impression in the county, at least for a time. In the years that followed, local newspapers could—without any evident irony—celebrate the Lea family's role in the Klan and confusingly explain that the Union League had been "a sort of post–Civil War CIA ... made even more menacing by the fact that it enjoyed the favor and backing of the Federal Government."[44]

Lest too much be read into Henderson's passion for Stephens's tale, it must be noted that the predominant white Caswell attitude toward the county's Reconstruction history was a sort of bemused acceptance. That the period had been a time of unrest and corruption was a given, but that history seemed long past. "Chicken" Stephens as an individual no longer raised much ire, his life and death were seen as an incredible or intriguing episode rather than a defining moment in the county's history, and his story seemed set in stone rather than up for debate. After all, Stephens had lost. It was hard to muster too much outrage over a foe who had been vanquished. Jim Crow all but silenced local African American political power and Democrats held firm control over the county, and so in the years after Lea's confession was revealed local whites found more humor and satisfaction than trouble in the memories of the contested post–Civil War landscape.

Indeed, Yanceyville almost seemed too quiet a place to have ever been the center of such contention. It had become the stereotypical sleepy southern courthouse town by the time Lea's confession was published. (Hinting at this somnolence, one historian of the county titled a chapter covering the fifty years after the Kirk-Holden War "A Sluggish Half Century.")[45] In some respects, Caswell's backwards appearance by the late 1930s was as much a product of modern forces as evidence that they had passed by the region. Tobacco was again at the heart of affairs. After strong prices during World

War I, tobacco markets had declined through the 1920s, further impoverishing the region. Franklin D. Roosevelt's New Deal had sought to combat this agrarian malaise, most notably in the tobacco belt through the Agricultural Adjustment Act's commodities stabilization program. In 1933 it established a floor on tobacco prices and linked tobacco acreage and the right to grow the crop to specific farms to reduce competition. The result was tremendous dependence on tobacco as a cash crop, especially for small and poor farmers. This federal intervention prevented economic free fall across the Piedmont, but it also served to freeze the rural landscape in existing patterns rather than to promote alternate forms of development and ensured that tobacco would remain king in Caswell for at least a few more decades.[46]

This characterization of a "sluggish" southern tobacco town was best captured in the mythos that developed around a long-standing, prosaic local event: the Yanceyville card game. By the end of the 1930s, a town tradition years in the making—a standing card game that took place daily, either in the courthouse or on its lawn—drew national interest. First a federal photographer, Marion Post Wolcott, captured scenes of the card game during her documentary visits to Caswell in 1939 and 1940. Wolcott was working for the Farm Security Administration, a New Deal agency tasked with bettering conditions across rural America. In Caswell she captured images of poor farms, eroded fields, and hungry children, but she also seemed enamored of the lazy scenes she found in Yanceyville. A series of Wolcott photographs in 1939 captured vignettes of a "Saturday afternoon" in September, including the card game on the courthouse lawn. In 1940 she returned to town, taking pictures of an African American church picnic, the county fair, and a land use meeting, as well as more images of the regular card game. Through Wolcott's work, Yanceyville became one representation of the New Deal's documentary impulse that fixed the nation's gaze on the rural South.[47]

A year after Wolcott's second visit, a new courthouse ordinance that finally ended the game—at least on the building's grounds—attracted national news. An article in *Life* magazine reported that "it seems certain the game has been going on at least half a century" and traced the evolution of the hands from whist to rook to a version of euchre. "The game became part of the life of the town," the reporter noted, "like the creaking mule carts loaded with bright leaf tobacco."[48] Accompanying images included a scene of tobacco being transported by wagon and a picture of the courthouse. The caption for the latter mentioned that it had been built by slaves and, somewhat ambiguously, that "Union troops" had stolen its clock weights, but the "citizens have never replaced them."[49] The message seemed at once to be a

Thanks to its well-publicized daily card game under a shady tree in the courthouse's front yard, Yanceyville came to represent the classic sleepy southern town by 1940. Marion Post Wolcott, *Members of the Community Playing Cards in front of the Courthouse, Yanceyville, Caswell County, North Carolina,* Farm Security Administration— Office of War Information, 1940, Library of Congress.

bemused nostalgia for the end of a long tradition in a backward town and to highlight the notion that Yanceyville had changed little if any since the day its clock weights rode out of town in federal wagons. That the courthouse itself had once stood at the center of a bloody struggle over the future of the state did not enter into the sketch.

Despite its long duration, the card game was shorter lived than the "chicken" image of Stephens and state Republicans, which remained durable well past World War II. For example, Manly Wade Wellman's 1954 *Dead and Gone: Classic Crimes of North Carolina* was yet another profile of the assassination and the mystery that had long surrounded it. Wellman was a prolific science fiction and fantasy writer who also had an abiding interest in North Carolina history, and his book demonstrated how well he had absorbed the Lost Cause and Dunning School portrayals of Reconstruction in the state. In this "true crime" accounting, Stephens was a master "in the arts of swindling, terrorism, and ballot-box stuffing" and was but one of "the political pirates who administered North Carolina's graceless Reconstruction government."[50] Switching analogies, Wellman wrote that "Reconstruction came upon North Carolina like all ten of Egypt's plagues at once," with Stephens playing the part of one of the locusts.[51] He praised the Klan's secretive work and the conspirators' silence for so many years after the fact and argued that they had committed something "very close to the category of perfect crime."[52] A reader gets the sense that for Wellman, the perfection lay as much in the crime's aims as in its execution.

More official state histories adopted in schools continued to largely toe the "tragedy" line in their explanations of Reconstruction, and especially in their accounts of Stephens's assassination and the Kirk-Holden War. As previously noted, John Moore's *School History of North Carolina* painted quite a negative picture of both, as did Connor's later, multivolume state history that found adoption in college classrooms. Archibald Henderson updated Connor's scholarship in 1941 with a two-volume text: *North Carolina: The Old North State and the New*. Here, too, the Dunning and Hamilton characterizations of Reconstruction as a corrupt tragedy largely held sway. In Henderson's account of the Kirk-Holden War, his contorted narrative managed to completely avoid mention of the Klan violence that led to Holden's declaration of insurrection and martial law in Alamance and Caswell Counties: Wyatt Outlaw and Stephens never graced the pages. The Klan's victims may have been noticeably absent, but there was still plenty of blame to be cast. Kirk was a "ruthless soldier" with a reputation in the state that was "only less hateful than that of Sherman," and Holden's decision to declare martial law and arrest suspected Klansmen was simply "military terrorism."[53]

First appearing in 1954, and later revised and enlarged, Hugh Talmage Lefler and Albert Ray Newsome's *North Carolina: The History of a Southern State* became the new standard textbook for advanced classes and remained influential into the 1980s. The two University of North Carolina professors retained Henderson's negative interpretation of the state's Union League and Holden's and Kirk's actions under martial law and criticized what they labeled a general "federal interference in North Carolina's politics." Stephens did appear in this book but bore his old label that Hamilton had so savored: in its pages readers were introduced to "John W. ('Chicken') Stephens."[54] After the passage of more than a century, Conservatives' slur and their portrayals of the era showed real staying power.

Even as many North Carolina students after World War II learned about Reconstruction from textbooks with a lineage tracing back to the late nineteenth-century Lost Cause, nationally the period was receiving a scholarly makeover. A wave of revisionist historians worked to sweep aside the entrenched "tragedy" narrative that Dunning and his students had popularized and erect a new interpretation in its place. In some instances, these historians had trained under Dunning scholars but rejected their interpretations of the period. Instead of a tragic era, they redefined Reconstruction as a time of noble efforts to remake American society and politics, even if this "unfinished revolution" failed to establish a more thorough or lasting equality.[55] The tragedy was not that Republicans held sway in the South for a few years, revisionists like John Hope Franklin and Kenneth Stampp noted, it was that Redemption so thoroughly undid their work and then cemented in its place white supremacy for generations to come. And even as Lefler and Newsome conveyed familiar accounts of a flawed Reconstruction imposed from the outside, other North Carolina faculty embraced, and sometimes led, revisionism. These intellectual shifts happened with relative rapidity. In 1930 Bowdoin College historian Howard Beale wrote a book attempting to rehabilitate Andrew Johnson's image and lamented that under congressional guidance "military rule and negro supremacy supplanted slowly reviving democratic institutions in the South." But just ten years later, now a University of North Carolina faculty member, he reversed course in the pages of the nation's most preeminent scholarly historical journal, advising fellow southern historians that it was time to approach "the history of Reconstruction without first assuming, at least subconsciously, that carpetbaggers and Southern white Republicans were wicked, that Negroes were illiterate incompetents, and that the whole white South owes a debt of gratitude to the restorers of 'white supremacy.'"[56] Following Beale, Joel Williamson took up the department torch, reframing the particularly harsh Dunning assessments of South Carolina's Reconstruction. And, it should be noted, the University of North Carolina Press brought a substantial amount of Reconstruction revisionism to print.[57] "Postrevisionists" modified these arguments in the following decades, to be revised again by historians sometimes styled "post-postrevisionists," with each generation steering further from the tragic era narrative.[58]

The most impressive effort to rewrite North Carolina's Reconstruction experience came from Otto Olsen, a scholar who focused in particular on Tourgée and North Carolina's Ku Klux Klan. Olsen studied under C. Vann Woodward at Johns Hopkins and taught on the faculty at the University of North Carolina before spending the majority of his career at Northern Illinois University. In numerous publications he recast Tourgée as a principled crusader, Holden as stubborn but misunderstood, and the African American struggle for rights as brave, democratic, and determined. In their way stood a violent, bigoted, and self-interested Klan, aided and abetted by the mass of Conservatives who looked the other way at illegal action. Olsen was the son of Norwegian immigrants and achieved scholarly prominence studying American race relations during the 1960s, and he directly connected Reconstruction and Jim Crow to the ongoing social change and civil rights movement of the era. His revision was thus a personal as well as a historiographical crusade, according to colleagues, who described him as "an activist at heart" with "a passion to right social wrongs that kept him active in progressive political movements" throughout his life.[59] Other sympathetic studies of Republican efforts in North Carolina appeared, based on Olsen's model, including scholarship redeeming Holden's tarnished image and, more recently, a burgeoning interest in Tourgée as a foundational civil rights figure.[60]

Many revisionists also emphasized what Du Bois had highlighted in *Black Reconstruction in America* back in 1935: that black people had been more than passive victims of Conservatives or supplicants to white Republican leadership. In North Carolina, as across the rest of the South, freedpeople had been active agents in pushing Reconstruction in the direction of greater political, social, and economic equality and had been bitterly disappointed when the wave of Redemption collapsed their progress on these fronts.[61] Several of these studies accorded newfound importance to Wyatt Outlaw in Union League and Republican efforts to broaden the political base in Alamance and Caswell Counties.[62]

The revisionists were almost as attracted to Stephens as had been the Dunning School, but for different purposes. Long one of the villains in the stories of his own life, he appeared in a number of the new scholarly histories as some combination of hero, martyr, and victim. Olsen described Stephens as a successful businessman and a political moderate. Allen Trelease believed that he had probably been an arsonist yet brushed aside the chicken imbroglio as "inconsequential" and claimed he had been a wartime Unionist. Edgar Folk and Bynum Shaw lamented the durability of his "chicken" nickname while misinforming readers that the senator had been shot to death in front of multiple witnesses. Richard Current thought he was a man of principle persecuted for his leadership abilities and organizational acumen, hated by Conservatives because of his success. Richard Zuber also claimed his faults were that he was "too successful" and "had too much influence" for his opponents to tolerate. And Gregory Downs labeled him a heroic figure who "fought to defend African Americans" and in so doing acted "courageously."[63] All in all, the transformation was a dramatic one, shifting the common take on Stephens from "scalawag" to principled moderate, a swing neatly mirroring the broader historiographical reframing of Reconstruction.

Academic historians at the national level may have enshrined Stephens in the pantheon of Reconstruction martyrs, but their narratives hardly made a dent in more general state histories. Within North Carolina and Caswell, the old stories clung on with tenacity, shrugging off the copious new historiography. The author of the most detailed history of Caswell County to date, William Powell, repeated many of the harshest Conservative critiques of Stephens in his 1977 book *When the Past Refused to Die*. A virtual repetition of Hamilton's characterization of Stephens more than a half century past, Powell's senator was a scheming opportunist, "a willing tool in the hands of Carpetbagger Albion W. Tourgée and other Republicans" for "herding blacks to the polls." Powell did not go so far as to praise the county's Klansmen for the murder, but he certainly reviled their victim and admired the perpetrators' cleverness in accomplishing the deed and successfully covering it up for more than fifty years.[64]

Powell's take might have mattered little had he not been such an esteemed state historian. He oversaw an extensive collection of state documents as librarian of the North Carolina Collection at the University of North Carolina and assumed the mantle of the leading Tar Heel expert on the state's local history after Hamilton's death. Powell wrote or coauthored several state history textbooks, as well as a large body of literature on local history. This included a manual instructing the state's students on how to thoroughly and ethically research their own local pasts (a book in which he labeled Congressional Reconstruction "retaliation" and advised students to read Hamilton's *Reconstruction in North Carolina* if they really wanted to understand the era). Prestigious publishing houses also printed Powell's scholarship, including New York trade press giants Norton and Scribner, as well as university presses at Columbia and the University of North Carolina.[65] In addition, Powell served as chairman of the state's Historical Commission into the twenty-first century, the post Grimes held decades earlier. And he exerted a good deal of influence on the identification and interpretation of prominent historical North Carolinians through his editorship of a state encyclopedia and biographical dictionary. (Luckily for Stephens's memory, another more sympathetic historian—Allen Trelease—wrote the senator's biographical entry for the dictionary.)[66] Typical of Powell's interpretation in his broader histories were the two pages he devoted to Stephens in his textbook *North*

Carolina: A Bicentennial History (1977). He noted the chicken episode, rumors that Stephens had killed his own mother, and the senator's supposed role in county arson. It was this slate of "countless dastardly deeds" that led to his death, even if Powell fell short of praising the Klan for his murder.[67]

The Conservative portrayal of Stephens remains largely in place locally today. A historical marker mentioning the assassination still stands in front of the old courthouse in Yanceyville's town square, near the monument to Confederate soldiers erected by the United Daughters of the Confederacy nearly a century ago. The new marker labels the occurrence a "murder" and names Stephens as the victim but provides no clue as to who committed the deed. Still, it is a better interpretation than the marker that stood by the courthouse into the 1930s, which referred to an "alleged ku klux murder" without naming a victim.[68] That the square now also includes a memorial honoring black county residents hints at their long struggle to contest celebratory visions of the Old South and raise up stories of overcoming injustice, a commemorative countercurrent found in many southern communities.[69] The juxtaposition suggests advances made in local race relations in recent years but also a failure to fully reconcile the past and the present. Some other modern local interpretations have been similarly ambiguous in their messages, from a short video documentary about "Chicken" Stephens produced at the local community college to Jim Wise's *Murder in the Courthouse,* a popular account of the assassination and the Kirk-Holden War by a Raleigh journalist.[70] Others adhere more closely to the old Dunning School script, as in 2018 when the local newspaper chose to reprint one of Powell's portrayals of Stephens as a dastardly scalawag, black Republican rule as a tragedy, and the assassination as an inevitable, understandable, and maybe even admirable event.[71]

The tombstones that mark Lea's and Stephens's graves also reflect the distortions of time. Stephens is buried in the cemetery of the Yanceyville Methodist Church. A marker was erected on the spot well after his death, carved with a deeply ironic message rewriting history. The stone, closely modeled on those of Confederate veterans, provides a spare epitaph: "Soldier—C.S.A.—Patriot." Only the last, perhaps, is accurate. It is unclear when the stone was erected, or by whom, although the garbled details suggest that it was a later addition to the gravesite. Lea's stone stands in Danville's Mountain View Cemetery, about twenty miles to the north. Deepening the irony, his headstone contains just birth and death dates, making no mention of his service to either Confederacy or Klan.[72]

In shaping the memory of the past, figures like Josiah Turner, J. G. de R. Hamilton, John Lea, and Tom Henderson had done their work well.

The original historical marker in front of the courthouse entirely
omitted Stephens's name and labeled the Ku Klux Klan as only
the "alleged" murderers. Marion Post Wolcott, *Sign in front of
Courthouse, Yanceyville, Caswell County, North Carolina*, Farm Security
Administration—Office of War Information, 1940, Library of Congress.

John Walter Stephens was both dead and a "chicken" (or at best, naively misguided), freedpeople had been pawns and perhaps criminals during Reconstruction, and Redeemers like Lea and Wiley had saved North Carolina from a period of darkness. Better yet, all this unpleasantness was safely in the past, as Bruce Baker has noted of Reconstruction memory elsewhere, the stuff of bemused local remembrance rather than intense fighting.[73] In the clear light of the early twenty-first century, Reconstruction seemed securely removed from the present, as poignant yet distant as news of Lee's surrender at Appomattox.

Epilogue

PROPTER HOC

The Nation was so elated with its achievement that it forgot all about the source from which the evil sprang. Already the new growth has borne fruit of Violence and Misrule. Can we afford to allow the roots to remain?

ALBION W. TOURGÉE, *An Appeal to Caesar* (1884)

y the mid-twentieth century, John Walter Stephens's life and death mattered more than ever before. Or, perhaps more accurately, his life and death had become stories impregnated with meaning about the American South in the aftermath of the Civil War. Stephens's actual self—his intentions, words, and actions—mattered little, for others commandeered his story as mercilessly as conspirators had taken his life. Lost Cause historians, most notably J. G. de Roulhac Hamilton, cast Stephens as the archetypal scalawag, a villain whose death freed Caswell County of corruption and misrule and prompted sweeping reforms across North Carolina. His blood brought redemption, and in his death the white South had been reborn. History textbook authors, including R. D. W. Connor, Archibald Henderson, and William Powell, made these interpretations part of North Carolina's educational instruction. Bored students no doubt scribbled notes about "Republican misrule" and "scalawags" during long afternoons in schoolhouses across the state. Whites intent on maintaining segregation and racial supremacy drew analogies between Reconstruction and the burgeoning civil rights movement, at times embracing the first Klan as a force for the maintenance of social order in the face of "agitators" like Stephens. In each of these ways an imagined Stephens lived on, serving various ends.

These stories contrasted and came into conflict with other emerging narratives. Black and white historians intent on revising the Dunning narratives portrayed Stephens as heroic, a white man martyred for his efforts to advance racial equality. Like the better-known John Brown, Stephens came to represent a man willing to surrender his life for a higher cause.[1] The antagonists in these stories, meanwhile, became John G. Lea, Frank Wiley, and their fellow Klansmen, but also the subsequent historians who glorified or made apologies for the Klan and Redemption. Revisionists argued that Hamilton and his ilk covered up history rather than unearthed it, no matter how detailed their footnotes. This perspective became the dominant one, at least in academic circles, after World War II and was firmly established as the nation moved from the twentieth to the twenty-first century. Esteemed synthetic histories of Reconstruction and its legacy, such as those of Eric Foner, Steven Hahn, Leon Litwack, and David Blight, thoroughly discarded any traces of Dunning historiography and portrayed the work of men like Stephens with a great deal of sympathy. In these and similar histories, the murdered senator shape-shifted into an early civil rights leader.

Stephens, as best the fragmentary record shows, was none of these things. Or perhaps more accurately, he was little bits of all of them. He did often act like a man on the make, as his critics claimed. He was quick to seize opportunities for personal advancement whenever they presented themselves, even if it meant switching parties and careers, issuing a bribe, or embracing dangerous situations. His surviving letters suggest a willingness to shake down allies like Governor Holden for money, even as they expressed his willingness to stay the political course in the face of violent opposition. Not particularly educated, he was hardly stupid. No idealist, neither was he a coward (no matter how often his enemies applied the "chicken" label). Even if the worst accusations of corruption are discounted as politically motivated, he seemed far from pure. Like most human beings, he fell somewhere in that vast middle ground between villain and hero.

In his flawed humanity, Stephens is a poignant emblem of Reconstruction in the United States. The endeavor was fraught with contradiction and ambiguity. Foner has famously characterized the period as an "unfinished revolution," in the sense that the nation failed to follow through on the promise of emancipation by providing true equal rights to African Americans.[2] In asserting the ongoing struggle for civil rights Foner is certainly correct, as today's national conversations prompted by the Black Lives Matter movement and critical race theory remind us. Vital promises of the time were left unfulfilled and to this day remain a part of the era's legacy. Yet racial equality was only a part of Reconstruction's agenda, rightly or wrongly. Many white Americans of the time were more interested in questions of reconciliation, healing, economic restructuring, and political power, which they believed of at least equal importance. They sought to prevent a new, bloody rebellion more than they pursued a social revolution. Caswell County whites, including Stephens and Lea, were as interested in defining the terms of reconciliation as they were in questions of race, and the same was true for governments in Raleigh and Washington, DC.[3] Stephens sought political influence and economic opportunity, even as he may have harbored class resentment and truly believed that freedpeople deserved more political voice. Lea felt threatened by the economic and political challenges of men like Stephens, perhaps more than he feared African American power. These entwined motivations were rarely separable, something as true in the stories of individual Americans as in the national narrative. What appears obvious on the national scale was terribly messy in local communities.

The assassination thus illustrates the powerful influence of local and state history on how Reconstruction played out on the ground. North Carolina's politics had been particularly competitive and convoluted before and during the Civil War, a partisanship that remained during Reconstruction. A significant portion of Holden's postwar troubles stemmed from the divisive legacy he had built as an editor and war dissenter prior to the Confederacy's surrender. And men like Wiley and Lea built community standing during the war and were loath to have their personal influence eroded by the new order shaping up in Reconstruction. In local communities, then as now, reputations mattered: building them, and sometimes destroying them, was serious work.

Perhaps one of the least surprising elements of this story is that such sober work would turn to violence. The Civil War had taken multitudinous lives—perhaps as many as 750,000 Americans died in the conflict—cheapening death in the process. In both the Union and Confederate armies, roughly one in four soldiers who marched off to war had perished in a span of just four years. Many more returned home physically disabled or emotionally scarred by what they had seen.[4] "Death," historian Drew Gilpin Faust observes, "created the modern American union," and, by extension, killing would almost naturally be used as a tool to try to shape what that union would look like in the war's immediate aftermath.[5] Participants in postwar struggles—many of them veterans of the conflict—simply returned to the methods they had so recently used to settle political impasse. How thin the veil must have seemed between state-sanctioned killing and criminal murder to men who had seen so much recent blood.

My personal assessment is that Stephens was on the right side of history, and thus his redeemers are probably closer to the "truth" than his critics. The slight hesitancy of the preceding statement highlights the numerous ambiguities of this book. Here I must admit to something of a crisis of confidence concerning the preceding portrayal of Stephens's life, death, and memory. This story undid much that I took for granted as a historian. The discipline emphasizes the ways in which careful research in primary sources and reading other historians' accounts bring a fuller and more accurate understanding of past events. (This despite the relativism that postmodernists contend shapes all historical practice.) I entered this study with several assumptions: that Stephens's story was worth telling, that its details could be teased out, and that the resulting profile would tell us more about the victim, his killers, and life in North Carolina after the Civil War. I trust that the preceding pages have accomplished these aims to some extent.

And yet I leave the story less certain about some things than when I started researching it more than a decade ago. The basic framework that I assumed to be firm—that Stephens struggled for what was politically and socially right and was murdered for that work by a group of Klansmen led by John G. Lea—now appears shaky. Stephens himself seems as easily interpreted as an opportunist and a grifter as a brave martyr, at times damned by his own words and actions as much as by the accusations of others. (Accusations, to be clear, that were often water drawn from a poisoned well.) To some extent, this did not shock me. Politicians have their flaws, just like the rest of us, and Stephens could both be of questionable moral character *and* have fought for the right cause. By and large I think that is true in this case. Taken as a whole, the direct evidence is too thin to say for certain exactly what sort of man he was, and the accounts of his life are all biased in particular ways. Leaving his legacy on such unsettled ground seems unsatisfying but honest.

But I have also grown to question Lea's place in the story. Here as in many previous accounts of these events, the revelation of his confession in 1935 serves as a culminating moment when the curtain is pulled back, providing clarity on a murder sixty-five years in the past and putting to bed old rumors and questions. In some ways his matter-of-fact testimony is as shocking as the assassination itself, providing today's readers with an unfiltered glimpse into the world of Jim Crow white supremacy firmly in control of the early twentieth-century South. But I found myself with a nagging question: Is Lea a trustworthy source? Almost every historian of the subject has accepted his confession to the North Carolina Historical Commission as gospel truth, providing details that had long been hidden, but there is, I think, some reason to be suspicious. After all, his was at least the third confession to the killing, and the first two almost certainly included some deception. It had been rumored that Wiley confessed involvement on his deathbed, and he had certainly told many lies about that day's events in the preceding years. Felix Roan likewise provided details about the killing, although if Lea is to be believed, Roan omitted a number of co-conspirators from his telling (including Lea himself). Lea, in turn, omitted mention of Roan in his list of conspirators. By virtue of his confessing last, no one remained alive to contradict Lea's version of events when it was unveiled. He was at liberty to draft the final "firsthand" version of the story. And he testified at a moment in time when the first Klan had grown in respectability and mystique across the white South, providing moral capital to men like Lea who could claim credit for its birth. Many details of Lea's confession do match those from other sources, but those details were widely known, especially in Caswell County.[6] He had listened to testimony at the trial in Raleigh, seen the speculative newspaper accounts, and almost assuredly had read Albion Tourgée's version in *A Fool's Errand*. He must also have been familiar with Roan's confession.

I learned, too, that Lea seemed fond of mythmaking. I had run across his penchant for framing historical memory when researching an earlier book on the history of bright leaf tobacco. In 1886 Lea, who at that time worked as a tobacco dealer in Danville, Virginia, told a story of the "invention" of the lucrative bright variety of the crop. In that tale, he credited the Slade family of Caswell County with its discovery in 1839. A slave named Stephen had stumbled across the curing technique to make fine quality tobacco, Lea stated, and his white master then perfected the system that generated so much regional wealth. The story was picked up by a local newspaper and then reprinted in *Progressive Farmer*, an influential North Carolina–based agricultural magazine. It remains the "origin story" of bright tobacco to this day, despite its simplistic nature that ignores multiple innovators and much trial and error over the years.[7] Here, as in his account of Stephens's murder, Lea seemed intent on crediting white Caswell planters with mastery of people and place to local advantage.

These details about Lea raise suspicions. Was a young Lea really the head of the Caswell Klan and the architect of Stephens's assassination? Did he, by virtue of his family name, direct the actions of more experienced and politically prominent men like Frank Wiley and Felix Roan? Many corroborating stories, such as the local accounts of Tom Henderson, were created after the confession and drew heavily on it. They prove Lea's later influence rather than certify the accuracy of his claims. Was Lea rather a participant in the events of the time who in his last years inflated his role? He would not be the first old man to layer the glory a little thick on his youth. Certainty on these questions is probably impossible. The very questions themselves reveal something important about the killing and the memory of it, however. As much as men like Wiley, Roan, and Lea attempted to tell their own stories about the murder of Stephens, their tales would forever be entangled in local, state, regional, and national accounts of Reconstruction. In killing the senator, they birthed competing stories that took on lives of their own.

John Stephens was one figure in this history who never had the chance to recount the murder and, like Lea, remains blurred by the passage of time. In one last attempt to get a better handle on the slippery man at the center of the story, I returned to his haunts in February 2020, a day's side journey on a trip to a workshop in Durham. On this day, with ominous-looking storm clouds scuttling across the sky as I set out in the morning, I sought a few more bits and pieces of information. The trip took me back and forth across many of the landscapes where Stephens's life and death had played out: the small towns of Wentworth and Yanceyville, the state capital in Raleigh, the rural countryside of forest and farms in between. Much had changed in the intervening century and a half. Raleigh now sits at the heart of North Carolina's "Research Triangle," a region undergoing explosive growth rooted in higher education, health care, and technology. It is a city with haute cuisine, microbreweries, and software companies. To the west the "Triad" cities of Greensboro, High Point, and Winston-Salem experienced their own booms in the twentieth century, growing into manufacturing hubs of tobacco, furniture, and textiles.

But Yanceyville and Wentworth remain fairly small and quiet, seemingly still as sleepy as in Marion Post Wolcott's documentary photographs from the 1930s. To their north, the once important tobacco hub of Danville is settling into a long senescence. The "golden weed" still dominates the local agrarian economy, if not to the extent it once did. Most of the laborers in the fields are now Mexican migrant workers, and the curing barns are built of sheet metal rather than pine logs, resembling mobile homes more than log cabins.[8] Tobacco farming has changed in other ways as well. The New Deal price stabilization program had served to keep tobacco profits—and with them, small family farms—relatively strong for decades, although it and other federal programs had favored white over black farmers in various ways.[9] But the stability the program furnished ended in 2004 with the Tobacco Transition Payment Program, a federal plan that eliminated the quota system and price support. It was part of an effort to shift farmers in North Carolina and other tobacco-growing states away from the production of a crop so costly to human health, but so far it has produced farm consolidation rather than tobacco's elimination. Larger operations have replaced the small farms supported by the tobacco program, and no viable agricultural alternative has emerged to take tobacco's place.[10] The scene of Stephens's murder, the elaborate Italianate courthouse that tobacco built, remains standing at the heart of Yanceyville. It is neatly painted and well-cared for, looking like a fancily frosted wedding cake, but it no longer serves as the seat of county government; instead, it houses an assortment of municipal offices. Altogether the region is an eclectic mix of modern and historic, dignified and down-on-its-luck, high-tech and agrarian.

On the trip I first hoped to find some legal records of a case involving Stephens in Rockingham County, an action that may have led to his move to Caswell shortly after the Civil War. How accurate was the "chicken" story? I had discovered a contemporary account in the National Archives from a Freedmen's Bureau agent who claimed to have reviewed the files and had reprinted a transcription of the indictment, but I hoped to see the original court papers for myself. My first stop, Rockingham's impressive modern Judicial Center (combining a county jail with the functions of the court), proved a dead end. After I shed my belt, shoes, keys, and coat to pass through the metal detectors, I soon discovered that the clerk's office held no old court records. Staffers were uncertain where they might have gotten to; a clerk suggested that perhaps they had been sent to the state archives (where I also had no luck finding the case in question in a later search). Disappointed, I then drove east to Yanceyville with the rain falling intermittently and the wind picking up. Cattle and winter-fallowed tobacco fields scrolled by the car windows as the radio broadcasted a flash flood warning for the region.

I had been to Yanceyville on several occasions, searching for records in the new courthouse and inspecting the historical markers outside of the old one, trying to get a feel for the place where Stephens had been killed. Today I wanted another look at the old courthouse and to tour a small museum operated by the county's historical society, which advertised among its attractions two pistols that had been taken from Stephens's dead body and a shelf of local history resources. The museum's website promised that it would open at two o'clock, but I arrived at the charming town square a little more than an hour early. The rain had tapered off, and so I wandered the courthouse grounds; behind them, a historic jailhouse and school lured me a little farther from my car. Then, with a roaring wind gust, the heavens opened up with a veritable wall of rain—more August gully washer than winter storm. I sprinted for the car but arrived completely soaked. With heater and defroster on full blast I tried to dry out, still waiting for the museum to open. The opening hour came and passed, but no lights came on, and the "closed" sign remained in place. Giving it another thirty minutes, I then exited my car—still quite damp— and approached the entrance, only to find a sign saying that the museum was actually supposed to open at 1:00 p.m., yet clearly no one would be coming in today.

The rain began again at a more measured pace that promised to continue for quite a while. With no new revelations concerning John Stephens forthcoming, I threw in the figurative towel (wishing for a real one) and called it a day. Driving north out of town, the radio announced that the worst of the storm line had passed, swept off to the east by a cold front. From south and east of Caswell reports trickled in of multiple tornadoes on the ground. The damage the storm line had done as it moved across the state awaited full accounting. But, as has long been the case in North Carolina, tomorrow promised change.

Notes

ABBREVIATIONS

AWTP Albion W. Tourgée Papers, Chautauqua County Historical
Society and McClurg Museum, Westfield, NY

BRFAL Records of the Bureau of Refugees, Freedmen, and Abandoned Lands,
Record Group 105, National Archives at Atlanta, Morrow, GA

CCHAC Caswell County Historical Association Collection, Southern
Historical Collection, University of North Carolina, Chapel Hill

Duke Special Collections, Duke University, Durham, NC

GASR General Assembly Session Records, November 1870–April 1871,
North Carolina State Archives, Raleigh

GPO Government Printing Office

JGLC John G. Lea's Confession, Reconstruction Papers, 1868–1973,
Private Collection 872, North Carolina State Archives, Raleigh

JSH *Journal of Southern History*

NAA National Archives at Atlanta, Morrow, GA

NCHR *North Carolina Historical Review*

NCSA North Carolina State Archives, Raleigh

SHC Southern Historical Collection, University
of North Carolina, Chapel Hill

INTRODUCTION

1. The central multimedia article, Carli Brosseau, "In a Small Town, a Battle for Racial Justice Confronts a Bloody Past and an Uncertain Future," can be found at Pro-Publica, May 19, 2021, www.propublica.org/article/small-town-battle-for-racial-justice-confronts-bloody-past-uncertain-future.

2. David Harvey quoted in Susan Eva O'Donovan, *Becoming Free in the Cotton South* (Cambridge, MA: Harvard University Press, 2007), 9. The best overarching study of

Reconstruction, environment, and land use is Erin Stewart Mauldin, *Unredeemed Land: An Environmental History of Civil War and Emancipation in the Cotton South* (New York: Oxford University Press, 2018). There are some good studies of the connection between particular southern crop cultures and Reconstruction: for examples from the cotton, sugar, and rice districts, see O'Donovan, *Becoming Free in the Cotton South*; John C. Rodrigue, *Reconstruction in the Cane Fields: From Slavery to Free Labor in Louisiana's Sugar Parishes, 1862–1880* (Baton Rouge: Louisiana State University Press, 2001); and Mart A. Stewart, *"What Nature Suffers to Groe": Life, Labor, and Landscape on the Georgia Coast, 1680–1920* (Athens: University of Georgia Press, 1996), chap. 5.

3. William A. Blair, *The Record of Murders and Outrages: Racial Violence and the Fight over Truth at the Dawn of Reconstruction* (Chapel Hill: University of North Carolina Press, 2021), 4–5.

4. There are a number of excellent works on tobacco in North Carolina. Crucial older histories of the crop include Joseph Clarke Robert, *The Tobacco Kingdom: Plantation, Market, and Factory in Virginia and North Carolina, 1800–1860* (Durham, NC: Duke University Press, 1938); and Nannie May Tilley, *The Bright-Tobacco Industry, 1860–1929* (Chapel Hill: University of North Carolina Press, 1948). More recent studies that trace North Carolina tobacco's local particularities and global reach include Sarah Milov, *The Cigarette: A Political History* (Cambridge, MA: Harvard University Press, 2019); Nan Enstad, *Cigarettes, Inc.: An Intimate History of Corporate Imperialism* (Chicago: University of Chicago Press, 2018); Evan P. Bennett, *When Tobacco Was King: Families, Farm Labor, and Federal Policy in the Piedmont* (Gainesville: University Press of Florida, 2014); Barbara Hahn, *Making Tobacco Bright: Creating an American Commodity, 1617–1937* (Baltimore, MD: Johns Hopkins University Press, 2011); and Peter Benson, *Tobacco Capitalism: Growers, Migrant Workers, and the Changing Face of a Global Industry* (Princeton, NJ: Princeton University Press, 2011). For tobacco in Caswell County specifically, see Drew A. Swanson, *A Golden Weed: Tobacco and Environment in the Piedmont South* (New Haven, CT: Yale University Press, 2014).

5. Among notable efforts to explain Reconstruction as a continuation of the war and its violent methods are Megan Kate Nelson, *The Three-Cornered War: The Union, the Confederacy, and Native Peoples in the Fight for the West* (New York: Scribner, 2020); Gregory P. Downs, *After Appomattox: Military Occupation and the Ends of War* (Cambridge, MA: Harvard University Press, 2015); Adam Wesley Dean, *An Agrarian Republic: Farming, Antislavery Politics, and Nature Parks in the Civil War Era* (Chapel Hill: University of North Carolina Press, 2015), chaps. 4 and 5; Elizabeth R. Varon, *Appomattox: Victory, Defeat, and Freedom at the End of the Civil War* (New York: Oxford University Press, 2014); Ari Kelman, *A Misplaced Massacre: Struggling over the Memory of Sand Creek* (Cambridge, MA: Harvard University Press, 2013); Paul A. Cimbala and Randall M. Miller, *The Great Task Remaining before Us: Reconstruction as America's Continuing Civil War* (New York: Fordham University Press, 2010); Heather Cox Richardson, *West from Appomattox: The Reconstruction of America after the Civil War* (New Haven, CT: Yale University Press, 2007); Douglas R. Egerton, *The Wars of Reconstruction: The Brief, Violent History of America's Most Progressive Era* (New York: Bloomsbury Press, 2014); Carole Emberton, *Beyond Redemption: Race, Violence, and the American South after the Civil War* (Chicago: University of Chicago Press, 2013); Hannah Rosen, *Terror in the Heart of Freedom: Citizenship, Sexual Violence, and the Meaning of Race in the Postemancipation South* (Chapel Hill: University of North Carolina Press, 2009); Nicholas Lemann, *Redemption: The Last Battle of the Civil War* (New York: Farrar, Straus

and Giroux, 2006); James K. Hogue, *Uncivil War: Five New Orleans Street Battles and the Rise and Fall of Radical Reconstruction* (Baton Rouge: Louisiana State University Press, 2006); James M. Smallwood, Barry A. Crouch, and Larry Peacock, *Murder and Mayhem: The War of Reconstruction in Texas* (College Station: Texas A&M University Press, 2003); Noel C. Fisher, *War at Every Door: Partisan Politics and Guerrilla Violence in East Tennessee, 1860–1869* (Chapel Hill: University of North Carolina Press, 1997); Richard Zuczek, *State of Rebellion: Reconstruction in South Carolina* (Columbia: University of South Carolina Press, 1996); and George C. Rable, *But There Was No Peace: The Role of Violence in the Politics of Reconstruction* (Athens: University of Georgia Press, 1984).

6. Justin Behrend, "When Neighbors Turn against Neighbors: Irregular Warfare and the Crisis of Democracy in the Civil War Era," in *Beyond Freedom: Disrupting the History of Emancipation,* ed. David W. Blight and Jim Downs (Athens: University of Georgia Press, 2017), 97.

7. The four studies referenced here are T. H. Breen and Stephen Innes, *"Myne Owne Ground": Race and Freedom on Virginia's Eastern Shore, 1640–1676* (New York: Oxford University Press, 1980); Turk McClesky, *The Road to Black Ned's Forge: A Story of Race, Sex, and Trade on the Colonial American Frontier* (Charlottesville: University of Virginia Press, 2014); Michael Wayne, *Death of an Overseer: Reopening a Murder Investigation from the Plantation South* (New York: Oxford University Press, 2001); and Chris Meyers Asch, *The Senator and the Sharecropper: The Freedom Struggles of James O. Eastland and Fannie Lou Hamer* (New York: New Press, 2008).

8. Microhistories that explore and personalize the intersection of race and violence in the South include Karen L. Cox, *Goat Castle: A True Story of Murder, Race, and the Gothic South* (Chapel Hill: University of North Carolina Press, 2017); Jason Morgan Ward, *Hanging Bridge: Racial Violence and America's Civil Rights Century* (New York: Oxford University Press, 2016); Joshua D. Rothman, *Flush Times and Fever Dreams: A Story of Capitalism and Slavery in the Age of Jackson* (Athens: University of Georgia Press, 2012); J. William Harris, *The Hanging of Thomas Jeremiah: A Free Black Man's Encounter with Liberty* (New Haven, CT: Yale University Press, 2011); Edwin T. Arnold, *What Virtue There Is in Fire: Cultural Memory and the Lynching of Sam Hose* (Athens: University of Georgia Press, 2009); Laura Wexler, *Fire in a Canebrake: The Last Mass Lynching in America* (New York: Scribner, 2003); Kenneth C. Barnes, *Who Killed John Clayton? Political Violence and the Emergence of the New South, 1861–1893* (Durham, NC: Duke University Press, 1998); and Winthrop D. Jordan, *Tumult and Silence at Second Creek: An Inquiry into a Civil War Slave Conspiracy* (Baton Rouge: Louisiana State University Press, 1993). Many more tragic yet exceptional histories might be added to this list.

9. Bryant Simon, *The Hamlet Fire: A Tragic Story of Cheap Food, Cheap Government, and Cheap Lives* (New York: New Press, 2017); Claude A. Clegg III, *Troubled Ground: A Tale of Murder, Lynching, and Reckoning in the New South* (Urbana: University of Illinois Press, 2010); Suzanne Lebsock, *A Murder in Virginia: Southern Justice on Trial* (New York: W. W. Norton, 2003); Henry Wiencek, *The Hairstons: An American Family in Black and White* (New York: St. Martin's Press, 1999); Eric W. Rise, *The Martinsville Seven: Race, Rape, and Capital Punishment* (Charlottesville: University of Virginia Press, 1998); Richard B. Sherman, *The Case of Odell Waller and Virginia Justice, 1940–1942* (Knoxville: University of Tennessee Press, 1992).

10. On memory of the era as a whole, see Bruce Baker, *What Reconstruction Meant: Historical Memory in the American South* (Charlottesville: University of Virginia Press, 2007). For a recent examination of the evolving public memory of another moment of Reconstruction

violence, Louisiana's Colfax Massacre (1873), see David T. Ballantyne, "Remembering the Colfax Massacre: Race, Sex, and the Meanings of Reconstruction Violence," *JSH* 87, no. 3 (August 2021): 427–66.

11. For examples of the many books examining and debating the legacies of these three men, see R. Blakeslee Gilpin, *John Brown Still Lives! America's Long Reckoning with Violence, Equality, and Change* (Chapel Hill: University of North Carolina Press, 2011); Francis D. Cogliano, *Thomas Jefferson: Reputation and Legacy* (Charlottesville: University of Virginia Press, 2008); and Thomas L. Connelly, *The Marble Man: Robert E. Lee and His Image in American Society* (Baton Rouge: Louisiana State University Press, 1978).

12. One inspiration here is Michel-Rolph Trouillot, *Silencing the Past: Power and the Production of History* (Boston: Beacon Press, 1995). My thanks to Bruce Baker for pointing me toward this work.

13. For the overall political situation in the state, see Paul D. Escott, *Many Excellent People: Power and Privilege in North Carolina, 1850–1900* (Chapel Hill: University of North Carolina Press, 1985); and an insightful examination of white political divisions in Reconstruction North Carolina, albeit largely focused on the western mountains, is Steven E. Nash, *Reconstruction's Ragged Edge: The Politics of Postwar Life in the Southern Mountains* (Chapel Hill: University of North Carolina Press, 2016). An excellent study of the divisions between poor and wealthy white southerners in general is Keri Leigh Merritt, *Masterless Men: Poor Whites and Slavery in the Antebellum South* (Cambridge: Cambridge University Press, 2017).

14. Robert Penn Warren, *Night Rider* (1939; repr., New York: Bantam, 1968), 47.

CHAPTER ONE

1. The narrative of Byrd's survey was first published more than a century later: William Byrd, "History of the Dividing Line: Run in the Year 1728," in Byrd's *The Westover Manuscripts: Containing the History of the Dividing Line betwixt Virginia and North Carolina; a Journey to the Land of Eden, A.D. 1733; and a Progress to the Mines*, ed. Edmund Ruffin (Petersburg, VA: Edmund and Julian C. Ruffin, 1841), 1–102. An engaging study of the Piedmont environment that Byrd encountered is in Stephen Conrad Ausband, *Byrd's Line: A Natural History* (Charlottesville: University of Virginia Press, 2002), 76–135.

2. Christopher E. Hendricks, *The Backcountry Towns of Colonial Virginia* (Knoxville: University of Tennessee Press, 2006), 64–69; William Byrd, *William Byrd's Natural History of Virginia, or the Newly Discovered Eden*, ed. Richard Croom Beatty and William Mulloy (Richmond, VA: Dietz Press, 1940).

3. Richard Beeman, *The Evolution of the Southern Backcountry: A Case Study of Lunenburg County, Virginia, 1746–1832* (Philadelphia: University of Pennsylvania Press, 1989), 21–23; Allan Kulikoff, *Tobacco and Slaves: The Development of Southern Cultures in the Chesapeake, 1680–1800* (Chapel Hill: University of North Carolina Press, 1986), 141–44; Maud Carter Clement, *The History of Pittsylvania County, Virginia* (Lynchburg, VA: J. P. Bell, 1929), 35–37, 46–47.

4. On the absence of Native American populations in Caswell County at the time of settlement, see William Powell, *When the Past Refused to Die: A History of Caswell County, North Carolina, 1777–1977* (Durham, NC: Moore Publishing, 1977), 23–24. There are many accounts of Bacon's Rebellion, but for an accessible treatment that places an emphasis on

Native American perspectives, see James D. Rice, *Tales from a Revolution: Bacon's Rebellion and the Transformation of Early America* (New York: Oxford University Press, 2012).

5. *Return of the Whole Number of Persons within the Several Districts of the United States* (Philadelphia, 1793), 53; J. D. B. DeBow, *Statistical View of the United States, Embracing Its Territory, Population . . . Being a Compendium of the Seventh Census* (Washington, DC: A. O. P. Nicholson, 1854), 278. The absolute decline of Caswell's white population is explained in part by the creation of Person County from its eastern half in 1792.

6. On the slow development of towns in the backcountry, see Charles J. Farmer, *In the Absence of Towns: Settlement and Country Trade in Southside Virginia, 1730–1800* (Lanham, MD: Rowman and Littlefield, 1993); Carville Earle and Ronald Hoffman, "Urban Development in the Eighteenth-Century South," *Perspectives in American History* 10 (1976): 5–78.

7. On the early years of Danville as a regional commercial hub, see Frederick Siegel, *The Roots of Southern Distinctiveness: Tobacco and Society in Danville, Virginia, 1780–1865* (Chapel Hill: University of North Carolina Press, 1987).

8. On the decline of Chesapeake farms, see Richard Lyman Bushman, *The American Farmer in the Eighteenth Century: A Social and Cultural History* (New Haven, CT: Yale University Press, 2018), chaps. 11 and 12; James D. Rice, *Nature and History in the Potomac Country: From Hunter-Gatherers to the Age of Jefferson* (Baltimore, MD: Johns Hopkins University Press, 2009), chap. 13; Timothy Silver, *A New Face on the Countryside: Indians, Colonists, and Slaves in South Atlantic Forests, 1500–1800* (New York: Cambridge University Press, 1990), chap. 6; Carville Earle, "The Myth of the Southern Soil Miner: Macrohistory, Agricultural Innovation, and Environmental Change," in *The Ends of the Earth: Perspectives on Modern Environmental History*, ed. Donald Worster (New York: Cambridge University Press, 1988), 175–210; and Avery Craven, *Soil Exhaustion as a Factor in the Agricultural History of Virginia and Maryland, 1606–1860* (1926; repr., Columbia: University of South Carolina Press, 2007).

9. "The Bible Cause, in the County of Caswell, North Carolina," *Boston Recorder and Religious Telegraph* 14, no. 51 (December 16, 1829): 201.

10. For a local discussion, see "Going to Texas," *Milton Chronicle*, August 3, 1842, 2.

11. On Jeffreys's agricultural improvement activities, see Drew A. Swanson, *A Golden Weed: Tobacco and Environment in the Piedmont South* (New Haven, CT: Yale University Press, 2014). On southern improvement in general, see Benjamin R. Cohen, *Notes from the Ground: Science, Soil, and Society in the American Countryside* (New Haven, CT: Yale University Press, 2009); Lynn A. Nelson, *Pharsalia: An Environmental Biography of a Southern Plantation, 1780–1880* (Athens: University of Georgia Press, 2007); Edmund Ruffin, *Nature's Management: Writings on Landscape and Reform, 1822–1859*, ed. Jack Temple Kirby (Athens: University of Georgia Press, 2000); Jack Temple Kirby, *Poquosin: A Study of Rural Landscape and Society* (Chapel Hill: University of North Carolina Press, 1995); and William M. Matthew, *Edmund Ruffin and the Crisis of Slavery in the Old South: The Failure of Agricultural Reform* (Athens: University of Georgia Press, 1988). On the intrinsic differences between southern and northern forms of improvement, see Ariel Ron, *Grassroots Leviathan: Agricultural Reform and the Rural North in the Slaveholding Republic* (Baltimore, MD: Johns Hopkins University Press, 2020); Emily Pawley, *The Nature of the Future: Agriculture, Science, and Capitalism in the Antebellum North* (Chicago: University of Chicago Press, 2020); and Steven Stoll, *Larding the Lean Earth: Soil and Society in Nineteenth-Century America* (New York: Hill and Wang, 2002).

12. On Jeffreys's relationship with Jefferson and agricultural society membership, see Powell, *When the Past Refused to Die*, 474–75; quote from Diary of George Washington Jeffreys, 1842–1848, January 30, 1845, box 1, folder 7, William Bethell Williamson Papers, SHC.

13. H. P. Womack to Pleasant H. Womack, August 19, 1847, box 2, Hatchett Family Papers, Duke.

14. For other examples, see the cultivation requirements outlined in the rental contracts between Caswell landowners William Armistead and Thomas Bruce and their tenants. Contract between William H. Armistead and H. C. Moon and Parham Moon, January 1, 1846, box 1, folder 1840–1846, and Contract between Thomas Bruce and A. B. Spooner, July 25, 1853, box 1, folder 1850–1855, both in Philip H. Howerton Papers, Duke.

15. J. S. Totten Account Book, 1832–1858, series 17, box 1, folder 2; and Indenture between William M. Gwin and Joseph S. Totten, April 27, 1840, both in series 17, box 1, folder 2, Joseph Silas Totten Papers, CCHAC, SHC.

16. There is a substantial body of recent literature arguing for the capitalist nature of antebellum slavery. For examples, see the list of sources in chapter 1, note 48 below.

17. David Hackett Fischer and James C. Kelly, *Bound Away: Virginia and the Westward Movement* (Charlottesville: University of Virginia Press, 2000), esp. chaps. 3–5.

18. Earle, "Myth of the Southern Soil Miner," 175–210; Craven, *Soil Exhaustion.*

19. For typical critiques of tobacco as a soil-destroying crop, see Address of James C. Bruce to the Mecklenberg and Granville Agricultural Clubs, July 14, 1847, 7–15, Bruce Family Papers, in Kenneth M. Stampp, ed., *Records of Ante-bellum Southern Plantations from the Revolution through the Civil War* (Frederick, MD: University Publications of America, 1985–), series E, part 3, reel 14; John Hartwell Cocke, "Tobacco, the Bane of Virginia Husbandry," *Southern Planter* 18 (1858): 716–19; and Ruffin, *Nature's Management*, 325.

20. Agricola [George Jeffreys], *A Series of Essays on Agriculture and Rural Affairs; in Forty-Seven Numbers* (Raleigh, NC: Joseph Gales, 1819), 5.

21. Agricola, *Series of Essays*, 16.

22. Swanson, *Golden Weed*, chap. 2; Barbara Hahn, *Making Tobacco Bright: Creating an American Commodity, 1617–1937* (Baltimore, MD: Johns Hopkins University Press, 2011), 13–14, 138; Jerome E. Brooks, *Green Leaf and Gold: Tobacco in North Carolina* (Raleigh, NC: State Department of Archives and History, 1962), 18–20; Nannie May Tilley, *The Bright-Tobacco Industry, 1860–1929* (Chapel Hill: University of North Carolina Press, 1948), 24–26.

23. Swanson, *Golden Weed*, chap. 2.

24. Swanson, *Golden Weed*, chap. 2.

25. Powell, *When the Past Refused to Die*, 128.

26. Powell, *When the Past Refused to Die*, 114–28; E. S. Yarbrough, "Yarbrough's Foundry," unpublished manuscript, 1960, 5–6, box 1, folder 10, Yarbrough Foundry Papers, CCHAC.

27. Advertisement draft of Philip Howerton and Thomas Easley, November 12, 1851, box 2, folder "receipts and bills, undated"; and D. M. Reese to Philip Howerton, June 17, 1857, box 2, folder "correspondence and papers, 1870–1879," both in Duke.

28. D. Garland to John T. Garland, May 22, 1846, series 2, folder 9, Glenn Family Papers, CCHAC; William L. Plummer [?] to Dabney Cosby, January 26, 1843, folder 1, Dabney Cosby Papers, SHC.

29. Receipt of William Hatchett, January 1, 1855, Receipt of William R. Hatchett, February 3, 1855, and September 10, 1857, box 1, Hatchett Family Papers; Diary of George Washington Jeffreys, 1842–1848, February 21, 1845.

30. *The Somerville Female Institute, Leasburg, Caswell County, N.C.* (Raleigh, NC: A. M. Gorman, 1855), 10, from the University of North Carolina Chapel Hill Library, available online at https://archive.org/details/catalogueofsomer1855some/page/n3/mode/2up (accessed November 22, 2022).

31. John T. Garland to William T. Sutherlin, March [?], 1857, box 1, folder 3, William Thomas Sutherlin Papers, SHC; Thomas Lindsey to John Sutherlin, April 26, 1858, folder "1846–1858," William Thomas Sutherlin Papers, Duke; Armistead T. Moore to William T. Sutherlin, April 26, 1860, box 1, folder 5 William Thomas Sutherlin Papers, SHC; B. Brown to William Thomas Sutherlin, May 35, 1860, box 1, folder 6, William Thomas Sutherlin Papers, SHC.

32. J. B. Killebrew and Herbert Myrick, *Tobacco Leaf: Its Culture and Cure, Marketing and Manufacture* (New York: Orange Judd Company, 1897), 10–11; W. Edward Hearn and Frank P. Drane, *Soil Survey of Caswell County, North Carolina* (Washington, DC: GPO, 1910), 9; Powell, *When the Past Refused to Die,* 110.

33. H. P. Womack to Pleasant H. Womack, April 24, 1853, box 2, Hatchett Family Papers; Paul D. Escott, *Many Excellent People: Power and Privilege in North Carolina, 1850–1900* (Chapel Hill: University of North Carolina Press, 1985), 8–9.

34. Killebrew and Myrick, *Tobacco Leaf,* 11.

35. DeBow, *Statistical View of the United States,* 278; Joseph C. G. Kennedy, *Population of the United States in 1860; Compiled from the Original Returns of the Eighth Census under the Direction of the Secretary of the Interior* (Washington, DC: GPO, 1864), 349, 355.

36. Powell, *When the Past Refused to Die,* 113.

37. "List of Negroes Belonging to the Estate of Isabella Glenn," n.d. (1840s), box 1, folder 9, Glenn Family Papers, CCHAC.

38. Compiled from the 1860 Federal Population Census, Slave Schedule for Caswell County, NC, M653, roll 921, NAA; and Hairston Family Plantation Records, books 1 and 3, box 8, folders 104 and 106, Peter Wilson Hairston Papers, SHC. On the Hairston family's complex plantation enterprise, see Henry Wiencek, *The Hairstons: An American Family in Black and White* (New York: St. Martin's Press, 1999).

39. Slave Census Schedule for Caswell County, 1860.

40. Powell, *When the Past Refused to Die,* 82, 94–95, 151–52.

41. The foundational study of free black people in North Carolina remains John Hope Franklin, *The Free Negro in North Carolina, 1790–1860* (Chapel Hill: University of North Carolina Press, 1943).

42. Patricia Phillips Marshall and Jo Ramsay Leimenstoll, *Thomas Day: Master Craftsman and Free Man of Color* (Chapel Hill: University of North Carolina Press, 2010). Other work on Day includes Rodney Barfield and Patricia P. Marshall, *Thomas Day: African American Furniture Maker* (Raleigh: North Carolina Office of Archives and History, 2005); Rodney D. Barfield, "Thomas and John Day and the Journey to North Carolina," *NCHR* 78, no. 1 (January 2001): 1–31; Patricia Phillips Marshall, "The Legendary Thomas Day: Debunking the Popular Mythology of an African American Craftsman," *NCHR* 78, no. 1 (January 2001): 32–66; and W. A. Robinson et al., "Thomas Day and His Family," *Negro History Bulletin* 13 (March 1950): 123–26, 140.

43. For the full text of the petition, see "Petition from the Citizens of Milton on behalf of Thomas Day, 1830," appendix B in Marshall and Leimenstoll, *Thomas Day,* 200.

44. DeBow, *Statistical View of the United States,* 278; Kennedy, *Population of the United States in 1860,* 351. The majority of the county's free black people (164) in 1860 were described,

like Thomas Day, as "mulatto," as were 966 enslaved people (Kennedy, *Population of the United States in 1860*, 358).

45. Good explorations of the racial dynamics of the 1930s effort by the Federal Writers' Project to collect the narratives of former slaves can be found in Catherine A. Stewart, *Long Past Slavery: Representing Race in the Federal Writers' Project* (Chapel Hill: University of North Carolina Press, 2016); and George P. Rawick, "General Introduction," in *The American Slave: A Composite Autobiography*, Supplement, Series 1, ed. George P. Rawick, Jan Hillegas, and Ken Lawrence (Westport, CT: Greenwood Press, 1977), ix–li.

46. George P. Rawick, ed., *The American Slave: A Composite Autobiography*, vol. 15, *North Carolina Narratives, Part 2* (Westport, CT: Greenwood Publishing, 1972), 44–50.

47. Rawick, *American Slave*, 15:44–50.

48. The literature on the expanding cotton South is vast, but recent influential syntheses that focus on the dynamic capitalist nature of the region include Edward E. Baptist, *The Half Has Never Been Told: Slavery and the Making of American Capitalism* (New York: Basic Books, 2016); Sven Beckert and Seth Rockman, eds., *Slavery's Capitalism: A New History of American Economic Development* (Philadelphia: University of Pennsylvania Press, 2016); Sven Beckert, *Empire of Cotton: A Global History* (New York: Alfred A. Knopf, 2015); Calvin Schermerhorn, *The Business of Slavery and the Rise of American Capitalism, 1815–1860* (New Haven, CT: Yale University Press, 2015); Walter Johnson, *River of Dark Dreams: Slavery and Empire in the Cotton Kingdom* (Cambridge, MA: Belknap/Harvard University Press, 2013); and Joshua D. Rothman, *Flush Times and Fever Dreams: A Story of Capitalism and Slavery in the Age of Jackson* (Athens: University of Georgia Press, 2012). On the bright tobacco district's similarities, see Swanson, *Golden Weed*, 115–18.

49. DeBow, *Statistical View of the United States*, 282; Joseph C. G. Kennedy, *Agriculture of the United States in 1860; Compiled from the Original Returns of the Eighth Census, under the Direction of the Secretary of the Interior* (Washington, DC: GPO, 1864), 104–11.

50. Hinton Rowan Helper, *The Impending Crisis of the South: How to Meet It* (New York: Burdick Brothers, 1857), 56. On the book's contemporary impact, see David Brown, *Southern Outcast: Hinton Rowan Helper and "The Impending Crisis of the South"* (Baton Rouge: Louisiana State University Press, 2006), chaps. 6 and 7.

51. George Fitzhugh's *Sociology for the South, or the Failure of Free Society* (Richmond, VA: A. Morris, 1854) had laid out his philosophy of slavery three years prior to Helper's publication, and his second and even more influential work, *Cannibals All! or, Slaves without Masters* (Richmond, VA: A. Morris, 1857), appeared the same year as *The Impending Crisis*. Where most white southerners came to see Helper as traitorous, the most ardent "fire-eaters" believed Fitzhugh to be their champion.

52. On Helper's gold rush experience, see Hinton R. Helper, *The Land of Gold: Reality versus Fiction* (Baltimore, MD: Henry Taylor, 1855); and Brown, *Southern Outcast*, chap. 2.

53. Powell, *When the Past Refused to Die*, 177; "Caswell County Courthouse," Historic American Buildings Survey, HABS NC-192, July 1, 1983, available at the Library of Congress website, www.loc.gov/pictures/item/nc0015/ (accessed November 22, 2022); H. G. Jones, "National Register of Historic Places Inventory—Nomination Form," April 3, 1973, available online at http://files.nc.gov/ncdcr/nr/CS0001.pdf (accessed November 22, 2022); *Milton Chronicle* quote on p. 4.

54. Powell, *When the Past Refused to Die*, 179–82; David Brown, "North Carolina Ambivalence: Rethinking Loyalty and Disaffection in the Civil War Piedmont," in *North Carolinians*

in the Era of the Civil War and Reconstruction, ed. Paul D. Escott (Chapel Hill: University of North Carolina Press, 2008), 13.

55. William T. Auman, *Civil War in the North Carolina Quaker Belt: The Confederate Campaign against Peace Agitators, Deserters and Draft Dodgers* (Jefferson, NC: McFarland, 2014), 33.

56. Powell, *When the Past Refused to Die*, 187–88, 203–4, quote on 191.

57. Powell, *When the Past Refused to Die*, 191, 194–95, 199–200.

58. Bartlett Yancey Malone, "The Diary of Bartlett Yancey Malone," ed. William Whatley Pierson Jr., *James Sprunt Historical Publications* 16, no. 2 (1919): 5, 9.

59. Malone, "Diary of Bartlett Yancey Malone," 43–58, quotes on 44.

60. Powell, *When the Past Refused to Die*, 188–89, 207–10.

61. Judkin Browning, *Shifting Loyalties: The Union Occupation of Eastern North Carolina* (Chapel Hill: University of North Carolina Press, 2011); Barton Myers, *Executing Daniel Bright: Race, Loyalty, and Guerrilla Violence in a Coastal Carolina Community, 1861–1865* (Baton Rouge: Louisiana State University Press, 2009); Martin Crawford, *Ashe County's Civil War: Community and Society in the Appalachian South* (Charlottesville: University of Virginia Press, 2001); John C. Inscoe and Gordon B. McKinney, *The Heart of Confederate Appalachia: Western North Carolina in the Civil War* (Chapel Hill: University of North Carolina Press, 2000); William R. Trotter, *Bushwhackers: The Civil War in North Carolina; The Mountains* (Winston-Salem, NC: John F. Blair, 1991); Phillip Shaw Paludan, *Victims: A True Story of the Civil War* (Knoxville: University of Tennessee Press, 1981). Although it has little to say about North Carolina, an accessible general history of southern opposition to the war is William W. Freehling, *The South vs. the South: How Anti-Confederate Southerners Shaped the Course of the Civil War* (New York: Oxford University Press, 2001).

62. Victoria E. Bynum, *The Long Shadow of the Civil War: Southern Dissent and Its Legacies* (Chapel Hill: University of North Carolina Press, 2010), chap. 2; Brown, "North Carolina Ambivalence," 9–12, 15–23, 27–28; Auman, *Civil War in the North Carolina Quaker Belt*, 32–33, 165–66.

63. David Silkenat, *Driven from Home: North Carolina's Civil War Refugee Crisis* (Athens: University of Georgia Press, 2016), chap. 1.

64. Richard M. Reid, *Freedom for Themselves: North Carolina's Black Soldiers in the Civil War Era* (Chapel Hill: University of North Carolina Press, 2008), xiv–xv.

65. The famous phrasing is James C. Scott's, *Weapons of the Weak: Everyday Forms of Peasant Resistance* (New Haven, CT: Yale University Press, 1985).

66. William C. Harris, *William Woods Holden: Firebrand of North Carolina Politics* (Baton Rouge: Louisiana State University Press, 1987), 6–10; Carole Watterson Troxler and William Murray Vincent, *Shuttle and Plow: A History of Alamance County, North Carolina* (n.p.: Alamance County Historical Association, 1999), 324–25; Edgar E. Folk and Bynum Shaw, *W. W. Holden: A Political Biography* (Winston-Salem, NC: John F. Blair, 1982).

67. Escott, *Many Excellent People*, 90.

68. Harris, *William Woods Holden*, 11–21, quote on 56.

69. Harris, *William Woods Holden*, chaps. 6 and 7; James Alex Baggett, *The Scalawags: Southern Dissenters in the Civil War and Reconstruction* (Baton Rouge: Louisiana State University Press, 2003), 90–92.

70. Barton A. Myers, *Rebels against the Confederacy: North Carolina's Unionists* (New York: Cambridge University Press, 2014), 114–20; Carole Emberton, *Beyond Redemption: Race,*

Violence, and the American South after the Civil War (Chicago: University of Chicago Press, 2013), 160; Scott Reynolds Nelson, "Red Strings and Half Brothers: Civil Wars in Alamance County, North Carolina, 1861–1871," in *Enemies of the Country: New Perspectives on Unionists in the Civil War South*, ed. John C. Inscoe and Robert C. Kenzer (Athens: University of Georgia Press, 2001), 43; Paul Escott, "White Republicanism and Ku Klux Klan Terror: The North Carolina Piedmont during Reconstruction," in *Race, Class, and Politics in Southern History: Essays in Honor of Robert F. Durden*, ed. Jeffrey J. Crow, Paul D. Escott, and Charles L. Flynn Jr. (Baton Rouge: Louisiana State University Press, 1989), 17–19; J. G. de Roulhac Hamilton, *Reconstruction in North Carolina* (New York: Columbia University Press, 1914), 63–64.

71. Chandra Manning, "'The Order of Nature Would Be Reversed: Soldiers, Slavery, and the North Carolina Gubernatorial Election of 1864," in Escott, *North Carolinians in the Era of the Civil War and Reconstruction*, 101–28; James M. McPherson, *Battle Cry of Freedom: The Civil War Era* (New York: Oxford University Press, 1988), 696–98, quote on 698.

72. Swanson, *Golden Weed*, 133, 139–40; Powell, *When the Past Refused to Die*, 215–21.

73. Brown, "North Carolina Ambivalence," 9–12, 15–23, 27–28; Manning, "Order of Nature Would Be Reversed," 105.

74. Editorial, *Milton Chronicle*, November 9, 1863, 2.

75. John M. Worth to Jonathan Worth, February 16, 1865, in *The Correspondence of Jonathan Worth*, 2 vols., ed. Joseph G. de Roulhac Hamilton (Raleigh, NC: Edwards and Broughton, 1909), 1:348–49, quote on 348.

76. Silkenat, *Driven from Home*, chap. 4.

77. John Majewski, *Modernizing a Slave Economy: The Economic Vision of the Confederate Nation* (Chapel Hill: University of North Carolina Press, 2009), 147, table 6.

78. George G. Kundahl, ed., *The Bravest of the Brave: The Correspondence of Stephen Dodson Ramseur* (Chapel Hill: University of North Carolina Press, 2010), 3, 173, 175; Gary W. Gallagher, *Stephen Dodson Ramseur: Lee's Gallant General* (Chapel Hill: University of North Carolina Press, 1985), 84–85.

79. Inscoe and McKinney, *Heart of Confederate Appalachia*, 243–57. For an outraged and quite partisan take on Sherman's actions in North Carolina and the uncertainty that the close of the war generated in the Piedmont, see Cornelia Phillips Spencer, *The Last Ninety Days of the War in North-Carolina* (New York: Watchman, 1866), 51–64, 197; and on Spencer's influence, see John C. Inscoe, "To Do Justice to North Carolina: The War's End according to Cornelia Phillips Spencer, Zebulon B. Vance, and David L. Swain," in Escott, *North Carolinians in the Era of the Civil War and Reconstruction*, 129–54. (Spencer's brother, Samuel Phillips, would prosecute dozens of suspected North Carolina Klansmen under the Ku Klux Act in the early 1870s as assistant US district attorney, men who might have heartily agreed with Spencer's harsh assessments of federal actions in the state. Archibald Henderson, *North Carolina: The Old North State and the New*, 2 vols. [Chicago: Lewis Publishing Co., 1941], 2:335.)

CHAPTER TWO

1. On freedpeople moving to Danville, see John Richard Dennett, *The South as It Is: 1865–1866* (1965; repr., Baton Rouge: Louisiana State University Press, 1995), 98. On rumors of land division at the end of the year in the state, see Sharon Ann Holt, *Making Freedom Pay: North Carolina Freedpeople Working for Themselves, 1865–1900* (Athens: University of Georgia Press, 2000), 52–54; William S. Powell, *North Carolina through Four Centuries* (Chapel Hill: University of North Carolina Press, 1989), 383; Paul D. Escott, *Many Excellent People:*

Power and Privilege in North Carolina, 1850–1900 (Chapel Hill: University of North Carolina Press, 1985), 133–34; and, more broadly, Mark Wahlgren Summers, *A Dangerous Stir: Fear, Paranoia, and the Making of Reconstruction* (Chapel Hill: University of North Carolina Press, 2009), chap. 3.

2. Elizabeth R. Varon, *Appomattox: Victory, Defeat, and Freedom at the End of the Civil War* (New York: Oxford University Press, 2014), 192; Hans L. Trefousse, "Andrew Johnson and the Freedmen's Bureau," in *The Freedmen's Bureau and Reconstruction: Reconsiderations*, ed. Paul A. Cimbala and Randall M. Miller (New York: Fordham University Press, 1999), 31; William C. Harris, *William Woods Holden: Firebrand of North Carolina Politics* (Baton Rouge: Louisiana State University Press, 1987), chap. 8; Richard L. Zuber, *North Carolina during Reconstruction* (Raleigh, NC: Division of Archives and History, 1969), 2–4; Kenneth M. Stampp, *The Era of Reconstruction, 1865–1877* (New York: Alfred A. Knopf, 1965), 67–68.

3. J. T. Trowbridge, *The South: A Tour of Its Battle-Fields and Ruined Cities* (Hartford, CT: L. Stebbins, 1866), 580–81, quote on 581.

4. Dennett, *South as It Is*, 103–4, quote on 103.

5. Whitelaw Reid, *After the War: A Southern Tour* (Cincinnati, OH: Moore, Wilstach and Baldwin, 1866), 21–27.

6. Steven E. Nash, *Reconstruction's Ragged Edge: The Politics of Postwar Life in the Southern Mountains* (Chapel Hill: University of North Carolina Press, 2016), 77; Richard Nelson Current, *Those Terrible Carpetbaggers* (New York: Oxford University Press, 1988), 102.

7. Although Conservatives were an amalgamation of former party loyalties, the pages that follow will use "Democrat" and "Conservative" interchangeably, as was the practice for a time in the postwar years. The coalition would eventually readopt Democrat as its party name by Reconstruction's end.

8. *Report of the Joint Committee on Reconstruction, at the First Session Thirty-Ninth Congress*, 4 parts (Washington, DC: GPO, 1866), 2:186; George R. Bentley, *A History of the Freedmen's Bureau* (New York: Octagon Books, 1970), 73. For specific analyses of the composition of bureau agents in two states, Arkansas and Georgia, see Randy Finley, "The Personnel of the Freedmen's Bureau in Arkansas," in Cimbala and Miller, *Freedmen's Bureau and Reconstruction*, 93–118; and Paul A. Cimbala, *Under the Guardianship of the Nation: The Freedmen's Bureau and the Reconstruction of Georgia, 1865–1870* (Athens: University of Georgia Press, 1997), 42–45.

9. Roberta Sue Alexander, *North Carolina Faces the Freedmen: Race Relations during Presidential Reconstruction, 1865–67* (Durham, NC: Duke University Press, 1985); Bentley, *History of the Freedmen's Bureau*, 58, 128–32, 216; J. G. de Roulhac Hamilton, *Reconstruction in North Carolina* (New York: Columbia University Press, 1914), 321–24; "Freedmen's Bureau Personnel in North Carolina," Smithsonian Online Virtual Archives, https://sova.si.edu/record/NMAAHC.FB.M1909#Freedmen's%20Bureau%20Personnel%20in%20North%20Carolina (accessed November 22, 2022). North Carolina's assistant commissioners were, in order, Whittlesey, Ruger, John Robinson, James Bomford, Nelson Miles, Jacob Chur, and Compton.

10. On Helper's postwar career, see David Brown, *Southern Outcast: Hinton Rowan Helper and "The Impending Crisis of the South"* (Baton Rouge: Louisiana State University Press, 2006), chaps. 9 and 10.

11. Hinton Rowan Helper, *Nojoque; A Question for a Continent* (New York: George W. Carleton, 1867), v.

12. Hinton Rowan Helper, *The Negroes in Negroland; the Negroes in America; and Negroes Generally* (New York: G. W. Carleton, 1868), title page, viii.

13. Hinton Rowan Helper, *Noonday Exigencies in America* (New York: Bible Brothers, 1871), 15.

14. Deborah Beckel, *Radical Reform: Interracial Politics in Post-emancipation North Carolina* (Charlottesville: University of Virginia Press, 2011), 48–49; Gregory P. Downs, *Declarations of Dependence: The Long Reconstruction of Popular Politics in the South, 1861–1908* (Chapel Hill: University of North Carolina Press, 2011), 83–84; James Alex Baggett, *The Scalawags: Southern Dissenters in the Civil War and Reconstruction* (Baton Rouge: Louisiana State University Press, 2003), 181, 266; Harris, *William Woods Holden*, chap. 8; Richard L. Zuber, *Jonathan Worth: A Biography of a Southern Unionist* (Chapel Hill: University of North Carolina Press, 1965), esp. chaps. 16 and 17; Hamilton, *Reconstruction in North Carolina*, quote on 191.

15. 1850 Federal Population Census, Free Schedule for Rockingham County, NC, M432, roll 643, NAA; 1860 Federal Population Census, Free Schedule for Rockingham County, NC, M653, roll 912, NAA; Nonpopulation Census Schedules for North Carolina, 1850–1880, 1870 Mortality Schedules, M1805, roll 3, NAA. There is some contention over Stephens's year of birth, though 1834 is the most common claim; see John H. Wheeler, *Reminiscences and Memoirs of North Carolina and Eminent North Carolinians* (Columbus, OH: Columbus Printing Works, 1884), 111; and A. J. Stedman, *Murder and Mystery: History of the Life and Death of John W. Stephens, State Senator of North Carolina, from Caswell County* (Greensboro, NC: Patriot, 1870), 6. For more on Stedman as a source, see chapter 3.

16. 1860 Census, page 174; Luther M. Carlton, "Assassination of John Walter Stephens," in *An Annual Publication of Historical Papers: Legal and Biographical Studies*, Series 2 (Durham, NC: Historical Society of Trinity College, 1898), 1–2; Stedman, *Murder and Mystery*, 7. Stedman gives John's first wife's name as "Nancy."

17. John W. Moore, *Roster of North Carolina Troops in the War between the States*, 4 vols. (Raleigh, NC: Ash and Gatling, 1882), 1:480, 484, 486, 500, 507; Carlton, "Assassination of John Walter Stephens," 2; Stedman, *Murder and Mystery*, 8–9. Moore's list of North Carolina Confederate servicemen does include one John W. Stephens. He enlisted in coastal Beaufort County in 1861, and the likelihood that he is the John in question seems minimal (1:152).

18. Carlton, "Assassination of John Walter Stephens," 4; 1860 Federal Population Census, Free Schedule for Caswell County, NC, M653, roll 891, NAA.

19. Jonathan Worth to A. M. Tomlinson and Sons, February 17, 1866, 1:501–2, quote on 502, and W. H. Bagley to Rev. Drury Lacy, March 21, 1867, 2:917, both in *The Correspondence of Jonathan Worth*, 2 vols., ed. Joseph G. de Roulhac Hamilton (Raleigh, NC: Edwards and Broughton, 1909).

20. For recent biographies of Tourgée, see Carolyn L. Karcher, *A Refugee from His Race: Albion W. Tourgée and His Fight against White Supremacy* (Chapel Hill: University of North Carolina Press, 2016); Mark Elliott, *Color-Blind Justice: Albion Tourgée and the Quest for Racial Equality from the Civil War to Plessy v. Ferguson* (New York: Oxford University Press, 2006), details of Tourgée tutoring Stephens are found on 136. An older account is Richard Stiller, *The White Minority: Pioneers for Racial Equality* (New York: Harcourt Brace Jovanovich, 1977).

21. Charles Wolff to W. B. Bowe, August 27, 1866, Letters Sent and a Register of Letters Received, August 1866–December 1867; Isaac Porter to Charles Wolff, August 25, 1866, Letters Received, September 1866–December 1867, both in Graham (Assistant Subassistant Commissioner), M1909, roll 18, BRFAL. These records may be found in multiple locations, including the National Archives and Records Administration, College Park, MD,

on microfilm at its branch offices, and portions of them are now online at the Smithsonian's National Museum of African American History and Culture's website at https://sova .si.edu/record/NMAAHC.FB.M1909. Research for this book was conducted at the National Archives at Atlanta, located in Morrow, Georgia, and on the Smithsonian site. The citations that follow include the manuscript and roll call numbers for the National Archives records in microfilm form. The Smithsonian site is searchable, although its optical recognition software is imperfect at recognizing the various handwriting of the records.

22. F. W. Liedtke to J. W. Stephens, May 29, 1868, Letters Sent, March–December 1868, Graham (Assistant Subassistant Commissioner), M1909, roll 18, BRFAL; J. W. Stephens to F. W. Liedtke, May 14, 1868, and F. W. Liedtke to [?], May 14, 1868, both in Register of Letters Received and Endorsements Sent, May–December 1868, Graham (Assistant Subassistant Commissioner), M1909, roll 18, BRFAL. Entries recording Stephens acting as an "Assistant Agent" of the bureau through early May 1869 may be found in Register of Complaints, March–November 1868, Graham (Assistant Subassistant Commissioner), M1909, roll 18, BRFAL. The register also contains an intriguing entry noting the case of *Jerry Niece vs. Civil Authorities*, May 21, 1868, in which a freedman pressed assault charges against "Stephens, [a] white [man]." A magistrate arrested Stephens, who was released on bail and failed to appear before the superior court, and the matter was ultimately dropped. The case title suggests the possibility that the defendant was John Stephens, accused of wrongdoing in his role as justice of the peace. If so, this might help explain his dismissal from the bureau post at roughly the same time. Stephens may have been appointed by Manchester Weld, who served as the agent in charge of the Graham office between the original commander, Isaac Porter, and Liedtke. On the civilian agents and the fee system in general, see Bentley, *History of the Freedmen's Bureau*, 73.

23. Douglas R. Egerton, *The Wars of Reconstruction: The Brief, Violent History of America's Most Progressive Era* (New York: Bloomsbury Press, 2014), 293; Steven Hahn, *A Nation under Our Feet: Black Political Struggles in the Rural South from Slavery to the Great Migration* (Cambridge, MA: Belknap Press, 2003), 177–89; Scott Reynolds Nelson, *Iron Confederacies: Southern Railways, Klan Violence, and Reconstruction* (Chapel Hill: University of North Carolina Press, 1999), 49; Michael W. Fitzgerald, *The Union League Movement in the Deep South: Politics and Agricultural Change during Reconstruction* (Baton Rouge: Louisiana State University Press, 1989); Eric Foner, *Reconstruction: America's Unfinished Revolution, 1863–1877* (New York: Harper and Row, 1988), 283–85.

24. Harris, *William Woods Holden*, 223; Bentley, *History of the Freedmen's Bureau*, 192; Hamilton, *Reconstruction in North Carolina*, 336–37.

25. Hahn, *Nation under Our Feet*, 183.

26. For Reconstruction labor arrangements in the tobacco belt, see Evan P. Bennett, *When Tobacco Was King: Families, Farm Labor, and Federal Policy in the Piedmont* (Gainesville: University Press of Florida, 2014), esp. chap. 1; Adrienne Monteith Petty, *Standing Their Ground: Small Farmers in North Carolina since the Civil War* (New York: Oxford University Press, 2013), chap. 2; Jeffrey Kerr-Ritchie, *Freedpeople in the Tobacco South: Virginia, 1860–1900* (Chapel Hill: University of North Carolina Press, 1999); and Lynda J. Morgan, *Emancipation in Virginia's Tobacco Belt, 1850–1870* (Athens: University of Georgia Press, 1992). For a general summary of the emergence of sharecropping, see Ralph Shlomowitz, "The Origins of Southern Sharecropping," *Agricultural History* 53, no. 3 (July 1979): 563–65. A sampling of primary sources on labor arrangements in the months following emancipation may be found in Steven Hahn et al., eds., *Freedom: A Documentary History of Emancipation, 1861–1867,*

Series 3: Vol. 1, *Land and Labor, 1865* (Chapel Hill: University of North Carolina Press, 2008). Daniel Novak has argued that North Carolina's codes were less restrictive than those in most Deep South states, although the state did make a practice of leasing the labor of freedpeople arrested under vagrancy laws into the 1870s: Daniel A. Novak, *The Wheel of Servitude: Black Forced Labor after Slavery* (Lexington: University Press of Kentucky, 1978), 7, 28.

27. Charles Wolff [?] to Col. M. Cogswell, March 23, 1867, Letters Sent and a Register of Letters Received, August 1866–December 1867, Graham (Assistant Subassistant Commissioner), M1909, roll 18, BRFAL.

28. The most thorough study of North Carolina's Reconstruction apprenticeships is found in Karin L. Zipf, *Labor of Innocents: Forced Apprenticeship in North Carolina, 1715–1919* (Baton Rouge: Louisiana State University Press, 2005), esp. chaps. 2–5. See also James D. Schmidt, *Free to Work: Labor Law, Emancipation, and Reconstruction, 1815–1880* (Athens: University of Georgia Press, 1998), 186, 188; Laura F. Edwards, *Gendered Strife and Confusion: The Political Culture of Reconstruction* (Urbana: University of Illinois Press, 1997), 47–54; and Alexander, *North Carolina Faces the Freedmen*, 112–19. The language of the apprenticeship code drafted in 1868 was race-blind but still left the power to bind apprentices to county probate judges. See Victor C. Barringer, Will B. Rodman, and Albion W. Tourgée, *The Code of Civil Procedure of North Carolina, to Special Proceedings* (Raleigh, NC: N. Paige, 1868), 177–79.

29. Roger L. Ransom and Richard Sutch, *One Kind of Freedom: The Economic Consequences of Emancipation* (Cambridge: Cambridge University Press, 1977).

30. F. W. Liedtke to William W. Holden, September 22, 1868, in *The Papers of William Woods Holden*, 2 vols., ed. Horace W. Raper and Thornton W. Mitchell (Raleigh: North Carolina Division of Archives and History, 2000), 1:374–75.

31. For numerous examples of these disputes from Caswell and Alamance, see Register of Complaints, October–December 1867, Graham (Assistant Subassistant Commissioner), M1909, roll 18, BRFAL.

32. *Message of the President of the United States, Communicating, in Compliance with the Resolution of the Senate of the 16th of December, 1870, Information in Relation to Outrages Committed by Disloyal Persons in North Carolina and Other Southern States*, Senate Executive Document Number 16, part 1, 41st Congress, 3rd Session, January 13, 1871; Alexander, *North Carolina Faces the Freedmen*, chap. 6.

33. The best study of this record keeping and its contestation is William A. Blair, *The Record of Murders and Outrages: Racial Violence and the Fight over Truth at the Dawn of Reconstruction* (Chapel Hill: University of North Carolina Press, 2021). For a discussion of the bureau's record-keeping practices and the silences in the documents, see Jim Downs, "Emancipating the Evidence: The Ontology of the Freedmen's Bureau Records," in *Beyond Freedom: Disrupting the History of Emancipation*, ed. David W. Blight and Jim Downs (Athens: University of Georgia Press, 2017), 160–80.

34. George P. Rawick, ed., *The American Slave: A Composite Autobiography*, vol. 15, *North Carolina Narratives, Part 2* (Westport, CT: Greenwood Publishing, 1972), 254–55.

35. George P. Rawick, ed., *The American Slave: A Composite Autobiography*, vol. 14, *North Carolina Narratives, Part 1* (Westport, CT: Greenwood Publishing, 1972), 224–28.

36. Gregory P. Downs, "Anarchy at the Circumference: Statelessness and the Reconstruction of Authority in Emancipation North Carolina," in *After Slavery: Race, Labor, and Citizenship in the Reconstruction South*, ed. Bruce E. Baker and Brian Kelly (Gainesville: University Press of Florida, 2013), 100.

37. Rawick, *American Slave*, 14:160.

38. Andrew Mahony to Charles Wolff, September 1, 1867, and G. B. Carse to R. S. Lacey, April 27, 1867, both in Letters Received, September 1866–December 1867, Graham (Assistant Subassistant Commissioner), MS 1909, roll 18, BRFAL.

39. Wilson Carey to Charles Wolff, July 24, 1867, and J. C. Griffith to Charles Wolff, August 15, 1867, both in Letters Received, September 1866–December 1867, Graham (Assistant Subassistant Commissioner), M1909, roll 18, BRFAL.

40. Manchester W. Weld to Thomas Wilhelm, May 11, 1868, Endorsements Sent and Received, March–May 1868, Graham (Assistant Subassistant Commissioner), M1909, roll 18, BRFAL.

41. "Evidence of W. T. Ector to Asa Teal, Assistant Superintendent of Freedmen, District of Greensboro, NC," and "Trial of Edward Glass (Colored), August 1, 1865," Records Relating to Court Cases, February 1865–December 1868, Records of the Field Offices for the State of North Carolina, M1909, roll 21, BRFAL, quote in the latter.

42. Depositions in the Case of US Government vs. James Hunt, February 1, 1866, Contracts, Indentures, and Papers Regarding Cases, Danville Field Office, M1913, roll 72, BRFAL.

43. A letter sent from F. W. Liedtke to J. S. Griffith, July 5, 1867, Letters Sent and a Register of Letters Received, August 1866–December 1867, Graham (Assistant Subassistant Commissioner), M1909, roll 18, BRFAL.

44. Charles Wolff to [?], July 26, 1867, Letters Sent and a Register of Letters Received, August 1866–December 1867, Graham (Assistant Subassistant Commissioner), M1909, roll 18, BRFAL.

45. Charles Wolff [?] to David Burch, April 11, 1867, Letters Sent and a Register of Letters Received, August 1866–December 1867, Graham (Assistant Subassistant Commissioner), M1909, roll 18, BRFAL.

46. Federal Writers' Project, *Slave Narratives: A Folk History of Slavery in the United States from Interviews with Former Slaves*, vol. 11, *North Carolina Narratives*, part 2, (Washington, DC: Federal Writers' Project, 1941), 11, available at the Library of Congress, www.loc.gov /resource/mesn.112/?sp=15&r=-0.517,0.323,2.035,1.021,0 (accessed November 27, 2022).

47. Karin Zipf, "No Longer under Cover(ture): Marriage, Divorce, and Gender in the 1868 Constitutional Convention," in *North Carolinians in the Era of the Civil War and Reconstruction*, ed. Paul D. Escott (Chapel Hill: University of North Carolina Press, 2008), 194–95; Mark L. Bradley, *Bluecoats and Tar Heels: Soldiers and Civilians in Reconstruction North Carolina* (Lexington: University Press of Kentucky, 2009), 181; Powell, *North Carolina through Four Centuries*, 392–94. For a general assessment of the convention, see Richard L. Hume and Jerry B. Gough, *Blacks, Carpetbaggers, and Scalawags: The Constitutional Conventions of Radical Reconstruction* (Baton Rouge: Louisiana State University Press, 2008), chap. 5.

48. Hume and Gough, *Blacks, Carpetbaggers, and Scalawags*, 116; Robert C. Kenzer, *Enterprising Southerners: Black Economic Success in North Carolina, 1865–1915* (Charlottesville: University Press of Virginia, 1997), 87–88; Frenise A. Logan, "Black and Republican: Vicissitudes of a Minority Twice Over in the North Carolina House of Representatives, 1876–1877," *NCHR* 61, no. 3 (July 1984): 344; Leonard Bernstein, "The Participation of Negro Delegates in the Constitutional Convention of 1868 in North Carolina," *Journal of Negro History* 34, no. 4 (October 1949): 391. The roll calls that record Carey's and Hodnett's votes can be found throughout the *Journal of the Constitutional Convention of the State of North-Carolina, at Its Session 1868* (Raleigh, NC: Joseph W. Holden, 1868). Carey would also serve in the state's 1875 Constitutional Convention.

49. Baggett, *Scalawags*, 190–91; Harris, *William Woods Holden*, 223–33; Allen W. Trelease, "Republican Reconstruction in North Carolina: A Roll-Call Analysis of the State House of Representatives, 1868–1870," *JSH* 42, no. 3 (August 1976): 321; R. D. W. Connor, *A Manual of North Carolina, Issued by the North Carolina Historical Commission, for the Use of Members of the General Assembly, Session 1913* (Raleigh, NC: E. M. Uzzell and Co., 1913), 475, 832. Joseph was the *Standard's* editor while his father served as interim governor and would again head the paper for a time in 1870. See Edgar E. Folk and Bynum Shaw, *W. W. Holden: A Political Biography* (Winston-Salem, NC: John F. Blair, 1982), 198, 206, 222.

50. Brown was also a surgeon who described his medical work for a national audience, submitting regular treatises to the *American Journal of the Medical Sciences*, among other publications. For examples, see Bedford Brown, "Case of Extensive Compound Fracture of the Cranium. Severe Laceration and Destruction of a Portion of the Brain, Followed by Fungus Cerebri, and Terminating in Recovery," *American Journal of the Medical Sciences* 39, no. 80 (October 1860): 399–403; Bedford Brown, "Some Remarks on the Adynamic Type of Remittent Fever and Its Treatment with Nitric Acid," *American Journal of the Medical Sciences* 39, no. 77 (January 1860): 43–51; Bedford Brown, "On the State of the Nutritive Functions during the Progress of Continued Fever," *American Journal of the Medical Sciences* 38, no. 75 (July 1859): 78–84.

51. Connor, *Manual of North Carolina*, 926–29; Houston G. Jones, "Bedford Brown: State Rights Unionist, Part I: The Senator," *NCHR* 32, no. 3 (July 1955): 321–45; Houston G. Jones, "Bedford Brown: State Rights Unionist, Part II: The Conciliator," *NCHR* 32, no. 4 (October 1955): 483–511.

52. *Report of the Joint Committee on Reconstruction*, 2:261–65, quote on 264.

53. Bradley, *Bluecoats and Tar Heels*, 182, 184, 200.

54. F. W. Liedtke to Lieut. H. R. Anderson, June 17, 1868, and F. W. Liedtke to Lieut. H. R. Anderson, June 19, 1868, both in Letters Sent book, 1868, Graham (Assistant Subassistant Commissioner), M1909, roll 18, BRFAL. Quote in the June 17 report. See exhibit G of the June 17 letter for Willis's affidavit. On Conservative efforts to disenfranchise African Americans through criminal convictions, see Pippa Holloway, *Living in Infamy: Felon Disfranchisement and the History of American Citizenship* (New York: Oxford University Press, 2014), chap. 2.

55. Frederick W. Liedtke to J. S. Griffith, July 5, 1867, Letters Sent and a Register of Letters Received, August 1866–December 1867, Graham (Assistant Subassistant Commissioner), M1909, roll 18, BRFAL.

56. Jonathan Worth to Thomas Settle, October 22, 1867, Jonathan Worth to John Kerr, January 1, 1868, and Jonathan Worth to B. S. Hedrick, January 8, 1868, all in *Correspondence of Jonathan Worth*, 2:1056, 1100–1102, 1120–23.

57. F. W. Liedtke to H. R. Anderson, June 17, 1868.

58. *Laws and Resolutions Passed by the General Assembly of the State of North Carolina, at the Special Session, Begun and Held in the City of Raleigh on the First of July, 1868* (Raleigh, NC: N. Paige, 1868), 92, 98, 107; *Public Laws of the State of North Carolina, Passed by the General Assembly at Its Session 1868-'69* (Raleigh, NC: M. S. Littlefield, 1869), 804; Trelease, "Republican Reconstruction in North Carolina," 320; Hamilton, *Reconstruction in North Carolina*, 351. Stephens would use the same appeal in communication with Albion Tourgée in an effort to have a number of Caswell Conservatives evicted from county offices in 1868. See J. W. Stephens to Albion W. Tourgée, August 25, 1868, document #875, AWTP. Thanks to an ambitious digitization project, images of Tourgée's papers may be found on the Chautauqua County Historical Society's website, at https://mcclurgmuseum.org

/collection/archives/albion_w_tourgee_papers/albion_w_tourgee_papers.html (accessed November 27, 2022).

59. Katherine Kerr Kendall, *Caswell County, 1777–1877: Historical Abstracts of Minutes of Caswell County, North Carolina* (Raleigh, NC: Multiple Images Press, 1976), 102.

CHAPTER THREE

1. This story is assembled from the following sources: Luther M. Carlton, "Assassination of John Walter Stephens," in *An Annual Publication of Historical Papers: Legal and Biographical Studies*, Series 2 (Durham, NC: Historical Society of Trinity College, 1898), 2–4; John W. Wheeler, *Reminiscences and Memoirs of North Carolina and Eminent North Carolinians* (Columbus, OH: Columbus Printing Works, 1884), 111; A. J. Stedman, *Murder and Mystery: History of the Life and Death of John W. Stephens, State Senator of North Carolina, from Caswell County* (Greensboro, NC: Patriot, 1870), 9–11; Copy of indictment of John W. Stephens in F. W. Liedtke to Liet. H. R. Anderson, June 17, 1868, exhibit A, in Letters Sent book, 1868, Graham (Assistant Subassistant Commissioner), M1909, roll 18, BRFAL. Stedman also includes a copy of the indictment and settlement. (My search at the Rockingham Judicial Center and in the Rockingham County court records held at the North Carolina State Archives failed to produce a surviving copy.)

2. Hyman Rubin III, *South Carolina Scalawags* (Columbia: University of South Carolina Press, 2006); James Alex Baggett, *The Scalawags: Southern Dissenters in the Civil War and Reconstruction* (Baton Rouge: Louisiana State University Press, 2003).

3. J. G. de Roulhac Hamilton, *Reconstruction in North Carolina* (New York: Columbia University Press, 1914), 258n4.

4. For a repetition of this tale, see *Papers of Randolph Abbott Shotwell*, 3 vols., ed. Joseph G. de Roulhac Hamilton with Rebecca Cameron, 3 vols. (Raleigh: North Carolina Historical Commission, 1929–36), 2:327.

5. On the evolution of popular perceptions of Longstreet, see William Garrett Piston, *Lee's Tarnished Lieutenant: James Longstreet and His Place in Southern History* (Athens: University of Georgia Press, 1987). On the elevation of Lee and Jackson, see Thomas L. Connelly, *The Marble Man: Robert E. Lee and His Image in American Society* (Baton Rouge: Louisiana State University Press, 1978); and Wallace Hettle, *Inventing Stonewall Jackson: A Civil War Hero in History and Memory* (Baton Rouge: Louisiana State University Press, 2011).

6. "Rockingham Court," *Greensboro Register*, July 7, 1869, 2.

7. Richard L. Zuber, *North Carolina during Reconstruction* (Raleigh, NC: Division of Archives and History, 1969), 23.

8. *Journal of the Senate of the General Assembly of the State of North Carolina, at Its Session of 1868* (Raleigh, NC: M. Paige, 1868), 58, 96, 126, 256–57, 260.

9. *Executive and Legislative Documents Laid before the General Assembly of North-Carolina* (Raleigh, NC: William E. Pell, 1869), document 21, 1–2; *Journal of the Senate of the General Assembly of the State of North Carolina, at Its Session of 1868–69* (Raleigh, NC: M. S. Littlefield, 1869), 235–37, 243–46, 608–11; *Read and Circulate!* (pamphlet, North Carolina, 1872?), 4–5, North Carolina Collection, UNC–Chapel Hill, located at Docsouth, http://docsouth.unc.edu/nc/readcirculate/readcirculate.html (accessed November 27, 2022); Hamilton, *Reconstruction in North Carolina*, 379.

10. Allen W. Trelease, "Republican Reconstruction in North Carolina: A Roll-Call Analysis of the State House of Representatives, 1868–1870," *JSH* 42, no. 3 (August 1976): 320; John

Herbert Roper Sr., "Ransack Roulhac and Racism: Joseph Grégoire de Roulhac Hamilton and Dunning's Questions of Institution Building and Jim Crow," in *The Dunning School: Historians, Race, and the Meaning of Reconstruction*, ed. John David Smith and J. Vincent Lowery (Lexington: University Press of Kentucky, 2013), 188–89; David Silkenat, *Moments of Despair: Suicide, Divorce, and Debt in Civil War Era North Carolina* (Chapel Hill: University of North Carolina Press, 2011), 169–72; Laura F. Edwards, *Gendered Strife and Confusion: The Political Culture of Reconstruction* (Urbana: University of Illinois Press, 1997), 53–54; Hamilton, *Reconstruction in North Carolina*, 351; Monroe N. Work et al., "Some Negro Members of Reconstruction Conventions and Legislatures and of Congress," *Journal of Negro History* 5, no. 1 (January 1920): 76.

11. *Journal of the Senate of the General Assembly of the State of North Carolina, at Its Session of 1868–69*, 37, 299, 360–61; *Journal of the Senate of the General Assembly of the State of North Carolina, at Its Session of 1869–70* (Raleigh, NC: M. S. Littlefield, 1870), 20, 24, 37, 50, 423.

12. Mark Wahlgren Summers, *The Ordeal of Reunion: A New History of Reconstruction* (Chapel Hill: University of North Carolina Press, 2014), 287–90; Richard Nelson Current, *Those Terrible Carpetbaggers* (New York: Oxford University Press, 1988), 211, 236; Hamilton, *Reconstruction in North Carolina*, 378–79, 430–32, 448–51; W. M. Shipp, J. B. Batchelor, and Jas. G. Martin, *Report of the Commission to Investigate Charges of Fraud and Corruption, under Act of Assembly, Session 1871-'72*, North Carolina General Assembly Document No. 11, Session 1871-'72 (Raleigh, NC: James H. Moore, 1872). On antebellum concerns about southern railroads and corrupt bargains, see John Majewski, *Modernizing a Slave Economy: The Economic Vision of the Confederate Nation* (Chapel Hill: University of North Carolina Press, 2009), chap. 3.

13. *Public Laws of the State of North Carolina, Passed by the General Assembly at the Sessions of 1866 '67* (Raleigh, NC: William E. Pell, 1867), 167–74.

14. Shipp, Batchelor, and Martin, *Report of the Commission to Investigate Charges of Fraud*, 515. It should be noted that this report of the loan came as hearsay from M. W. Churchill, who worked at the *Raleigh Standard*, and was made after Stephens's death to a rather partisan fraud investigation committee. Churchill claimed that Stephens pledged to redeem the loan with funds from his per diem but withdrew and spent that allowance as well.

15. *Journal of the Senate of the General Assembly of the State of North Carolina, at Its Session of 1868–69*, 58, 527; *Journal of the Senate of the General Assembly of the State of North Carolina, at Its Session of 1869–70*, 20, 49; *Public Laws of the State of North Carolina, Passed by the General Assembly at Its Session 1868-'69* (Raleigh, NC: M. S. Littlefield, 1869), 84.

16. J. W. Stephens to A. W. Tourgée, September 6, 1869, document #1194; J. W. Stephens to A. W. Tourgée, April 27, 1869, in Letterbook, document #1472, both in AWTP.

17. J. W. Stephens to [William W. Holden?], October 12, 1868, Reconstruction Papers, 1868–1973, NCSA; *Executive and Legislative Documents Laid before the General Assembly of North Carolina, Session 1869–70* (Raleigh, NC: Joseph W. Holden, 1870), document no. 3, 46.

18. J. W. Stephens to William W. Holden, June 20, 1868, in *The Papers of William Woods Holden*, 2 vols., ed. Horace W. Raper and Thornton W. Mitchell (Raleigh: North Carolina Division of Archives and History, 2000), 1:314–15.

19. For the earlier assessment, see Charles Wolff to [?], July 26, 1867, Letters Sent and a Register of Letters Received, August 1866–December 1867, Graham (Assistant Subassistant Commissioner), M1909, roll 18, BRFAL.

20. F. W. Liedtke to Jacob F. Chur, November 15, 1868, Letters Sent, March–December 1868, Graham (Assistant Subassistant Commissioner), M1909, roll 18, BRFAL.

21. John W. Stephens to William W. Holden, August 29, 1868, in *Papers of William Woods Holden*, 1:364–65.

22. Affidavit of Jacob Pass, before John W. Stephens, November 14, 1868, in *Papers of William Woods Holden*, 1:406.

23. Elaine Frantz Parsons, *Ku-Klux: The Birth of the Klan during Reconstruction* (Chapel Hill: University of North Carolina Press, 2016); Scott Reynolds Nelson, *Iron Confederacies: Southern Railways, Klan Violence, and Reconstruction* (Chapel Hill: University of North Carolina Press, 1999), chap. 5; Wyn Craig Wade, *The Fiery Cross: The Ku Klux Klan in America* (London: Simon and Schuster, 1987), esp. chaps. 1 and 2; Allen W. Trelease, *White Terror: The Ku Klux Klan Conspiracy and Southern Reconstruction* (Westport, CT: Greenwood Press, 1979); *Journal of the Senate of the General Assembly of the State of North Carolina, at Its Session of 1870–71* (Raleigh, NC: James H. Moore, 1871), 33.

24. 1860 Federal Population Census, Free Schedule for Caswell County, NC, M653 roll 891, NAA; Jeannine D. Whitlow, ed., *The Heritage of Caswell County, North Carolina* (Winston-Salem, NC: Hunter Publishing, 1985), 350–56.

25. John W. Moore, *Roster of North Carolina Troops in the War between the States*, 4 vols. (Raleigh, NC: Ash and Gatling, 1882), 3:153; 1870 Federal Population Census, Caswell County, NC, M593, roll 1128, NAA; Confederate Pension Rolls, Veterans and Widows, collection #CP-3_171, roll 171, roll description: City of Danville (surnames Co-Wi), Library of Virginia, Richmond. Historian William Powell lists a John G. Lea as donor of land for the New Hope Methodist Church and member of the Caswell Agricultural Society before the war, but given his age, this was an older relative: William Powell, *When the Past Refused to Die: A History of Caswell County, North Carolina, 1777–1977* (Durham, NC: Moore Publishing, 1977), 442, 475. The Klan leader should not be confused with another John G. Lea from Caswell—perhaps the same individual who donated the church land—who enlisted in Company A of the 13th North Carolina Infantry in April 1861, rose to the rank of sergeant, and was wounded at South Mountain: Moore, *Roster of North Carolina Troops*, 1:474.

26. Michael W. Fitzgerald, "Ex-Slaveholders and the Ku Klux Klan: Exploring the Motivations of Terrorist Violence," in *After Slavery: Race, Labor, and Citizenship in the Reconstruction South*, ed. Bruce E. Baker and Brian Kelly (Gainesville: University Press of Florida, 2013), 156.

27. A. W. Fisher, Circular of Detectives' Instructions, April 3, 1869, box 10, GASR, NCSA. For a summary of Holden's detectives program, see Stephen E. Massengill, "The Detectives of William W. Holden, 1869–1870," *NCHR* 62, no. 4 (October 1985): 448–87.

28. Detective Salary Account Sheet, May 28, 1869, and Account Sheet of Detectives' Expenses, 1869–1870, both in box 10, GASR.

29. R. H. Wray to A. W. Tourgée, December 9, 1868, Letterbook, document #1472, AWTP; "Rockingham Court," 2.

30. J. W. Stephens to A. W. Fisher, April 22, 1869; J. W. Stephens to William W. Holden, May 15, 1869; J. W. Stephens to W. W. Holden, June 1, 1869 (first quote); J. W. Stephens to W. W. Holden, July 12, 1869 (second quote); all in box 10, GASR.

31. Telegraph message from John W. Stephens to A. W. Fisher, May 28, 1869; J. W. Stephens to (A. W. Fisher?), May 24, 1869, quotes in the latter, underlined in the original, both in box 10, GASR.

32. For examples, see J. W. Stephens to W. W. Holden, July 12, 1869; J. W. Stephens to William W. Holden, May 15, 1869; J. W. Stephens to A. W. Fisher, April 22, 1869; quote in J. W. Stephens to (A. W. Fisher?), May 24, 1869; all in box 10, GASR.

33. Detective Salary Account Sheet, May 28, 1869, and Account Sheet of Detectives' Expenses, 1869–1870; Massengill, "Detectives of William W. Holden," 477–78. Stephens's death was the most likely reason no payments were issued for his work in 1870, especially if his widow failed to petition the state.

34. Stedman, *Murder and Mystery*, 35–36; "The State against F. A. Wiley," *Raleigh Weekly Standard*, August 31, 1870. The *Raleigh Standard* changed names throughout its print run (1834-1870). On the date ranges of the newspaper's various titles, see "The Weekly North-Carolina Standard (Raleigh, N.C.) 186?-1869," Library of Congress, Chronicling America, www.loc.gov/item/sn85042148/ (accessed November 28, 2022).

35. Diary of Jacob Doll, 1868–1871, box 1, folder 3, Jacob Doll Diaries, SHC. For examples of the rumor later appearing in print, see "Murder of J. W. Stephens," *Raleigh Semi-Weekly Sentinel*, May 25, 1870; "The Murder of Senator Stephen's [*sic*] Confirmed," *Raleigh Weekly Standard*, June 1, 1870; and Wheeler, *Reminiscences and Memoirs of North Carolina and Eminent North Carolinians*, 111.

36. JGLC.

37. "Murder of J. W. Stephens." See also "Meeting in Yanceyville," *Raleigh Semi-Weekly Sentinel*, May 28, 1870.

38. "Jacobin Clubs and Loyal Leagues," *Raleigh Semi-Weekly Sentinel*, May 14, 1870.

39. Trelease, *White Terror*, 195–97.

40. *Testimony Taken by the Joint Select Committee to Inquire into the Condition of Affairs in the Late Insurrectionary States*, vol. 2, North Carolina (Washington, DC: GPO, 1872), 250–51.

41. "Large Meeting at Yanceyville," *Raleigh Weekly Standard*, June 1, 1870; quote in "Rockingham Court," italics in the original.

42. *Argument in the Impeachment Trial of W. W. Holden, Governor of North Carolina* (Raleigh, NC: James H. Moore, 1871), 2405.

43. For examples, see Shawn Leigh Alexander, ed., *Reconstruction Violence and the Ku Klux Klan Hearings* (Boston: Bedford/St. Martin's, 2015), 80, 89; *Testimony Taken by the Joint Select Committee to Inquire into the Condition of Affairs in the Late Insurrectionary States*, vol. 5, South Carolina (Washington, DC: GPO, 1872), 1295, 1427–28, 1683; *Testimony Taken by the Joint Select Committee to Inquire into the Condition of Affairs in the Late Insurrectionary States*, vol. 8, Alabama (Washington, DC: GPO, 1872), 58, 158.

44. The body of literature on southerners' use of fire is substantial. Some good places to start include Albert G. Way, *Conserving Southern Longleaf: Herbert Stoddard and the Rise of Ecological Land Management* (Athens: University of Georgia Press, 2011), chap. 2; Jack Temple Kirby, *Mockingbird Song: Ecological Landscapes of the South* (Chapel Hill: University of North Carolina Press, 2008), chap. 3; Stephen J. Pyne, *Fire in America: A Cultural History of Wildland and Rural Fire* (Seattle: University of Washington Press, 1997), esp. 143–60; Michael Williams, *Americans and Their Forests: A Historical Geography* (Cambridge: Cambridge University Press, 1992), esp. part 2; and Carville Earle, "The Myth of the Southern Soil Miner: Macrohistory, Agricultural Innovation, and Environmental Change," in *The Ends of the Earth: Perspectives on Modern Environmental History*, ed. Donald Worster (New York: Cambridge University Press, 1988), 175–210.

45. "Letter from the Courthouse," *Danville Register*, October 5, 1870.

46. Catherine W. Bishir and Michael T. Southern, *A Guide to the Historic Architecture of Piedmont North Carolina*, Richard Hampton Jenrette Series in Architecture and Decorative Arts (Chapel Hill: University of North Carolina Press, 2003), 182–83; Ruth Little-Stokes, *An Inventory of Historic Architecture, Caswell County, North Carolina: The Built Environment*

of a Burley and Bright-Leaf Tobacco Economy (Yanceyville, NC: Caswell County Historical Association, 1979), 20–106; John Fraser Hart and Eugene Cotton Mather, "The Character of Tobacco Barns and Their Role in the Tobacco Economy of the United States," *Annals of the Association of American Geographers* 51, no. 3 (September 1961): 274, 288–93; William Tatham, *An Historical and Practical Essay on the Culture and Commerce of Tobacco* (London: Vernor and Hood, 1800), 29–34.

47. On the racial implications of tobacco work and culture, see Drew A. Swanson, *A Golden Weed: Tobacco and Environment in the Piedmont South* (New Haven, CT: Yale University Press, 2014), esp. chap. 5. On the destruction and vandalism of farm resources as a form of slave resistance, see Eugene Genovese, *The Political Economy of Slavery: Studies in the Economy and Society of the Slave South* (New York: Pantheon, 1961), part 2.

48. Erin Stewart Mauldin, *Unredeemed Land: An Environmental History of Civil War and Emancipation in the Cotton South* (New York: Oxford University Press, 2018); R. Douglas Hurt, *Agriculture and the Confederacy: Policy, Productivity, and Power in the Civil War South* (Chapel Hill: University of North Carolina Press, 2015); Lisa Brady, *War upon the Land: Military Strategy and the Transformation of Southern Landscapes during the American Civil War* (Athens: University of Georgia Press, 2012); Megan Kate Nelson, *Ruin Nation: Destruction and the American Civil War* (Athens: University of Georgia Press, 2012).

49. JGLC.

50. On Tourgée's military service, see Mark Elliott, *Color-Blind Justice: Albion Tourgée and the Quest for Racial Equality from the Civil War to* Plessy v. Ferguson (New York: Oxford University Press, 2006), chap. 4; and Albion W. Tourgée, *The Story of a Thousand* (Buffalo, NY: S. McGerald and Son, 1896). For Tourgée's thoughts on Sherman's and Sheridan's destructive campaigns, see Albion W. Tourgée, *The Veteran and His Pipe* (Chicago: Belford, Clarke and Co., 1888), 114–17.

51. Chris J. Hartley, *Stoneman's Raid, 1865* (Winston-Salem, NC: John F. Blair, 2010); John C. Inscoe and Gordon B. McKinney, *The Heart of Confederate Appalachia: Western North Carolina in the Civil War* (Chapel Hill: University of North Carolina Press, 2000), 243–57; Cornelia Phillips Spencer, *The Last Ninety Days of the War in North-Carolina* (New York: Watchman, 1866), 197.

52. Barton Myers, *Executing Daniel Bright: Race, Loyalty, and Guerrilla Violence in a Coastal Carolina Community, 1861–1865* (Baton Rouge: Louisiana State University Press, 2009), especially chap. 3.

53. Scott C. Cole, *34th Battalion Virginia Cavalry* (Lynchburg, VA: H. E. Howard, 1993), 64–65. See also William R. Trotter, *Bushwhackers: The Civil War in North Carolina; The Mountains* (Winston-Salem, NC: John F. Blair, 1991); Inscoe and McKinney, *Heart of Confederate Appalachia.*

54. These sorts of actions proved common in Kentucky's and Tennessee's burley tobacco belt in an episode known as the "black patch war," which took place during the first decade of the twentieth century. See Barbara Hahn, *Making Tobacco Bright: Creating an American Commodity, 1617–1937* (Baltimore, MD: Johns Hopkins University Press, 2011), 147–57; Christopher Waldrep, *Night Riders: Defending Community in the Black Patch, 1890–1915* (Durham, NC: Duke University Press, 1993); and Suzanne Marshall, *Violence in the Black Patch of Kentucky and Tennessee* (Columbia: University of Missouri Press, 1994). The most famous representation of plant bed scraping and arson in the black patch war is Robert Penn Warren's novel *Night Rider* (Boston: Houghton Mifflin, 1939).

55. William Faulkner, *The Hamlet* (New York: Random House, 1940).

56. Lisa Brady has made a version of this point for the war period in *War upon the Land*.

57. Scott Reynolds Nelson, "Red Strings and Half Brothers: Civil Wars in Alamance County, North Carolina, 1861–1871," in *Enemies of the Country: New Perspectives on Unionists in the Civil War South*, ed. John C. Inscoe and Robert C. Kenzer (Athens: University of Georgia Press, 2001), 37–53; Carole Watterson Troxler, "'To Look More Closely at the Man': Wyatt Outlaw, a Nexus of National, Local, and Personal History," *NCHR* 77, no. 4 (October 2000): 403–33; Nelson, *Iron Confederacies*, 100–4, 108.

58. Nelson, *Iron Confederacies*, 112; Otto H. Olsen, "The Ku Klux Klan: A Study in Reconstruction Politics and Propaganda," *NCHR* 39, no. 3 (July 1962): 355; Samuel A'Court Ashe, *History of North Carolina*, vol. 2 (Raleigh, NC: Edwards and Broughton, 1925), 1110; Hamilton, *Reconstruction in North Carolina*, 467.

59. Samuel B. McGuire, "'Rally Union Men in Defence of Your State!': Appalachian Militiamen in the Kirk-Holden War, 1870," *Appalachian Journal* 39, nos. 3/4 (Spring/Summer 2012): 296; Nelson, *Iron Confederacies*, 112–13; C. P. McTaggart to Col. S. B. Hayman, March 4, 1870, box 10, GASR, NCSA; *Message of the President of the United States, Communicating, in Further Compliance with the Resolution of the Senate of the 16th of December, 1870, Additional Information in Relation to the Existence of Disloyal Organizations in the State of North Carolina*, Senate Executive Document Number 16, Part 2, 41st Congress, 3rd Session, January 17, 1871, 13, 38–39, 59–61, quote on 38; Statement of James M. Stockard, n.d., document #1475, AWTP.

60. "The Attempt to Assassinate Senator Shoffner," *Raleigh Weekly Standard*, August 24, 1870; Mark L. Bradley, *Bluecoats and Tar Heels: Soldiers and Civilians in Reconstruction North Carolina* (Lexington: University Press of Kentucky, 2009), 212–13; Carole Watterson Troxler and William Murray Vincent, *Shuttle and Plow: A History of Alamance County, North Carolina* (n.p.: Alamance County Historical Association, 1999), 329; Trelease, *White Terror*, 203.

61. The bureau would limp along for two more years before Congress completely disbanded it in the summer of 1872, but it had been a shadow of its former self since the start of 1870. George R. Bentley, *A History of the Freedmen's Bureau* (New York: Octagon Books, 1970), 211–12.

62. *Message of the President of the United States, Communicating, in Compliance with the Resolution of the Senate of the 16th of December, 1870, Information in Relation to Outrages Committed by Disloyal Persons in North Carolina and Other Southern States*, Senate Executive Document Number 16, part 1, 41st Congress, 3rd Session, January 13, 1871, 6; *Message of the President of the United States*, January 17, 1871, 38–41, quote on 41; William Gillette, *Retreat from Reconstruction, 1869–1879* (Baton Rouge: Louisiana State University Press, 1979), 91; Ashe, *History of North Carolina*, 2:1111.

63. A Citizen of Caswell, "Letter from Yanceyville—Incidents Connected with the Death of John W. Stephens," *Raleigh Semi-Weekly Sentinel*, May 28, 1870; Carlton, "Assassination of John Walter Stephens," 5; Trelease, *White Terror*, 211.

64. J. W. Stephens to A. W. Tourgée, April 20, 1870, document #1270, AWTP.

65. "Jacobin Clubs and Loyal Leagues."

66. "Murder of J. W. Stephens." See also "Meeting in Yanceyville."

67. "Rumored Death of Mr. Stephens," *Raleigh Semi-Weekly Sentinel*, May 25, 1870.

68. "Large Meeting at Yanceyville."

69. For the definitive Conservative take, see Hamilton, *Reconstruction in North Carolina*, 339, 473; and for a more sympathetic treatment, see Trelease, *White Terror*, 192, 212–13. See also Massengill, "Detectives of William W. Holden," 478; and Ashe, *History of North Carolina*, 2:1111.

70. Carlton, "Assassination of John Walter Stephens," 5–6.

71. "State against F. A. Wiley." More descriptions of the witness testimony are found in the next chapter of this book.

72. "State against F. A. Wiley"; *Impeachment Trial of W. W. Holden*, 2359.

73. "State against F. A. Wiley"; Stedman, *Murder and Mystery*, 29–31.

74. May 21 and 22, 1870, entries, Diary of Jacob Doll, 1868–1871, box 1, folder 3, Jacob Doll Diaries.

CHAPTER FOUR

1. On the duties, function, and evolution of southern coroners and their juries, see the fascinating web project *CSI: Dixie*, an eHistory University of Georgia project created by Stephen Berry, at https://csidixie.org/ (accessed November 27, 2022).

2. Coroner's Court of Inquest in the case of John W. Stephens, May 26, 1870, reprinted in A. J. Stedman, *Murder and Mystery: History of the Life and Death of John W. Stephens, State Senator of North Carolina, from Caswell County* (Greensboro, NC: Patriot, 1870), 20–27.

3. "Rumored Death of Mr. Stephens," *Raleigh Semi-Weekly Sentinel*, May 25, 1870.

4. "The Kuklux Organization," *Raleigh Weekly Standard*, June 1, 1870.

5. Albion Tourgée to Joseph C. Abbott, May 24, 1870, in *Undaunted Radical: The Selected Writings and Speeches of Albion W. Tourgée*, ed. Mark Elliott and John David Smith (Baton Rouge: Louisiana State University Press, 2010), 47–51.

6. "Murder of J. W. Stephens," *Raleigh Semi-Weekly Sentinel*, May 25, 1870.

7. A Citizen of Caswell, "Letter from Yanceyville—Incidents Connected with the Death of John W. Stephens," *Raleigh Semi-Weekly Sentinel*, May 28, 1870, first quote; "Who Killed Stephens," *Raleigh Semi-Weekly Sentinel*, June 1, 1870, second quote, italics in the original.

8. Yanceyville, "Affairs in Caswell," *Raleigh Semi-Weekly Sentinel*, June 1, 1870.

9. "Meeting in Yanceyville," *Raleigh Semi-Weekly Sentinel*, May 28, 1870.

10. "Official Turpitude," *Raleigh Semi-Weekly Sentinel*, June 8, 1870, first quote; Yanceyville, "Affairs in Caswell," second quote. The public notice is also reproduced in Stedman, *Murder and Mystery*, 39–40.

11. "The Murder of Senator Stephen's [*sic*] Confirmed," *Raleigh Weekly Standard*, June 1, 1870.

12. "J. W. Stephens," *Greensboro Patriot*, May 26, 1870, quote; "Murder of J. W. Stephens."

13. "Lex Talionis," and G. D. H., "Radicalism Doomed," both in *Greensboro Patriot*, May 26, 1870.

14. On Stedman's career, see David Winifred Gaddy, "Stedman, Andrew Jackson," in *Dictionary of North Carolina Biography*, 6 vols., ed. William S. Powell (Chapel Hill: University of North Carolina Press, 1994), 5:430–31.

15. Stedman, *Murder and Mystery*, 5. For Tourgée's contentious relationship with the *Patriot*, see Richard Nelson Current, *Those Terrible Carpetbaggers* (New York: Oxford University Press, 1988), 62–64, 199–200.

16. Stedman, *Murder and Mystery*, 7–18.

17. Stedman, *Murder and Mystery*, 27, 37–39.

18. *Trial of William Woods Holden*, Appendix No. 2 (1870), 16, 29, booklet, Reconstruction Papers, 1868–1973, NCSA.

19. "A Proclamation by His Excellency, the Governor of North Carolina," June 6, 1870, reprinted in W. W. Holden, *Answer to the Articles of Impeachment* (Raleigh, NC: n.p., 1870),

17–19. This Library of Congress holding is available digitally at https://babel.hathitrust .org/cgi/pt?id=loc.ark:/13960/t1khovs5k&view=1up&seq=5 (accessed November 27, 2022).

20. Holden, *Answer to the Articles of Impeachment*, 20.

21. No title, *Greensboro Republican*, July 14, 1870.

22. Steven E. Nash, *Reconstruction's Ragged Edge: The Politics of Postwar Life in the Southern Mountains* (Chapel Hill: University of North Carolina Press, 2016), 133–35; Samuel B. McGuire, "The Making of a Black Militia Company: New Bern Troops in the Kirk-Holden War, 1870," *NCHR* 91, no. 3 (July 2014): 288–322; Samuel B. McGuire, "'Rally Union Men in Defence of Your State!': Appalachian Militiamen in the Kirk-Holden War, 1870," *Appalachian Journal* 39, nos. 3/4 (Spring/Summer 2012): 296. Mark L. Bradley has painstakingly reconstructed Holden's decision-making process and the movement of militia and federal troops during this "Kirk-Holden War" in *Bluecoats and Tar Heels: Soldiers and Civilians in Reconstruction North Carolina* (Lexington: University Press of Kentucky, 2009), 223–33.

23. Gordon B. McKinney, *Southern Mountain Republicans, 1865–1900: Politics and the Appalachian Community* (Chapel Hill: University of North Carolina Press, 1978), esp. chap. 2; McGuire, "Rally Union Men," 294–323; John C. Inscoe and Gordon B. McKinney, *The Heart of Confederate Appalachia: Western North Carolina in the Civil War* (Chapel Hill: University of North Carolina Press, 2000), 134–36, 242–43. It must be noted that Inscoe and McKinney conclude that western North Carolina was not as "Unionist" as often claimed: the region's opposition to the war stemmed more from internal state divisions than from any abiding love for the Union. McGuire's articles are the most thorough examination of the composition of Kirk's force. Also worth noting are two very good master's theses: Jim D. Brisson, "The Kirk-Holden War of 1870 and the Failure of Reconstruction in North Carolina" (MA thesis, University of North Carolina Wilmington, 2010); and Bradley David Proctor, "The Reconstruction of White Supremacy: The Ku Klux Klan in Piedmont, North Carolina, 1868–1872" (MA thesis, University of North Carolina at Chapel Hill, 2009).

24. Michael C. Hardy, *Kirk's Civil War Raids along the Blue Ridge* (Charleston, SC: History Press, 2018); Noel C. Fisher, *War at Every Door: Partisan Politics and Guerrilla Violence in East Tennessee, 1860–1869* (Chapel Hill: University of North Carolina Press, 1997), 68, 87; Nash, *Reconstruction's Ragged Edge*, 22; Phillip Shaw Paludan, *Victims: A True Story of the Civil War*, 7th ed. (Knoxville: University of Tennessee Press, 2008), 102, 108; Inscoe and McKinney, *Heart of Confederate Appalachia*, 273–74.

25. McGuire, "Rally Union Men," 308–14; J. G. de Roulhac Hamilton, *Reconstruction in North Carolina* (New York: Columbia University Press, 1914), 496–533; *Message of the President of the United States, Communicating, in Further Compliance with the Resolution of the Senate of the 16th of December, 1870, Additional Information in Relation to the Existence of Disloyal Organizations in the State of North Carolina*, Senate Executive Document Number 16, Part 2, 41st Congress, 3rd Session, January 17, 1871, quote on 27; "A Michigander on Kirk," *Greensboro Patriot*, September 8, 1870.

26. *The Correspondence of Jonathan Worth*, 2 vols., ed. Joseph G. de Roulhac Hamilton (Raleigh, NC: Edwards and Broughton, 1909), 2:887n1; John W. Moore, *Roster of North Carolina Troops in the War between the States*, 4 vols. (Raleigh, NC: Ash and Gatling, 1882), 1:480; *Message of the President of the United States, Communicating, in Compliance with the Resolution of the Senate of the 16th of December, 1870, Information in Relation to Outrages Committed by Disloyal Persons in North Carolina and other Southern States*, Senate Executive Document Number 16, part 1, 41st Congress, 3rd Session, January 13, 1871, 10; "The Habeas Corpus Cases," *Raleigh Weekly Standard*, August 24, 1870.

27. *Trial of William Woods Holden*, Appendix No. 2, 32.

28. Luther M. Carlton, "Assassination of John Walter Stephens," in *An Annual Publication of Historical Papers: Legal and Biographical Studies*, Series 2 (Durham, NC: Historical Society of Trinity College, 1898), 10.

29. JGLC, 7. A transcript of the confession may also be found online at Civil War Era NC, https://cwnc.omeka.chass.ncsu.edu/items/show/22 (accessed November 27, 2022).

30. Scott Reynolds Nelson, *Iron Confederacies: Southern Railways, Klan Violence, and Reconstruction* (Chapel Hill: University of North Carolina Press, 1999), 105–8, 113–14; Stephen E. Massengill, "The Detectives of William W. Holden, 1869–1870," *NCHR* 62, no. 4 (October 1985): 459–60.

31. "Jacobin Clubs," *Raleigh Sentinel*, May 4, 1870.

32. Nash, *Reconstruction's Ragged Edge*, 135; Bradley, *Bluecoats and Tar Heels*, 226; Hamilton, *Reconstruction in North Carolina*, 524.

33. *Journal of the Constitutional Convention of the State of North-Carolina, at Its Session 1868* (Raleigh, NC: Joseph W. Holden, 1868), 224, quote on 229.

34. *Speech of Hon. James H. Harris on the Militia Bill, Delivered in the North Carolina House of Representatives Monday, January 17th, 1870* (Raleigh, NC: Raleigh Standard, 1870), North Carolina Collection, University of North Carolina at Chapel Hill, available online at https://archive.org/details/speechofhonjames00harr/page/n1/mode/2up (accessed November 27, 2022).

35. "Habeas Corpus Cases"; numerous 1868 party campaign flyers and tickets located in Reconstruction Papers, 1868–1973, NCSA; Bradley, *Bluecoats and Tar Heels*, 227–29; James Alex Baggett, *The Scalawags: Southern Dissenters in the Civil War and Reconstruction* (Baton Rouge: Louisiana State University Press, 2003), 89–90.

36. Otto H. Olsen, "North Carolina: An Incongruous Presence," in *Reconstruction and Redemption in the South*, ed. Otto H. Olsen (Baton Rouge: Louisiana State University Press, 1980), 182; Gregory P. Downs, *Declarations of Dependence: The Long Reconstruction of Popular Politics in the South, 1861–1908* (Chapel Hill: University of North Carolina Press, 2011), 125; *Trial of William Woods Holden*, Appendix No. 2, 13–17; quote in "Habeas Corpus Cases."

37. Nash, *Reconstruction's Ragged Edge*, 135; Bradley, *Bluecoats and Tar Heels*, 232; William Gillette, *Retreat from Reconstruction, 1869–1879* (Baton Rouge: Louisiana State University Press, 1979), 91–92; *Trial of William Woods Holden*, Appendix No. 2, 36–38.

38. State v. F. A. Wiley and others, 64 NC 821, 1870 WL 1889 (NC), NC 1870.

39. *State v. F. A. Wiley*; *Journal of the Senate of the General Assembly of the State of North Carolina, at Its Session of 1870–71* (Raleigh, NC: James H. Moore, 1871), 35; quotes in "Habeas Corpus Cases." This article is divided into two sections, each with the same title, and located on the same page of the newspaper. The last two men were likely S. P. Hill and Nathaniel Roan, among the Caswell men arrested by Kirk.

40. Unless otherwise noted, the details of the hearing that follow come from a transcription of the trial by a reporter for the *Raleigh Weekly Standard*, published as "The State against F. A. Wiley," in the *Raleigh Weekly Standard*, August 31, 1870. For the list of the coroner's inquest witnesses, see Stedman, *Murder and Mystery*, 20. Felix Roan was the sole defendant who did not testify in that inquiry.

41. William C. Harris, *William Woods Holden: Firebrand of North Carolina Politics* (Baton Rouge: Louisiana State University Press, 1987), 296.

42. A transcript of the earlier testimony is found in Stedman, *Murder and Mystery*, 22.

43. "Kirk's Prisoners," *Greensboro Patriot*, August 25, 1870.

44. Details of the decision found in *State v. F. A. Wiley*; and "State vs. F. A. Wiley and Others," *Raleigh Weekly Standard*, September 7, 1870. Quotes in both, punctuation from the former.

45. JGLC.

46. Otto H. Olsen, *Carpetbagger's Crusade: The Life of Albion Winegar Tourgée* (Baltimore, MD: Johns Hopkins Press, 1965), 169.

47. *Message of the President of the United States*, January 13, 1871; *Message of the President of the United States*, January 17, 1871; William A. Blair, *The Record of Murders and Outrages: Racial Violence and the Fight over Truth at the Dawn of Reconstruction* (Chapel Hill: University of North Carolina Press, 2021), 39–40. On Tourgée's role in stimulating this investigation, see Albion Tourgée to Joseph C. Abbott, May 24, 1870, in *Undaunted Radical: The Selected Writings and Speeches of Albion W. Tourgée*, ed. Mark Elliott and John David Smith (Baton Rouge: Louisiana State University Press, 2010), 47, 51; Carolyn Karcher, introduction to *Bricks without Straw: A Novel*, by Albion W. Tourgée, ed. Carolyn L. Karcher (Durham, NC: Duke University Press, 2009), 24.

48. *Message of the President of the United States*, January 13, 1871, 10; *Message of the President of the United States*, January 17, 1871, quote on 2.

49. *Message of the President of the United States*, January 17, 1871, 23, 59.

50. *Message of the President of the United States*, January 17, 1871, 5–6, quote on 6.

51. *Message of the President of the United States*, January 17, 1871, 8–9, quote on 6.

52. *Message of the President of the United States*, January 17, 1871, 13–14. This group of deponents specifically focused on outrages in Alamance County.

53. *Message of the President of the United States*, January 17, 1871, 13–14, 59, quotes on 13 and 14.

54. Kidada E. Williams, *I Saw Death Coming: A History of Terror and Survival in the War against Reconstruction* (New York: Bloomsbury, 2023); Kidada E. Williams, *They Left Great Marks on Me: African American Testimonies of Racial Violence from Emancipation to World War I* (New York: New York University Press, 2012).

55. *Message of the President of the United States*, January 17, 1871, 2.

56. *Message of the President of the United States*, January 13, 1871, 6, 10.

57. *Message of the President of the United States*, January 13, 1871, 6, first two quotes on 10, 11; *Message of the President of the United States*, January 17, 1871, 18–20, 29, quote on 23.

58. *Message of the President of the United States*, January 17, 1871, 23–27, quotes on 25, 27.

59. *Message of the President of the United States*, January 13, 1871, 11.

60. *Message of the President of the United States*, January 17, 1871, 61.

61. Bradley, *Bluecoats and Tar Heels*, 229–30, quote on 229; Hamilton, *Reconstruction in North Carolina*, 535; Elizabeth Balanoff, "Negro Legislators in the North Carolina General Assembly, July, 1868–February, 1872," *NCHR* 49, no. 1 (January 1972): 25.

62. *Rules for the Government of the Impeachment Trial*, North Carolina General Assembly Document 22, Session 1870-'71 (Raleigh, NC: James H. Moore, 1871), 3; *Proceedings of Impeachment*, North Carolina General Assembly Document 23, Session 1870-'71 (Raleigh, NC: James H. Moore, 1871), 2–4; *Journal of the Senate of the General Assembly of the State of North Carolina, at Its Session of 1870–71*, 187; *Trial of William Woods Holden*, Appendix No. 2; Allen W. Trelease, "Republican Reconstruction in North Carolina: A Roll-Call Analysis of the State House of Representatives, 1868–1870," *JSH* 42, no. 3 (August 1976): 321; Edgar E. Folk and Bynum Shaw, *W. W. Holden: A Political Biography* (Winston-Salem, NC: John F. Blair, 1982), 222; Deborah Beckel, *Radical Reform: Interracial Politics in Post-emancipation*

North Carolina (Charlottesville: University of Virginia Press, 2011), 76. (Confusingly, despite Joseph Holden's resignation, he was still listed as Speaker of the House in the *Proceedings of Impeachment* document.)

63. Harris, *William Woods Holden*, 302–8.

64. Hinton Rowan Helper, *The Negroes in Negroland; the Negroes in America; and Negroes Generally* (New York: G. W. Carleton, 1868), iii. On Merrimon's critiques of Confederate action in western North Carolina, see Paludan, *Victims*, 130.

65. *Argument in the Impeachment Trial of W. W. Holden, Governor of North Carolina* (Raleigh, NC: James H. Moore, 1871), 2359.

66. *Impeachment Trial of W. W. Holden*, 83, 2358–60, quote on 83 (the publication contains gaps in its pagination).

67. Holden, *Answer to the Articles of Impeachment*.

68. *Impeachment Trial of W. W. Holden*, 2501, quote on 2504.

69. *Impeachment Trial of W. W. Holden*, quote on 2564; Harris, *William Woods Holden*, 302–8; *Proceedings of Impeachment*, 3; R. D. W. Connor, *A Manual of North Carolina, Issued by the North Carolina Historical Commission, for the Use of Members of the General Assembly, Session 1913* (Raleigh, NC: E. M. Uzzell and Co., 1913), 475.

70. *Public Laws and Resolutions, Together with the Private Laws, of the State of North Carolina, Passed by the General Assembly at Its Session 1872–73* (Raleigh, NC: Stone and Uzzell, 1873), 298–300, quote on 299. For debates on the amnesty, see *Journal of the House of Representatives of the General Assembly of the State of North Carolina, at Its Session of 1872–73* (Raleigh, NC: Stone and Uzzell, 1873), 551–55; and *Journal of the Senate of the General Assembly of the State of North Carolina, at Its Session of 1872–73* (Raleigh, NC: Stone and Uzzell, 1873), 233–35, 498–99.

71. *Journal of the House of Representatives of the General Assembly of the State of North Carolina, at Its Session of 1874–75* (Raleigh, NC: Josiah Turner, 1875), 113–14, quote on 113 (Carey's name was spelled "Cary" in the journal); Olsen, *Carpetbagger's Crusade*, 186–87; Otto H. Olsen, "The Ku Klux Klan: A Study in Reconstruction Politics and Propaganda," *NCHR* 39, no. 3 (July 1962): 362.

CHAPTER FIVE

1. Eric Foner, *Reconstruction: America's Unfinished Revolution, 1863–1877* (New York: Harper and Row, 1988), 441.

2. R. D. W. Connor, *A Manual of North Carolina, Issued by the North Carolina Historical Commission, for the Use of Members of the General Assembly, Session 1913* (Raleigh, NC: E. M. Uzzell and Co., 1913), 546; Frenise A. Logan, "Black and Republican: Vicissitudes of a Minority Twice Over in the North Carolina House of Representatives, 1876–1877," *NCHR* 61, no. 3 (July 1984): 344.

3. Gregory P. Downs, *Declarations of Dependence: The Long Reconstruction of Popular Politics in the South, 1861–1908* (Chapel Hill: University of North Carolina Press, 2011), 126, 131–32; Paul Yandle, "Different Colored Currents of the Sea: Reconstruction North Carolina, Mutuality, and the Political Roots of Jim Crow, 1872–1875," in *North Carolinians in the Era of the Civil War and Reconstruction*, ed. Paul D. Escott (Chapel Hill: University of North Carolina Press, 2008), 230; John W. Wertheimer, *Law and Society in the South: A History of North Carolina Court Cases* (Lexington: University Press of Kentucky, 2009), 34; Heather Cox

Richardson, *The Death of Reconstruction: Race, Labor, and Politics in the Post–Civil War North, 1865–1901* (Cambridge, MA: Harvard University Press, 2001), 142; Otto H. Olsen, "North Carolina: An Incongruous Presence," in *Reconstruction and Redemption in the South*, ed. Otto H. Olsen (Baton Rouge: Louisiana State University Press, 1980), 156–201; Allen W. Trelease, "Who Were the Scalawags?," in *Reconstruction: An Anthology of Revisionist Writings*, ed. Kenneth M. Stampp and Leon F. Litwack (Baton Rouge: Louisiana State University Press, 1969), quote on 321. For a detailed yet clear summary of the long transition to Democratic dominance in the state and its subsequent uneasy reign, see Paul D. Escott, *Many Excellent People: Power and Privilege in North Carolina, 1850–1900* (Chapel Hill: University of North Carolina Press, 1985), 163–95.

4. Steven Hahn, *A Nation under Our Feet: Black Political Struggles in the Rural South from Slavery to the Great Migration* (Cambridge, MA: Belknap Press, 2003), 402–4; Jane Dailey, "Deference and Violence in the Postbellum Urban South: Manners and Massacres in Danville, Virginia," *JSH* 63, no. 3 (August 1997): 553–90; James Tice Moore, *Two Paths to the New South: The Virginia Debt Controversy, 1870–1883* (Lexington: University Press of Kentucky, 1974); Jack P. Maddex Jr., *The Virginia Conservatives, 1867–1879: A Study in Reconstruction Politics* (Chapel Hill: University of North Carolina Press, 1970).

5. On the evolution of attempts at interracial politics in the state after the war, see Deborah Beckel, *Radical Reform: Interracial Politics in Post-emancipation North Carolina* (Charlottesville: University of Virginia Press, 2011). For the Farmers' Alliance and populism in North Carolina, see Charles Postel, *The Populist Vision* (New York: Oxford University Press, 2007), 51–53, 197–200; Elizabeth Saunders, *Roots of Reform: Farmers, Workers, and the American State, 1877–1917* (Chicago: University of Chicago Press, 1999), 43, 50, 124, 127; Lala Carr Steelman, *The North Carolina Farmers' Alliance: A Political History, 1887–1893* (Greenville, NC: East Carolina University Publications, 1985); Dwight B. Billings Jr., *Planters and the Making of a "New South": Class, Politics, and Development in North Carolina, 1865–1900* (Chapel Hill: University of North Carolina Press, 1979), chap. 8; and Robert C. McMath Jr., *Populist Vanguard: A History of the Southern Farmers' Alliance* (Chapel Hill: University of North Carolina Press, 1975), 38–40, 147–50. On the racial tensions that accompanied early regional efforts at prohibition, see Richard F. Hamm, "The Killing of John R. Moffett and the Trial of J. T. Clark: Race, Prohibition, and Politics in Danville, 1887–1893," *Virginia Magazine of History and Biography* 101, no. 3 (July 1993): 375–404.

6. On the organization and methods of the committee, see *Report of the Joint Select Committee to Inquire into the Condition of Affairs in the Late Insurrectionary States*, 13 vols. (Washington, DC: GPO, 1872), 1:1–3. (Vols. 2 through 13 are titled *Testimony Taken by the Joint Select Committee to Inquire into the Condition of Affairs in the Late Insurrectionary States.*)

7. Richardson, *Death of Reconstruction*, quote on 91–92; Andrew F. Lang, *In the Wake of War: Military Occupation, Emancipation, and Civil War America* (Baton Rouge: Louisiana State University Press, 2017), 218–19.

8. For examples, see *Testimony Taken by the Joint Select Committee to Inquire into the Condition of Affairs in the Late Insurrectionary States*, vol. 2, *North Carolina* (Washington, DC: GPO, 1872), 103–4, 143, 242, 390.

9. *Testimony Taken by the Joint Select Committee*, 2:250–51.

10. *Testimony Taken by the Joint Select Committee*, 2:143.

11. Eric Foner, *Forever Free: The Story of Emancipation and Reconstruction* (New York: Knopf, 2005), 146–47, 173.

12. Richard Nelson Current, *Those Terrible Carpetbaggers* (New York: Oxford University Press, 1988), 65.

13. Henry Churton [Albion W. Tourgée], *Toinette: A Novel* (New York: J. B. Ford, 1874).

14. The most detailed study of Adaline Patillo is Naurice Frank Woods Jr., "Adaline and the Judge: An Ex-slave Girl's Journey with Albion W. Tourgée," *Elon Law Review* 5, no. 1 (July 2013): 199–222. Woods is a descendant of Adaline Patillo and ascribes the adoption to charitable notions on Tourgée's part. See also Mark Elliott, *Color-Blind Justice: Albion Tourgée and the Quest for Racial Equality from the Civil War to Plessy v. Ferguson* (New York: Oxford University Press, 2006), 136–37; Current, *Those Terrible Carpetbaggers*, 196–98, quote from the *Raleigh Sentinel* on 197; and Otto H. Olsen, "The Ku Klux Klan: A Study in Reconstruction Politics and Propaganda," *NCHR* 39, no. 3 (July 1962): 346. Intriguingly, Albert Patillo wrote to the Graham Freedmen's Bureau agent in July 1867 with a "request to return to him a col. girl that left his house." On August 8 he informed the agent that the runaway, perhaps Adaline, had "returned to him." See notes on pages 168 and 169 in the register of letters received section of Letters Sent and a Register of Letters Received, August 1866–December 1867, Graham (Assistant Subassistant Commissioner), M1909, roll 18, BRFAL.

15. J. W. Stephens to A. W. Tourgée, May 1, 1869, in Letterbook, document #1472; J. W. Stephens to A. W. Tourgée, September 6, 1869, document #1194, both in AWTP.

16. See throughout Woods, "Adaline and the Judge"; Elliott, *Color-Blind Justice*, 136–37; Current, *Those Terrible Carpetbaggers*, 196–98, quote from the *Raleigh Sentinel* on 197; Olsen, "Ku Klux Klan," 346.

17. See throughout Churton [Tourgée], *Toinette*.

18. Carolyn L. Karcher, introduction to *Bricks without Straw: A Novel*, by Albion W. Tourgée, ed. Carolyn L. Karcher (Durham, NC: Duke University Press, 2009), 29; Carolyn L. Karcher, *A Refugee from His Race: Albion W. Tourgée and His Fight against White Supremacy* (Chapel Hill: University of North Carolina Press, 2016), quote on 6. Lest too much be made of the Stowe comparison, later critics also hailed Thomas Dixon's *The Leopard's Spots* in the same manner. See Raymond A. Cook, *Thomas Dixon* (New York: Twayne, 1974), 66–67.

19. Albion W. Tourgée, *A Fool's Errand: A Novel of the South during Reconstruction*, ed. George M. Frederickson (New York: Harper and Row, 1966), see chap. 30, "A Thrice-Told Tale," 205–23, for the extended treatment of Walters's death.

20. Tourgée, *Fool's Errand*, 121–23, 205–23.

21. David W. Blight, *Race and Reunion: The Civil War in American Memory* (Cambridge, MA: Belknap Press, 2001), 221.

22. W. H. Stephens to A. W. Tourgée, October 21, 1872, document #1633; Statement of James M. Stockard, n.d., document #1475; W. H. Stephens to A. W. Tourgée, September 5, 1870; M. F. Stephens to A. W. Tourgée, July [?], 1870; the last two in Letterbook, document #1472, all four in AWTP. Incidentally, it seems likely that Fannie Stephens received at least some portion of the senator's life insurance policy. The 1870 census recorded her personal estate (under her first name, Martha) as worth a substantial $10,200. William remained living in her household a few months after the murder, his profession given as a "tobacconist." See 1870 Federal Population Census, Caswell County, NC, M593, roll 1128, NAA.

23. Affidavit of Patsie Burton before J. G. Hester as to Murder of J. W. Stephens, December 12, 1872, document #1639, AWTP. See also Sworn Statement of J. G. Hester, December 14, 1872, document #1640, AWTP. Otto Olsen and other historians drawing on his account give Patsie's last name as "Barton," but Tourgée recorded it as "Burton." Not only was Burton a

common Caswell County surname, but the 1870 census lists a twenty-three-year-old black woman, "Patsy Burton," who lived near Iverson Oliver. See 1870 Federal Population Census, Caswell County. For her part, Patsie signed the affidavit with an X, likely indicating her illiteracy and shedding no light on her preferred spelling.

24. Affidavit of Patsie Burton.

25. Tourgée, *Fool's Errand*, 252.

26. Tourgée, *Bricks without Straw*.

27. Karcher, *Refugee from His Race*, 6; Otto H. Olsen, introduction to *The Invisible Empire*, by Albion Winegar Tourgée (Baton Rouge: Louisiana State University Press, 1989), 1–5, 8–9; Tourgée, *Fool's Errand*, quotes on 252.

28. A partial list of Tourgée's books includes *Figs and Thistles: A Romance of the Western Reserve* (New York: Fords, Howard, and Hulbert, 1879); *A Royal Gentleman, and 'Zouri's Christmas* (New York: Fords, Howard, and Hulbert, 1881); *John Eax and Mamelon, or, The South without the Shadow* (New York: Fords, Howard, and Hulbert, 1882); *Hot Plowshares: A Novel* (New York: Fords, Howard, and Hulbert, 1883); and *An Appeal to Caesar* (New York: Fords, Howard, and Hulbert, 1884).

29. Elliott, *Color-Blind Justice*, 313–14, chap. 9; Karcher, *Refugee from His Race*, chap. 6; Olsen, introduction to *The Invisible Empire*, 8–9.

30. William L. Royall, *A Reply to "A Fool's Errand, by One of the Fools"* (New York: E. J. Hale and Son, 1880), 32–35, quote on 3.

31. "Charles Oscar Beasley," *Encyclopedia of Pennsylvania Biography*, vol. 15, ed. Thomas L. Montgomery (New York: Lewis Historical, 1924), 341; Charles Oscar Beasley, *Those American R's: Rule, Ruin, Restoration* (Philadelphia: Edward E. Wensley and Co., 1882). Like the initial edition of *A Fool's Errand*, the novel was published anonymously, the author listed tongue-in-cheek as "one who has been R'd."

32. Beasley, *Those American R's*, 174.

33. Beasley, *Those American R's*, 243–45.

34. Steven E. Nash, *Reconstruction's Ragged Edge: The Politics of Postwar Life in the Southern Mountains* (Chapel Hill: University of North Carolina Press, 2016), 112, 129, 148; Archibald Henderson, *North Carolina: The Old North State and the New*, 2 vols. (Chicago: Lewis Publishing Co., 1941), 2:335; *Papers of Randolph Abbott Shotwell*, 3 vols., ed. Joseph G. de Roulhac Hamilton with Rebecca Cameron (Raleigh: North Carolina Historical Commission, 1929–36), quotes in 2:327, 333, and 323.

35. John H. Wheeler, *Reminiscences and Memoirs of North Carolina and Eminent North Carolinians* (Columbus, OH: Columbus Printing Works, 1884), 110–11.

36. Jerome Dowd, *Sketches of Prominent Living North Carolinians* (Raleigh, NC: Edwards and Broughton, 1888); *Cyclopedia of Eminent and Representative Men of the Carolinas of the Nineteenth Century*, 2 vols. (Madison, WI: Brant and Fuller, 1892), vol. 2 focuses on North Carolina.

37. Luther M. Carlton, "Assassination of John Walter Stephens," in *An Annual Publication of Historical Papers: Legal and Biographical Studies*, Series 2 (Durham, NC: Historical Society of Trinity College, 1898), 2. For Carlton's relation to Stephens and publication of the Wake Forest essay, see Tom Henderson, "Murder of 'Chicken' Stephens," *The State* 6, no. 43 (March 25, 1939): 9.

38. Carlton, "Assassination of John Walter Stephens," 5.

39. Carlton, "Assassination of John Walter Stephens," 11–12.

40. Monroe Oliver and Wife and Others v. F. A. Wiley, Ex'r and H. F. Brandon, adm'r., 75 NC 320, 1876 WL 2802, June 1876. Perhaps suggesting a pattern of behavior, Wiley had been caught up in a similar suit in the late 1860s. In that instance he had been found guilty, and the court declared his management of the estate so poor as to be criminally suspect, stating that his actions displayed "gross negligence." See Franklin A. Wiley, Ex'r v. John H. Wiley, and Others, Phil.Law 131, 61 NC 131, 1867 WL 1319 (NC), January 1867; and Franklin A. Wiley, Ex'r v. John H. Wiley and Others, 63 NC 182, 1869 WL 1382 (NC), January 1869, quote in the latter.

41. "Murder Will Out," *Raleigh Signal*, December 10, 1891 (the article was also reprinted in the *Signal* on March 24, 1892, and March 31, 1892); Carlton, "Assassination of John Walter Stephens," 11; Henderson, "Murder of 'Chicken' Stephens," 19, 24.

42. "Murder Will Out." Unless otherwise noted, the details and quotes in the following paragraphs are drawn from this article.

43. It is worth noting that Roan's confession left out many of the names included in the Burton affidavit upon which Tourgée relied. Neither Mitchell nor Richmond appeared as participants in Burton's account, and she listed "Capt. Roan" rather than Felix Roan. (Burton did claim that she could not make out one of the names that Wiley mentioned to Oliver.)

44. David Zucchino, *Wilmington's Lie: The Murderous Coup of 1898 and the Rise of White Supremacy* (New York: Atlantic Monthly Press, 2020); John Herbert Roper Sr., "Ransack Roulhac and Racism: Joseph Grégoire de Roulhac Hamilton and Dunning's Questions of Institution Building and Jim Crow," in *The Dunning School: Historians, Race, and the Meaning of Reconstruction*, ed. John David Smith and J. Vincent Lowery (Lexington: University Press of Kentucky, 2013), 187–88; Beckel, *Radical Reform*, chap. 9; Timothy B. Tyson and David S. Cecelski, introduction to *Democracy Betrayed: The Wilmington Race Riot of 1898 and Its Legacy*, ed. David S. Cecelski and Timothy B. Tyson (Chapel Hill: University of North Carolina Press, 1998), 3–13; H. Leon Prather, *We Have Taken a City: The Wilmington Racial Massacre and Coup of 1898* (Rutherford, NJ: Farleigh Dickinson University Press, 1984).

45. John W. Moore, *School History of North Carolina, from 1584 to 1879* (Raleigh, NC: Alfred Williams and Co., 1879), 301–3, quote on 301–2. For a sketch of Moore's life and career, see James Elliott Moore, "Moore, John Wheeler," NCpedia, www.ncpedia.org/biography /moore-john-wheeler (accessed November 22, 2022).

46. John W. Moore, *School History of North Carolina, from 1584 to the Present Time*, 14th ed. (New York: American Book Company, 1901), 274.

47. Moore, *School History of North Carolina*, 14th ed., 274–75. Students did not, however, learn to correctly spell the colonel's name: Moore rendered it "Kirke" throughout the book.

48. Moore, *School History of North Carolina*, 14th ed., 276.

49. Moore, *School History of North Carolina*, 14th ed., 277–78.

50. Zebulon B. Vance, "Reconstruction in North Carolina," in *Why the Solid South? Or, Reconstruction and Its Results*, by Hilary A. Herbert et al. (Baltimore, MD: R. H. Woodward and Company, 1890), 70–84, quote on 84.

51. Michele K. Gillespie and Randal L. Hall, introduction to *Thomas Dixon Jr. and the Birth of Modern America*, ed. Michele K. Gillespie and Randal L. Hall (Baton Rouge: Louisiana State University Press, 2006), 1–22; Anthony Slide, *American Racist: The Life and Films of Thomas Dixon* (Lexington: University Press of Kentucky, 2004); Cook, *Thomas Dixon*.

52. Thomas Dixon, *Southern Horizons: The Autobiography of Thomas Dixon* (Alexandria, VA: IWV Publishing, 1984), 35, 47, 61–62.

53. William C. Harris, *William Woods Holden: Firebrand of North Carolina Politics* (Baton Rouge: Louisiana State University Press, 1987), 3; Thomas Dixon Jr., *The Clansman: An Historical Romance of the Ku Klux Klan* (New York: Doubleday, Page, 1905), quote on i.

54. William Rawlings, *The Second Coming of the Invisible Empire: The Ku Klux Klan of the 1920s* (Macon, GA: Mercer University Press, 2016), 50–53; Frank J. Wetta and Martin A. Novelli, *The Long Reconstruction: The Post-Civil War South in History, Film, and Memory* (New York: Routledge, 2014), esp. chap. 6; Charlene Regester, "The Cinematic Representation of Race in *The Birth of a Nation*: A Black Horror Film," in Gillespie and Hall, *Thomas Dixon Jr.*, 164–82; Nancy MacLean, *Behind the Mask of Chivalry: The Making of the Second Ku Klux Klan* (New York: Oxford University Press, 1994), 12–13; Wyn Craig Wade, *The Fiery Cross: The Ku Klux Klan in America* (London: Simon and Schuster, 1987), chap. 4. For Wilson's written take on Reconstruction, see Woodrow Wilson, "The Reconstruction of the Southern States," *Atlantic Monthly* 87, no. 519 (January 1901): 1–15; and on federal racial policies during Wilson's presidential administration, see Eric S. Yellin, *Racism in the Nation's Service: Government Workers and the Color Line in Woodrow Wilson's America* (Chapel Hill: University of North Carolina Press, 2013).

55. Myrta Lockett Avary, *Dixie after the War: An Exposition of Social Conditions Existing in the South, during the Twelve Years Succeeding the Fall of Richmond* (New York: Doubleday, Page, 1906), 263, 269.

56. Avary, *Dixie after the War*, 274, 275.

57. Avary, *Dixie after the War*, 278.

58. Mrs. T. J. [Mary Woodson] Jarvis, "The Ku-Klux Klans," *North Carolina Booklet* 2, no. 1 (May 1902): 3–26; Escott, *Many Excellent People*, 192–95.

59. Jarvis, "Ku-Klux Klans," quotes on 2, 23.

60. Frank Nash, "John Walter Stephens," in *Biographical History of North Carolina, from Colonial Times to the Present*, 8 vols., ed. Samuel A. Ashe (Greensboro, NC: Charles L. Van Noppen, 1905–17), 4:416–17.

61. Nash, "John Walter Stephens," 419–21, quote on 421.

62. Roper, "Ransack Roulhac and Racism," 179–201; Carole Watterson Troxler, "'To Look More Closely at the Man': Wyatt Outlaw, a Nexus of National, Local, and Personal History," *NCHR* 77, no. 4 (October 2000): 418; E. E. Moffitt, "J. G. de Roulhac Hamilton," *North Carolina Booklet* 6, no. 2 (October 1906): 154–55. The University of North Carolina's history department is currently housed in a building that bore Hamilton's name until July 2020. The department explains that the recent name change was provoked by "Hamilton's intellectually dishonest historical and archival work [which] promoted white supremacy." Although the department now refers to the structure as Pauli Murray Hall, it remains labeled Hamilton Hall on university campus maps, pending administrative review. See the explanatory statement at the bottom of the following web page: https://history.unc.edu/ (accessed November 22, 2022); and Hilary N. Green, "Enshrining Proud Shoes in Brick and Mortar: An Alumna Contemplates Pauli Murray Hall," *Southern Cultures* 26, no. 3 (Summer 2020): 172–75.

63. J. G. de Roulhac Hamilton, *Reconstruction in North Carolina* (New York: Columbia University Press, 1914), quotes on 473, 454. Hamilton initially published the core of his study in 1906 in a limited run with a Raleigh printer but then dramatically expanded its scope for a 1914 revision. It was this second edition that drew broad attention. For the first version, see J. G. de Roulhac Hamilton, *Reconstruction in North Carolina* (Raleigh, NC: Edwards and Broughton, 1906).

64. W. E. B. Du Bois, *Black Reconstruction in America* (1935; repr., New York: Oxford University Press, 2007), 589.

65. William A. Dunning, *Reconstruction, Political and Economic, 1865–1877* (New York: Harper and Brothers, 1907). In addition to Hamilton's work, state-specific Dunning School Reconstruction studies, some of which appeared before Dunning's synthesis, include James Wilford Garner, *Reconstruction in Mississippi* (New York: Macmillan, 1901); John S. Reynolds, *Reconstruction in South Carolina, 1865–1877* (Columbia, SC: The State, 1905); Walter L. Fleming, *Civil War and Reconstruction in Alabama* (New York: Columbia University Press, 1905); William Watson Davis, *The Civil War and Reconstruction in Florida* (New York: Columbia University Press, 1913); and Clara Mildred Thompson, *Reconstruction in Georgia: Economic, Social, Political, 1865–1872* (New York: Columbia University Press, 1915). A good summary of Dunning's importance and the historiographical responses to his and his students' work in the years that followed can be found in John David Smith, introduction to Smith and Lowery, *Dunning School*, 1–47. For an argument that historians ought to move away from giving the Dunning School such a prominent place in the historiography, see Elaine Frantz Parsons, "Can We Be Done with Dunning?," review of *Dunning School*, H-SHGAPE (April 2014), available at www.h-net.org/reviews/showrev.php?id=40901 (accessed November 22, 2022). I am sympathetic to Parsons's argument, but discussion of the Dunning School seems essential here since Hamilton (and figures to appear later) so closely identified with its methods and aims and were crucial to shaping public memory of Stephens.

66. Fleming, *Civil War and Reconstruction in Alabama*, 561–62, 565, quote on 553.

67. Garner, *Reconstruction in Mississippi*, 349–51.

68. Reynolds, *Reconstruction in South Carolina*, 183.

69. Thompson, *Reconstruction in Georgia*, 380, 388.

70. J. G. de Roulhac Hamilton, *History of North Carolina*, vol. 3, *North Carolina since 1860* (Chicago: Lewis Publishing, 1919), 140.

71. Samuel A'Court Ashe, *History of North Carolina*, 2 vols. (Raleigh, NC: Edwards and Broughton, 1925). In their attention to the Klan, Hamilton's and Ashe's volumes kept with progressive textbook patterns on the national level, though with more than typical admiration for the Klan's aims. See Elaine Parsons, "The Cultural Work of the Ku-Klux Klan in US History Textbooks, 1883–2015," in *Remembering Reconstruction: Struggles over the Meaning of America's Most Turbulent Era*, ed. Carole Emberton and Bruce E. Baker (Baton Rouge: Louisiana State University Press, 2017), 234–42.

72. William K. Boyd and J. G. de Roulhac Hamilton, *A Syllabus of North Carolina History, 1584–1876* (Durham, NC: Seeman Printery, 1913), 95–96, quote on 96.

73. Anderson, in Tom Henderson, *Ann of the Ku Klux Klan* (Yanceyville, NC: by the author, n.d.), 10.

74. Jeannine D. Whitlow, ed., *The Heritage of Caswell County, North Carolina* (Winston-Salem, NC: Hunter Publishing, 1985), 89.

75. George Anderson to [Edna Watkins?], January 22, 1914, folder 1, Watkins Family Papers, SHC.

76. George A. Anderson, *Caswell County in the World War, 1917–1918: Service Records of Caswell County Men* (Raleigh, NC: Edwards and Broughton Printing Co., 1921); James Hall, "Manhood, Duty, and Service: Conscription in North Carolina during the First World War," in *The American South and the Great War, 1914–1924*, ed. Matthew L. Downs and M. Ryan Floyd (Baton Rouge: Louisiana State University Press, 2018), 41–60; Kathelene McCarty Smith and Keith Phelan Gorman, "The Call to Duty in the Old North State: Patriotism,

Service, and North Carolina Women's Colleges during the Great War," in Downs and Floyd, *American South and the Great War*, 116–39.

77. Vanessa Siddle Walker, *Their Highest Potential: An African American School Community in the Segregated South* (Chapel Hill: University of North Carolina Press, 1996), 14–15, 17.

78. Francis A. Walker, *The Statistics of Wealth and Industry of the United States... Compiled, from the Original Returns of the Ninth Census (June 1, 1870), under the Direction of the Secretary of the Interior* (Washington, DC: GPO, 1872), 216, 220; Francis A. Walker and Charles W. Seaton, *Compendium of the Tenth Census (June 1, 1880), Compiled Pursuant to an Act of Congress Approved August 7, 1882*, part 1 (Washington, DC: GPO, 1883), 801. In 1870, county farmers cured 2,262,053 pounds of tobacco. Ten years later the figure was 4,336,664 pounds.

79. There are many studies of American cigarette production and the importance of the American Tobacco Company. Two excellent recent profiles are found in Sarah Milov, *The Cigarette: A Political History* (Cambridge, MA: Harvard University Press, 2019), chap. 1; and Nan Enstad, *Cigarettes, Inc.: An Intimate History of Corporate Imperialism* (Chicago: University of Chicago Press, 2018), esp. chaps. 1–3; while the most influential modern synthesis is that of Allan M. Brandt in *The Cigarette Century: The Rise, Fall, and Deadly Persistence of the Product That Defined America* (New York: Basic Books, 2007), chaps. 1 and 2. Also notable is Alfred D. Chandler Jr.'s enshrining of the American Tobacco Company as a prototypical business monopoly in his classic, *The Visible Hand: The Managerial Revolution in American Business* (Cambridge, MA: Belknap Press, 1977), chap. 12.

80. "Meeting of Caswell's Tobacco Growers," *Milton (NC) Herald*, January 11, 1900.

81. W. Edward Hearn and Frank P. Drane, *Soil Survey of Caswell County, North Carolina* (Washington, DC: GPO, 1910), 21, 26.

82. General ideas about changes in forested area and tree species composition can be drawn from comparing land surveys from Caswell over time. For example, 1880 surveys revealed fewer trees used as line markers than had been the case a century earlier, replaced by "pointers" used to denote boundaries in deforested areas. See Land Survey Book A, 1777–1783, and Deed Book NN, 1879–1881, Caswell County Courthouse, Yanceyville, NC.

83. Drew A. Swanson, *A Golden Weed: Tobacco and Environment in the Piedmont South* (New Haven, CT: Yale University Press, 2014), chap. 7; Adrienne Monteith Petty, *Standing Their Ground: Small Farmers in North Carolina since the Civil War* (New York: Oxford University Press, 2013), chap. 2.

84. B. E. Washburn, *As I Recall: The Hookworm Campaigns Initiated by the Rockefeller Sanitary Commission and the Rockefeller Foundation in the Southern United States and Tropical America* (New York: Rockefeller Foundation, 1960), 15–18, quotes on 16.

85. F. H. Jeter in Charles E. Landon, "The Tobacco Growing Industry of North Carolina," *Economic Geography* 10, no. 3 (July 1934): 253. The most authoritative study of tobacco troubles in the state during the New Deal is Anthony J. Badger, *Prosperity Road: The New Deal, Tobacco, and North Carolina* (Chapel Hill: University of North Carolina Press, 1980).

CHAPTER SIX

1. Linda Gordon, *The Second Coming of the KKK: The Ku Klux Klan of the 1920s and the American Political Tradition* (New York: Liveright, 2017), esp. chaps. 1 and 2; William Rawlings, *The Second Coming of the Invisible Empire: The Ku Klux Klan of the 1920s* (Macon: Mercer University Press, 2016), 87; Nan Elizabeth Woodruff, *American Congo: The African American*

Freedom Struggle in the Delta (Cambridge, MA: Harvard University Press, 2003), 91–94; David W. Blight, *Race and Reunion: The Civil War in American Memory* (Cambridge, MA: Belknap Press, 2001), quote on 9; Stewart E. Tolnay and E. M. Beck, *A Festival of Violence: An Analysis of Southern Lynching, 1882–1930* (Urbana: University of Illinois Press, 1995), 271–72; Nancy MacLean, *Behind the Mask of Chivalry: The Making of the Second Ku Klux Klan* (New York: Oxford University Press, 1994), 4–5, 23, 131; Wyn Craig Wade, *The Fiery Cross: The Ku Klux Klan in America* (London: Simon and Schuster, 1987), chap. 5. Note: Tolnay and Beck's estimate of 1919 lynching numbers included a census of just ten former Confederate states, omitting Texas and Virginia.

2. H. Leon Prather, *We Have Taken a City: The Wilmington Racial Massacre and Coup of 1898* (Rutherford, NJ: Fairleigh Dickinson University Press, 1984); David S. Cecelski and Timothy B. Tyson, eds., *Democracy Betrayed: The Wilmington Race Riot of 1898 and Its Legacy* (Chapel Hill: University of North Carolina Press, 1998); Paul D. Escott, *Many Excellent People: Power and Privilege in North Carolina, 1850–1900* (Chapel Hill: University of North Carolina Press, 1985), 254–55.

3. Vann R. Newkirk, *Lynching in North Carolina: A History, 1865–1941* (Jefferson, NC: McFarland and Co., 2009), 147–48; W. Fitzhugh Brundage, *Lynching in the New South: Georgia and Virginia, 1880–1930* (Urbana: University of Illinois Press, 1993), 34.

4. Elizabeth A. Herbin-Triant, *Threatening Property: Race, Class, and Campaigns to Legislate Jim Crow Neighborhoods* (New York: Columbia University Press, 2019), chap. 5; H. Leon Prather Sr., "We Have Taken a City: A Centennial Essay," 20, 29, and Michael Honey, "Class, Race, and Power in the New South: Racial Violence and the Delusions of White Supremacy," 176–77, both in Cecelski and Tyson, *Democracy Betrayed*; Jeffrey J. Crow, "An Apartheid for the South: Clarence Poe's Crusade for Rural Segregation," in *Race, Class, and Politics in Southern History: Essays in Honor of Robert F. Durden*, ed. Jeffrey J. Crow, Paul D. Escott, and Charles L. Flynn Jr. (Baton Rouge: Louisiana State University Press, 1989), 216–59.

5. J. G. de Roulhac Hamilton, *Reconstruction in North Carolina* (New York: Columbia University Press, 1914), 462.

6. The following details are drawn from JGLC.

7. See the letter of George Anderson in chap. 5, note 75.

8. A Caswell County genealogy site names one other listed co-conspirator, Pink Morgan, as living until 1930. See http://sites.rootsweb.com/~ncccha/biographies /senatorjohnstephens.html (accessed November 22, 2022).

9. Together the decisions in the *Slaughter-House Cases* (1873) and *United States v. Cruikshank* (1876), both originating in Louisiana, defined enforcement of the Fourteenth Amendment as largely a state responsibility, which meant that across the South the amendment would provide little practical protection for African Americans' rights. These decisions all but undermined the provisions of the Enforcement Acts designed to combat organizations like the Klan. See Pamela Brandwein, *Rethinking the Judicial Settlement of Reconstruction* (Cambridge: Cambridge University Press, 2011); Charles Lane, *The Day Freedom Died: The Colfax Massacre, the Supreme Court, and the Betrayal of Reconstruction* (New York: Henry Holt, 2008); LeeAnna Keith, *The Colfax Massacre: The Untold Story of Black Power, White Terror, and the Death of Reconstruction* (New York: Oxford University Press, 2008), 154–58; Ronald M. Labbe and Jonathan Lurie, *The Slaughterhouse Cases: Regulation, Reconstruction, and the Fourteenth Amendment* (Lawrence: University Press of Kansas, 2003); and Pamela Brandwein, *Reconstructing Reconstruction: The Supreme Court and the Production of Historical Truth* (Durham, NC: Duke University Press, 1999).

10. E. E. Moffitt, "Col. Fred. A. Olds," *North Carolina Booklet* 6, no. 2 (October 1906): 155; Fred A. Olds, "Colonial and Revolutionary Relics in the Hall of History," *North Carolina Booklet* 6, no. 2 (October 1906): 123.

11. "Meet the Statues," North Carolina Museum of History, www.ncmuseumofhistory .org/exhibits/meet-the-statues (accessed November 22, 2022). One of the other statues is of Thomas Day.

12. Maud Thomas Smith, "Grimes, John Bryan," NCPedia, www.ncpedia.org/biography /grimes-john-bryan (accessed November 22, 2022).

13. W. Fitzhugh Brundage, *The Southern Past: A Clash of Race and Memory* (Cambridge, MA: Belknap Press, 2005), 110–11, 126–27.

14. "How Secret of Ku Klux Klan Killing Defied Nosy Historians," *Raleigh News and Observer*, October 6, 1935 (clipping), Reconstruction Papers, 1868–1973, NCSA; R. D. W. Connor, *History of North Carolina: Volume 1, The Colonial and Revolutionary Periods, 1584–1783* (Chicago: Lewis Publishing, 1919); E. E. Moffitt, "Robert Diggs Wimberly Connor," *North Carolina Booklet* 6, no. 3 (January 1907): 206; R. D. W. Connor, *Improvement in Rural School Houses and Grounds, 1900–1906* (Raleigh, NC: State Superintendent of Public Instruction, 1907); Alex H. Poole, "The Strange Career of Jim Crow Archives: Race, Space, and History in the Mid-Twentieth-Century American South," *American Archivist* 77, no. 1 (Spring/Summer 2014): 35–36; Waldo Gifford Leland, "R. D. W. Connor, First Archivist of the United States," *American Archivist* 16, no. 1 (January 1953): 45–54.

15. R. D. W. Connor, *Race Elements in the White Population of North Carolina*, North Carolina State Normal and Industrial College Historical Publications, No. 1 (Raleigh: North Carolina State Normal and Industrial College, 1920).

16. R. D. W. Connor, *A Manual of North Carolina, Issued by the North Carolina Historical Commission, for the Use of Members of the General Assembly, Session 1913* (Raleigh, NC: E. M. Uzzell and Co., 1913), 545, 862n37.

17. R. D. W. Connor and Clarence Poe, *The Life and Speeches of Charles Brantley Aycock* (Garden City, NY: Doubleday, Page, and Co., 1912). On Connor's connections to the Dunning School beyond his friendship with Hamilton, see finding aid, "biographical information," R. D. W. Connor Papers, 1890–1950, Collection #02427, SHC, available online at https://finding-aids.lib.unc.edu/02427/ (accessed November 22, 2022); and Leland, "R. D. W. Connor," 47.

18. Brundage, *Southern Past*, chap. 3, quote on 117–18.

19. R. D. W. Connor, *Eighth Biennial Report of the North Carolina Historical Commission, December 1, 1918, to November 30, 1920* (Raleigh, NC: Edwards and Broughton, 1921), 10–29, 31–36.

20. R. D. W. Connor, *North Carolina: Rebuilding an Ancient Commonwealth, 1584–1925*, 4 vols. (Chicago: American Historical Society, 1928–29), 2:327. The final two volumes provided biographical profiles of important North Carolinians; John Stephens was not among them.

21. Confederate Pension Rolls, Veterans and Widows, collection CP-3_171, roll 171, roll description: City of Danville (surnames Co-Wi), Library of Virginia, Richmond; 1930 Census, Danville, Virginia, roll 2467, page 4B, enumeration district 10, image 421.0, Family History Library microfilm 2342201, found on Ancestry.com.

22. "How Secret of Ku Klux Klan Killing Defied Nosy Historians."

23. "How Secret of Ku Klux Klan Killing Defied Nosy Historians"; "Lea Statement Lay 16 Years in Archives," *Danville Bee*, October 1, 1935 (clipping), and "When Country Line

Creek Ran Red," *Danville Bee*, October 1, 1935 (clipping), both in Reconstruction Papers, NCSA. See also "65-Year-Old Homicide Is Solved," October 2, 1935, clipping in box 4, folder 24, CCHAC, SHC.

24. "Dying Klansman Tells of Yanceyville Assassination," *Daily Times-News* (Burlington, NC), October 1, 1935.

25. "Danville, Va. Now It Can Be Told," *Washington Post*, October 2, 1935 (clipping), and "Deathbed Deposition Reveals Secret of Carpetbag Slaying," *Washington Star*, October 1, 1935 (clipping), both in Reconstruction Papers, 1868–1973, NCSA.

26. "How Secret of Ku Klux Klan Killing Defied Nosy Historians." Not everyone agreed with the accuracy of the confession. George Ivey, a former Caswell resident living in Charlotte, North Carolina, in 1935, informed his city's newspaper that it was common knowledge that Republicans had killed Stephens to stir up trouble leading into the 1870 election. He believed Lea was simply stealing the credit after the fact. "Says J. W. Stephens Not a Carpetbagger," *Charlotte Observer*, October 13, 1935 (clipping), Reconstruction Papers, 1868–1973, NCSA.

27. Claude G. Bowers, *The Tragic Era: The Revolution after Lincoln* (Cambridge, MA: Riverside Press, 1929), 317.

28. Margaret Mitchell, *Gone with the Wind* (New York: Macmillan, 1936); *Gone with the Wind*, dir. Victor Fleming (Metro-Goldwyn-Meyer, 1939).

29. Francis Butler Simkins and Robert Hilliard Woody, *South Carolina during Reconstruction* (1932; repr., Gloucester, MA: Peter Smith, 1966).

30. W. E. B. Du Bois, *Black Reconstruction in America* (1935; repr., New York: Oxford University Press, 2007).

31. Justin Behrend, "Facts, Memories, and History: John R. Lynch and the Memory of Reconstruction in the Age of Jim Crow," in *Remembering Reconstruction: Struggles over the Meaning of America's Most Turbulent Era*, ed. Carole Emberton and Bruce E. Baker (Baton Rouge: Louisiana State University Press, 2017), 84–108.

32. Francis B. Simkins, "New Viewpoints on Southern Reconstruction," *JSH* 5, no. 1 (February 1939): 49–61; Howard K. Beale, "On Rewriting Reconstruction History," *American Historical Review* 45, no. 4 (July 1940): 807–27; John Hope Franklin, "Whither Reconstruction Historiography," *Journal of Negro Education* 17, no. 4 (Autumn 1948): 446–61. I am indebted to an essay by Elaine Parsons for this framework: "The Cultural Work of the Ku-Klux Klan in US History Textbooks, 1883–2015," in Emberton and Baker, *Remembering Reconstruction*, 227.

33. *Minutes of the Twenty-First Annual Convention of the United Daughters of the Confederacy, North Carolina Division* (Raleigh, NC: Capital Printing, 1917), 122.

34. On the importance of the United Daughters of the Confederacy in shaping Lost Cause memorialization, see Karen L. Cox, *Dixie's Daughters: The United Daughters of the Confederacy and the Preservation of Confederate Culture* (Gainesville: University Press of Florida, 2003); Gaines M. Foster, *Ghosts of the Confederacy: Defeat, the Lost Cause, and the Emergence of the New South* (New York: Oxford University Press, 1987), 127, 129, 158, 186–90; and Charles Reagan Wilson, *Baptized in Blood: The Religion of the Lost Cause, 1865–1920* (Athens: University of Georgia Press, 1983), 140–41, 144.

35. Jeannine D. Whitlow, ed., *The Heritage of Caswell County, North Carolina* (Winston-Salem, NC: Hunter Publishing, 1985), 17–18; William Powell, *When the Past Refused to Die: A History of Caswell County, North Carolina, 1777–1977* (Durham, NC: Moore Publishing, 1977), 222–23.

36. The description was B. E. Washburn's: Washburn, *As I Recall: The Hookworm Campaigns Initiated by the Rockefeller Sanitary Commission and the Rockefeller Foundation in the Southern United States and Tropical America* (New York: Rockefeller Foundation, 1960), 17.

37. Tom Henderson, *Ann of the Ku Klux Klan* (Yanceyville, NC: by the author, n.d.), 1.

38. Henderson, *Ann of the Ku Klux Klan*, 5.

39. Henderson, *Ann of the Ku Klux Klan*, 6.

40. Henderson, *Ann of the Ku Klux Klan*, 8–12, quote on 12.

41. Henderson, *Ann of the Ku Klux Klan*, 1–5, quotes on 5 and 3.

42. Henderson, *Ann of the Ku Klux Klan*, 1.

43. Tom Henderson, "Murder of 'Chicken' Stephens," *The State* 6, no. 43 (March 25, 1939): 9, 19, 24, quote spanning 19 and 24. It is unclear whether this is a garbled reference to Wiley's death.

44. "Caswell Night Riders . . . Lea Family Played Large Part in Ku Klux Klan Affairs," *Greensboro Daily News*, April 6, 1941 (clipping), and "Drama of 1870: 'Chicken' Stephens Executed by Klan," n,p, n.d. (1960s?) (clipping), both in Caswell County Historical Association Collection #05401, series 15, box 4, folder 24, SHC, quote in the latter.

45. Powell, *When the Past Refused to Die*, 253.

46. Evan P. Bennett, *When Tobacco Was King: Families, Farm Labor, and Federal Policy in the Piedmont* (Gainesville: University Press of Florida, 2014), 71–72; Paul K. Conkin, *A Revolution Down on the Farm: The Transformation of American Agriculture since 1929* (Lexington: University Press of Kentucky, 2008), 67–68; Roger Biles, *The South and the New Deal* (Lexington: University Press of Kentucky, 1994), 39; Pete Daniel, *Breaking the Land: The Transformation of Cotton, Tobacco, and Rice Cultures since 1880* (Urbana: University of Illinois Press, 1985), 110–11. The most thorough assessment of the New Deal's impact on North Carolina tobacco farming is Anthony J. Badger, *Prosperity Road: The New Deal, Tobacco, and North Carolina* (Chapel Hill: University of North Carolina Press, 1980). For a contemporary assessment of Caswell's farm economy, see Robert E. Graham, *Improving Low Incomes on Tobacco Farms, Caswell County, North Carolina* (Washington, DC: USDA Bureau of Agricultural Economics Cooperating with North Carolina Agricultural Experiment Station, 1941). The Supreme Court ruled the first Agricultural Adjustment Act unconstitutional in 1936, but its 1938 replacement would institute a similar tobacco program, and its mixture of price supports and production controls would continue with slight modification into the late 1990s.

47. Wolcott's Yanceyville images can be found on the Library of Congress's website at www.loc.gov/collections/fsa-owi-black-and-white-negatives/?q=Yanceyville+ (accessed November 22, 2022). Discussion of the Farm Security Administration's and Wolcott's conservation work in Caswell can be found in Drew A. Swanson, *A Golden Weed: Tobacco and Environment in the Piedmont South* (New Haven, CT: Yale University Press, 2014), 257–61. For an account of the card game as it was played in 1913, see Washburn, *As I Recall*, 16.

48. "The Yanceyville Card Game Is Ended by Law," *Life*, December 8, 1941, 59.

49. "Yanceyville Card Game," 60.

50. Manly Wade Wellman, *Dead and Gone: Classic Crimes of North Carolina* (Chapel Hill: University of North Carolina Press, 1954), 137. Some of Wellman's claims are demonstrably false and his account lacks notes, although he mentions reference to newspapers, local memories, A. J. Stedman's speculative pamphlet *Murder and Mystery*, and consultation with J. G. de R. Hamilton.

51. Wellman, *Dead and Gone*, 139.

52. Wellman, *Dead and Gone*, 153.

53. Archibald Henderson, *North Carolina: The Old North State and the New*, 2 vols. (Chicago: Lewis Publishing Co., 1941), 2:330–33, quotes on 330 and 331.

54. Hugh Talmage Lefler and Albert Ray Newsome, *North Carolina: The History of a Southern State*, rev. ed. (1954; Chapel Hill: University of North Carolina Press, 1963), 466–70, quotes on 466 and 470.

55. The iconic phrasing is Eric Foner's in *Reconstruction: America's Unfinished Revolution, 1863–1877* (New York: Harper and Row, 1988), in which he attempted to reconcile the revisionists and the historians who subsequently modified their arguments.

56. Kenneth M. Stampp, *The Era of Reconstruction, 1865–1877* (New York: Alfred A. Knopf, 1965); John Hope Franklin, *Reconstruction: After the Civil War* (1961; repr., Chicago: University of Chicago Press, 1994); Howard K. Beale, *The Critical Year: A Study of Andrew Johnson and Reconstruction* (New York: Harcourt, Brace, 1930), first quote on 1–2; Beale, "On Rewriting Reconstruction History," second quote on 808.

57. Joel Williamson, *After Slavery: The Negro in South Carolina during Reconstruction, 1861–1877* (Chapel Hill: University of North Carolina Press, 1965).

58. Quick introductions to the waves of historiographical revision of various Reconstruction debates can be found in the collected essays in John David Smith, ed., *Reconstruction* (Kent, OH: Kent State University Press, 2016); as well as in Bruce E. Baker and Elaine S. Frantz, "Against Synthesis: Diverse Approaches to the History of Reconstruction," in *Reinterpreting Southern Histories: Essays in Historiography*, ed. Craig Thompson Friend and Lorri Glover (Baton Rouge: Louisiana State University Press, 2020), 218–44.

59. Examples of Otto H. Olsen's work include "The Ku Klux Klan: A Study in Reconstruction Politics and Propaganda," *NCHR* 39, no. 3 (July 1962): 340–62; *Carpetbagger's Crusade: The Life of Albion Winegar Tourgée* (Baltimore, MD: Johns Hopkins Press, 1965); and "North Carolina: An Incongruous Presence," in *Reconstruction and Redemption in the South*, ed. Otto H. Olsen (Baton Rouge: Louisiana State University Press, 1980), 156–201. For Olsen's biographical information, see Joseph P. Reidy and Michael K. Honey, "In Memoriam: Otto H. Olsen," *Perspectives on History* 53, no. 3 (March 2015), available online at www.historians .org/publications-and-directories/perspectives-on-history/march-2015/in-memoriam -otto-olsen (accessed November 22, 2022).

60. Allen W. Trelease, "Who Were the Scalawags?," in *Reconstruction: An Anthology of Revisionist Writings*, ed. Kenneth M. Stampp and Leon F. Litwack (Baton Rouge: Louisiana State University Press, 1969), 299–322; Allen W. Trelease, "Republican Reconstruction in North Carolina: A Roll-Call Analysis of the State House of Representatives, 1868–1870," *JSH* 42, no. 3 (August 1976): 319–44; Allen W. Trelease, *White Terror: The Ku Klux Klan Conspiracy and Southern Reconstruction* (Westport, CT: Greenwood Press, 1979); Edgar E. Folk and Bynum Shaw, *W. W. Holden: A Political Biography* (Winston-Salem, NC: John F. Blair, 1982); Escott, *Many Excellent People*, chaps. 4–6; William C. Harris, *William Woods Holden: Firebrand of North Carolina Politics* (Baton Rouge: Louisiana State University Press, 1987); Richard Nelson Current, *Those Terrible Carpetbaggers* (New York: Oxford University Press, 1988); Mark Elliott, *Color-Blind Justice: Albion Tourgée and the Quest for Racial Equality from the Civil War to Plessy v. Ferguson* (New York: Oxford University Press, 2006); Mark Elliott and John David Smith, eds., *Undaunted Radical: The Selected Writings and Speeches of Albion W. Tourgée* (Baton Rouge: Louisiana State University Press, 2010); Carolyn L. Karcher, *A Refugee from His Race: Albion W. Tourgée and His Fight against White Supremacy* (Chapel Hill: University of North Carolina Press, 2016).

61. A few examples (with a particular eye toward North Carolina studies) include Adrienne Monteith Petty, *Standing Their Ground: Small Farmers in North Carolina since the Civil War* (New York: Oxford University Press, 2013), esp. chap 2; Carole Emberton, *Beyond Redemption: Race, Violence, and the American South after the Civil War* (Chicago: University of Chicago Press, 2013); Karin L. Zipf, *Labor of Innocents: Forced Apprenticeship in North Carolina, 1715–1919* (Baton Rouge: Louisiana State University Press, 2005); Steven Hahn, *A Nation under Our Feet: Black Political Struggles in the Rural South from Slavery to the Great Migration* (Cambridge, MA: Belknap Press, 2003); Sharon Ann Holt, *Making Freedom Pay: North Carolina Freedpeople Working for Themselves, 1865–1900* (Athens: University of Georgia Press, 2000); Robert C. Kenzer, *Enterprising Southerners: Black Economic Success in North Carolina, 1865–1915* (Charlottesville: University Press of Virginia, 1997); Roberta Sue Alexander, *North Carolina Faces the Freedmen: Race Relations during Presidential Reconstruction, 1865–67* (Durham, NC: Duke University Press, 1985); Leon Litwack, *Been in the Storm So Long: The Aftermath of Slavery* (New York: Vintage, 1980); and Williamson, *After Slavery*.

62. Steven E. Nash, *Reconstruction's Ragged Edge: The Politics of Postwar Life in the Southern Mountains* (Chapel Hill: University of North Carolina Press, 2016), 131; Scott Reynolds Nelson, "Red Strings and Half Brothers: Civil Wars in Alamance County, North Carolina, 1861–1871," in *Enemies of the Country: New Perspectives on Unionists in the Civil War South*, ed. John C. Inscoe and Robert C. Kenzer (Athens: University of Georgia Press, 2001), 37–53; Carole Watterson Troxler, "'To Look More Closely at the Man': Wyatt Outlaw, a Nexus of National, Local, and Personal History," *NCHR* 77, no. 4 (October 2000): 403–33; Scott Reynolds Nelson, *Iron Confederacies: Southern Railways, Klan Violence, and Reconstruction* (Chapel Hill: University of North Carolina Press, 1999), 98–114.

63. Olsen, "Ku Klux Klan," 356–57; Trelease, *White Terror*, 212–13, quote on 479n24; Folk and Shaw, *W. W. Holden*, 213; Current, *Those Terrible Carpetbaggers*, 203–4; Richard L. Zuber, *North Carolina during Reconstruction* (Raleigh, NC: Division of Archives and History, 1969), 29–33; Gregory P. Downs, *Declarations of Dependence: The Long Reconstruction of Popular Politics in the South, 1861–1908* (Chapel Hill: University of North Carolina Press, 2011), 124. See also mentions in Gregory P. Downs, *After Appomattox: Military Occupation and the Ends of War* (Cambridge, MA: Harvard University Press, 2015), 232; Hahn, *Nation under Our Feet*, 285; and Foner, *Reconstruction*, 427.

64. Powell, *When the Past Refused to Die*, 236–43, quote on 237.

65. William S. Powell, *North Carolina: A Bicentennial History* (New York: Norton, 1977); Hugh T. Lefler and William S. Powell, *Colonial North Carolina: A History* (New York: Scribner, 1973); William S. Powell, *North Carolina: A Students' Guide to Localized History* (New York: Teachers College, Columbia University, 1965), quote on 26; William S. Powell, *North Carolina through Four Centuries* (Chapel Hill: University of North Carolina Press, 1989).

66. William S. Powell, ed., *Encyclopedia of North Carolina* (Chapel Hill: University of North Carolina Press, 2006); Allen W. Trelease, "Stephens, John Walter," in *Dictionary of North Carolina Biography*, 6 vols., ed. William S. Powell (Chapel Hill: University of North Carolina Press, 1994), 5:439–40.

67. Powell, *North Carolina: A Bicentennial History*, 156–57, quote on 157.

68. Images of the new and old markers may be seen on the Caswell County Historical Association's website at http://sites.rootsweb.com/~ncccha/memoranda/historicalmarkers.html (accessed November 22, 2022).

69. For an example, see Ethan J. Kyle and Blain Roberts, *Denmark Vesey's Garden: Slavery and Memory in the Cradle of the Confederacy* (New York: New Press, 2018).

70. *The Murder of John Stephens*, series 15, VT-5401/1, Caswell County Historical Association Collection, SHC; Jim Wise, *Murder in the Courthouse: Reconstruction and Redemption in the North Carolina Piedmont* (Charleston, SC: History Press, 2010).

71. William S. Powell, "Caswell County History—The Death of 'Chicken' Stephens," *Caswell Messenger*, June 11, 2018. This article reprinted a section of Powell's older history of the county, *When the Past Refused to Die*.

72. An image of Lea's tombstone may be found at Find a Grave, www.findagrave.com /memorial/99787896/john-green-lea (accessed November 22, 2022).

73. Bruce Baker, "Wade Hampton's Last Parade: Memory of Reconstruction in the 1970 South Carolina Tricentennial," in Emberton and Baker, *Remembering Reconstruction*, 274.

EPILOGUE

1. On Brown's contested memory, see R. Blakeslee Gilpin, *John Brown Still Lives! America's Long Reckoning with Violence, Equality, and Change* (Chapel Hill: University of North Carolina Press, 2011); and David S. Reynolds, *John Brown, Abolitionist: The Man Who Killed Slavery, Sparked the Civil War, and Seeded Civil Rights* (New York: Knopf, 2005), chap. 18.

2. The subtitle of Foner's *Reconstruction* is *America's Unfinished Revolution*.

3. This is essentially Mark Wahlgren Summers's argument in *The Ordeal of Reunion: A New History of Reconstruction* (Chapel Hill: University of North Carolina Press, 2014), and to a lesser extent in his *A Dangerous Stir: Fear, Paranoia, and the Making of Reconstruction* (Chapel Hill: University of North Carolina Press, 2009).

4. Judkin Browning and Timothy Silver, *An Environmental History of the Civil War* (Chapel Hill: University of North Carolina Press, 2020), 136; "Civil War Casualties, The Cost of War: Killed, Wounded, Captured, and Missing," American Battlefield Trust, www.battlefields.org /learn/articles/civil-war-casualties (accessed November 28, 2022).

5. Drew Gilpin Faust, *This Republic of Suffering: Death and the American Civil War* (New York: Knopf, 2008), xiv.

6. The exception is Lea's assertion that the conspirators had thrown the key to the room where Stephens was murdered into Country Line Creek, although as chapter 5 notes this seems to have been rumored in Yanceyville prior to 1919. And the claim remains unproven, as the key was never recovered. Lea's mention of the key could as easily have been the repetition of an old rumor as confirmation of it.

7. "Bright Tobacco, an Old Negro the First to Cure It," *Progressive Farmer* 1, no. 10 (April 14, 1886): 4. For discussion of the origin myth, see Barbara Hahn, *Making Tobacco Bright: Creating an American Commodity, 1617–1937* (Baltimore, MD: Johns Hopkins University Press, 2011), 13–14, 138; and also Drew A. Swanson, *A Golden Weed: Tobacco and Environment in the Piedmont South* (New Haven, CT: Yale University Press, 2014), 46–49.

8. On the continued economic and cultural importance of tobacco in North Carolina, see Peter Benson, *Tobacco Capitalism: Growers, Migrant Workers, and the Changing Face of a Global Industry* (Princeton, NJ: Princeton University Press, 2011); Evan P. Bennett, *When Tobacco Was King: Families, Farm Labor, and Federal Policy in the Piedmont* (Gainesville: University Press of Florida, 2014), chap. 7 and conclusion; Drew Swanson, "Silver Screen, Bright Leaf: Hollywood's Cigarette Habit," in *Writing History with Lightning: Cinematic Representations of Nineteenth-Century America*, ed. Matthew C. Hulbert and John Inscoe (Baton Rouge: Louisiana State University Press, 2019), 279–88; *Bright Leaves*, dir. Ross McElwee (First Run Features, 2005); and Sarah Milov, *The Cigarette: A Political History* (Cambridge,

MA: Harvard University Press, 2019), esp. chap. 7 and conclusion. On the built environment of the county's tobacco economy, see Ruth Little-Stokes, *An Inventory of Historic Architecture, Caswell County, North Carolina: The Built Environment of a Burley and Bright-Leaf Tobacco Economy* (Yanceyville, NC: Caswell County Historical Association, 1979); and Catherine W. Bishir and Michael T. Southern, *A Guide to the Historic Architecture of Piedmont North Carolina*, Richard Hampton Jenrette Series in Architecture and Decorative Arts (Chapel Hill: University of North Carolina Press, 2003), 182–83.

9. For a summary of the discrimination woven into twentieth-century federal agricultural programs, see Greg A. Francis, *Just Harvest: The Story of How Black Farmers Won the Largest Civil Rights Case against the U.S. Government* (Brentwood, TN: Forefront Books, 2021); and Pete Daniel, *Dispossession: Discrimination against African American Farmers in the Age of Civil Rights* (Chapel Hill: University of North Carolina Press, 2013).

10. Milov, *Cigarette*, 287–95; Benson, *Tobacco Capitalism*, chap. 4; Allan M. Brandt, *The Cigarette Century: The Rise, Fall, and Deadly Persistence of the Product That Defined America* (New York: Basic Books, 2007), 434–40. The Tobacco Transition Payment Program was one outgrowth of the 1998 Master Settlement Agreement, in which an alliance of large tobacco companies settled existing state lawsuits by making financial and operational concessions.

Index

Printed in the USA
CPSIA information can be obtained
at www.ICGtesting.com
LVHW040757060823
754365LV00004B/391